A Little
Taste of
HEAVEN

DONIELLE INGERSOLL

DISCLAIMER
The information in this book is drawn largely from the imagination of the author. There are Bible texts at the end of each chapter to form a foundation, but the actual story is fictitious. In the Bible we read that our eyes have not seen, nor our ears heard neither can we even imagine the wonderful things the Lord has prepared for those who love Him. With that understanding, whatever the Lord has fashioned for us in the world to come will be a thousand times better than anything you or I can imagine. The doctrine contained in this book is based on the Bible and reflects the beliefs of no singular denomination. Several Bible texts are paraphrases of actual scriptures. I would invite you to look up those texts in your own Bible and study these things out for yourself. There is a heaven, but it may be far different than the one described in this book. Hopefully though it will be just a tiny bit like this. May God bless you as you seek a better understanding of Him and the hereafter and all we hope to attain through the grace of Jesus Christ.

Printed in the United States of America.

Springer Literary House LLC
6260 Lavender Cloud Place,
Las Vegas, Nevada 89122, USA

www.springerliteraryhouse.com

INTRODUCTION

"Jesus called a little child to him. He stood the child before the followers. Then he said, 'I tell you the truth. You must change and become like little children. If you don't do this, you will never enter the kingdom of heaven. The greatest person in the kingdom of heaven is the one who makes himself humble like this child. Whoever accepts a little child in my name accepts me.'"

Matthew 18:3-5

There are times in this old world when you get tired of the constant battle between right and wrong. You may even wish you were a child again, not having to bother with all the troubles you are called to endure. The circumstances surrounding you may be dark and gray. You long for sunny days and happy times, but they seldom come. If this is your experience now or has been in the past, you might want to fly away to a brighter, better world and rest for a while in a place where sin and suffering cannot exist. In this book you will be able to do just that. You will be allowed to leave the world behind and venture with two children, Joy and Trust, as they wander among the beauties of that glorious land far above the often, cloudy skies of your existence. There in that land beyond tomorrow, you will find rest for your soul.

So, set back and enjoy yourself as you get a little taste of Heaven.

The House of Trust and the Palace of Joy
(Prologue: An Allegory)

The place was heaven, the time, early in the twenty-first century. Jesus called a few of the twenty-four elders and a group of nearby angels to join Him for a short walk. He had just finished building the House of Trust and wanted to share it with some of His friends. The procession made their way over transparent streets of gold to the southern portion of the city. The homes Jesus had built here were very beautiful. He had taken the greatest care in fashioning each one. The House of Trust would prove to be no less a work of wonder. Those with the Savior would remark about this home for a long time to come. After several moments of travel, Jesus slowed, walked around a gigantic tree trunk, and pulled back some paradise foliage. There stood the house of Trust. It was breathtaking to say the least. Exclamations of wonder and amazement came from each being as they caught their first glimpse of this latest work of the Master Builder. It lay nestled in a blanket of colorful flowers. There was no golden sidewalk leading up to the silver door. There was only cobblestone like sections. Each one looked like a dark, shiny pool of silver glass.

"Master!" exclaimed one of the amazed angels. "What are these steppingstones made of? I have never seen anything like this in any of the other homes you have built."

"They are humility." replied the King. "On earth they would be recognized as hematite." The procession wondered at these pools of gleaming glass that seemed to beacon the travelers to turn aside and come into this house of rest.

Around the hematite Jesus had planted delicate strands of what on earth would be called Scottish and Irish moss. In heaven they were loveliness and holy longing.

The door of silver was very pretty. It had a little heart shaped window with red glass and golden letters that spelled the word LOVE. There were large spacious windows in this home. Each was trimmed in gold and silver. The walls were of a deep royal blue. The rock Jesus had chosen for them contained delicate patterns white mixed with strands of gold and silver.

"What are those beautiful walls made of?" asked one of the Elders.

Jesus answered. "They are made of truthfulness, Victory." Just as Trust was the essence of his own name so Victory was the essence and name of this particular elder, for he had obtained victory over the enemy through the blood of Jesus Christ.

"Trust will learn truthfulness in time, Victory, even as he will eventually learn to trust Me completely."

"Does he not trust you now Master?" questioned one of the angels? "No. Not yet. But he will. He surely will."

The group followed the Master up the silvery stones and paused a moment as Jesus looked up above the door and gently touched a grape like cluster of blue wisteria (as it would be known on earth). In heaven they were known as willingness and humble service. The vines were trained to curve around the door. There were two trunks that joined together in the center above the door. From the left and right side, two more branches trailed under the overhang along the top portion of the wall. It was a very creative work of art. The blue in the flowers perfectly complemented the deep royal color of the stone walls. Upon close examination, the walls were translucent. One could faintly see the beautiful images of the interior furnishings. Jesus touched the door and it quietly opened, receding into stone walls.

The interior was truly amazing. In the center of the room

was a glass table. On the table was a crystal bowl filled with the water of life. Around the bowl were matching crystal cups. Jesus dipped the cups in the water and gave one to each of the followers. They were grateful and thanked him sincerely. Every time they drank of this water they did so with wonder. It was a soft liquid that turned to a million bubbles when ingested. It entered each tiny cell, filling the body with energy and vitality. The crystal bowl and cups were golden in color. One could clearly see they were fashioned with much effort and care.

"What is the make-up of this crystal Master?", asked Triumph. "It is most exquisite and very delicate. The tiny carvings are created with painstaking effort. How could anyone create such a fine work of art as these?"

"You have analyzed them correctly, Triumph.", replied Jesus. "They were created most painstakingly, tear by tear, as Trust will face pain and sorrow on earth, but in the end his joy will be complete."

The followers finished their refreshing drink and put the cups of crystal back in their places. Next to the crystal was a lovely arrangement of flowers. They were living flowers that would never die or fade. They were flowers of joy, peace, longsuffering, gentleness, meekness, kindness, and love. Above the table was a lovely chandelier carved from the most precious jewels of the kingdom.

"These jewels are representative of the people Trust will influence to trust in Me," the King said softly. "See how they reflect the perfect light of the rainbow shining round the throne of God." It was amazing to see that rainbow through the roof. The King had covered the home with a golden substance. It was the golden rule. "Do unto others as you would have them do unto you." (Matthew 7:12.) Would Trust really appreciate all the flawless work his Creator had made for him? As if reading the thoughts of the questioner, Jesus answered.

"Yes, he will appreciate it greatly. He is a very humble

person. He will feel most unworthy to enter this place let alone live in it for eternity." The Master reflected on some private, far away thought as he looked out one of the large windows overlooking a beautiful garden. One could see the trim on these windows now very clearly and could tell they were created from strips of purest gold and silver. In heavens terms they would be noted as time well spent.

The garden was indeed beautiful. A small pool gleamed in the glorious light that shone from the heavens. Two, white swans glided gracefully on the water. Behind the swans a tall waterfall fell over quartz rock. It was speckled with flakes of gold, and silver hematite. The shiny pebbles of glass complemented the sparkling water of the pond. The water was flowing directly from the River of Life and was very clear. The river of life was the source of all the water in that celestial city. It never ran dry. Though some water had been taken from the crystal on the table, that bowl was now full again, waiting for the next traveler, or perhaps to remain there until Trust himself entered and drank.

There were thousands of furnishings in the wondrous palace. Many were so incredible; pen could never describe them. Not far from the table was a sofa of diligence and a chair of carefulness. Surrounding the windows were curtains of courtesy laced with golden threads of thoughtfulness. There was an entire room dedicated to reverence for God. In that room the king had carefully cushioned the floor with a material unlike anything else in the entire mansion.

"What is the floor made of?" asked one of the angels.

"It is faith," replied the King. "It only works when knelt on by the knees of prayer. When Trust meets with Me here to pray, if he uses faith, he will have access to all the treasures of heaven."

"Isn't that dangerous Master?", questioned a different angel. "Heaven has so many treasures. They do not belong on earth. If Trust can come here and remove whatever he wishes, what will he leave? He has already taken things that do not belong to him in his short stay on earth?"

"Trust will be trustworthy one day." responded the Master. "Whatever he takes from here will help him fashion his character for this better world. That is why I will freely give him all things. If he comes and takes those apples of honesty, will he not be the better for it? If he removes those diamonds of righteousness will not, he be more like his Maker? Everything in this kingdom is here for those who will occupy it someday. They can grasp hold of it by faith. Faith comes from hearing My Word, then kneeling in prayer to accept the blessings I freely offer. Every person who comes to Me, each home I build, I build using the materials they have gained while associating with Me from earth. To partake of the wonders of this kingdom, while still on earth, means they will never hunger and thirst again once they arrive in this heavenly place. What they take from Me they will keep. Everything else they receive will pass away. I freely offer all the riches of heaven to Trust because I love him more than anything here. He is worth more to Me than any of these treasures and I will freely give him all things to show him My love. Whatever he finds here he can have for it will never pass away. Earthly treasure will pass away. That is why I instructed My followers to not lay up for themselves treasures on earth where rust and moth destroy, and thieves break in and steal. I urged My beloved to lay up treasure here in heaven. (Matthew 6:19) Trust will do that someday. You will see. It will happen in time."

"You are most kind Master, and generous. Trust must love you greatly for doing all this for him."

"Yes," replied the King. "Trust will grow to love Me." but a look of sadness shadowed the face of Jesus.

The group now entered the dining room. It was spacious and lovely. On the walls were rare treasures gained from labor and heavy toil. There was a coat of armor hanging on the wall. It was the whole armor of God right down to the last piece. Trust could come here at any time and arm himself for battle with the enemy. There was a smooth stone resting on the counter. Mastery picked it up and examined it closely.

"What is this stone Jesus?", he asked.

"It is the stone that will bear the new name of Trust, Mastery." was His reply. (Mastery was another one of the elders who attended Jesus on this short walk.)

"But it is blank!" exclaimed the elder. "What will Trusts new name be?"

"Amanelohiym." was the reply.

"Whatever does it mean?"

"It means Trust in Jehovah." said Jesus. "This is the House of Trust and his name means just that, Trust."

As there were cups to drink upon entering, so now there was food to eat for any who were hungry. The fruit was of the same makeup as the flowers. It was the fruit of the Spirit, love, joy, peace longsuffering, etc. Some of those traveling with Jesus took up pieces of the food and refreshed themselves in its delicious flavor.

"Trust will come here soon and partake of this fruit." spoke Jesus almost in a whisper. "He will come soon."

There were other rooms in that pretty home. There was the crown room and the robe room. The procession noticed a beautiful garment of white hanging from a rack of gold. It radiated some of the glory of God, glowing faintly while illuminating the closet. They noticed a deep band of red along its base. None needed an explanation for this symbol. Both Triumph and Victory has similar boarders on their own garments. It was given to those who gave their lives as martyrs for the sake of Jesus.

"Is this Trust's robe? asked Victory.

"Yes, it is. It is the robe of My righteousness." replied Jesus.

"But it is so large, and he is so small." responded Triumph. "Will he ever measure up to your expectations? "asked one of the angels.

"My calling is My enabling." replied Jesus. "I have chosen and called him. He will come and bare much fruit and will be given this robe. Even now he has a portion of it but at the last trumpet. . ." Silence filled the room as Jesus paused in the middle of His sentence. He took a portion of His own robe and brushed away a tear. Looking ahead He saw the agony Trust would suffer for His name. Then Jesus repeated the last few words of His former sentence and continued. "But at the last trumpet, when he hears My voice calling him from his dusty grave, I will give him this robe in its entirety. It is not only the robe of My righteousness, but it is the robe of immortality for 'white robes were given to them and they were asked to wait a little while longer until the number of those who would shed their blood for the kingdom was completed.'" (Revelation 6:11)

As the heavenly throng exited the mansion, their attention was again called to the door. At the touch of Jesus, it closed again. One could clearly see it was made of tenderness. It glittered as the light, shining from the face of Jesus, illuminated it. For a moment, the group were lost in rapturous amazement for as they looked at the door, they saw reflecting back at them a perfect image of Christ.

"I am the door." Jesus spoke quietly. "No man can come to the Father except through Me. I am the Way, the Truth, and the Life. (John 14:6.) Trust will enter through this door and find salvation. He is almost ready to come. His home is prepared. Soon, very soon now, he will begin his journey to this glorious place and find it home. Now he is a stranger to earth, a pilgrim. This is his real home. This is the home that Trust built. Even now though he does not know it, he is looking for a city that has foundations, who's builder and maker is God. (Hebrews 11:10.) Even now his steps are approaching the narrow road for broad is the gate and wide the road that leads to destruction. (Matthew 7:13, 14) Many are on that road, but straight is the gate and narrow the road that Trust will choose. He is one of the few who will find it."

Before the group left the House of Trust each had a clear view of the foundation. They could see it was unbroken and built of a most durable material. The King had placed it there, block by block, in perfect order. The blocks were of truths carved from the Word of God. With such a foundation this house would stand forever and give glory to its Creator.

As the procession stepped back onto the silvery pools of stone, they looked again and saw that Jesus had taken great delight in landscaping the house. There were all kinds of fruit trees baring their royal harvest. Apples of honesty grew next to plums of mercy. There were oranges of compassion growing close to grapes of gratefulness. Tangerines of temperance mingled their beauty with pears of pure thought. Whatsoever things were pure, true, lovely and of good report, Trust would think on these things. (Philippians 4:8) He, as David, would set no wicked thing before his eyes. (Psalms 101:3) Somehow through the power of the Holy Spirit, he would learn how to close his eyes to the world around him and open them to heaven.

As the Creator made His way over the pebbles, the fragrant roses bent toward Him. He reached over and smelled an unusually brilliant one. For a moment He cupped it in His hand and smiled. On each rose was written "love for God and love for fellow man." Looking deep into the centers one could catch a glimpse of God's love for the sinner. The petals were trimmed in red while each center was of purest gold.

"Trials have planted these roses." remarked Jesus. "The more brilliant the flower, the greater the trial Trust will be called to bear. When he finally sets his foot in the gate, he will behold Me and by beholding, become changed. He will suffer much and sacrifice his life for Me. This is a trial he will bear."

"Why must you try him Master?" asked a nearby elder. "He is so small and if tried to deeply may not survive."

"Trust will survive, Victory, even as you survived your

struggle with Lucifer. When Trust is asked to enter this humble home, he will wear a crown of victory studded with a thousand jewels, for trust will give way to victory. Trust too will gain victory over his encounters with the enemy when he learns to truly trust Me. Why must I try him? Trials are my workmen to fashion him into a lovely vessel for service. Trust is a most precious agent. He is one of My chosen children. I have called him to do a work no other person can do. He was fashioned for a certain purpose. When he finishes his work, many will be blessed through him. In time the universe, when they hear his story, will also be blessed."

"You spoke of this mansion as humble, Master. Why? It seems more elaborate to me than most of the others you have built."

"Ah but it is humble," replied Jesus. "It is a small token of appreciation to Trust for what he will do for Me."

"What will Trust do for you?" inquired another elder.

"He will learn to love Me and choose to follow and trust Me. He will give a closing message of mercy during a time when many of My older servants will be confined to prison cells. The gift of speech will be taken from these older shepherds. When it is, Trust's voice will speak out. Thousands will hear his words and believe. They will tell others and the others will tell still others. The message Trust speaks will create a wave of souls who will enter in through the gates into this city. My Spirit will enter into him in a mighty way and he will speak out until at last his voice is silenced." Jesus lowered His head as He looked and saw the future fate of Trust.

The little group following Jesus bowed their heads also in reverence. They could not know the thoughts of the Creator nor the future of Trust, but they would trust his life in the hands of Jesus even as they had learned to trust their own lives with Him while on earth. Jesus would surely see this child through the severe trials he would be called to face. Trust would do the work he was chosen to do. Why else would Jesus spend such care in building his splendid home? Before they left his house, they could look in on Trust, down on earth. He was reading a murder mystery. His mind was far away from spiritual things. Those gathered around Jesus wondered at this. "Was this the boy Jesus was entrusting with eternal life? Was he the one who would inhabit this beautiful mansion? How could it be? When would the change come? But then again, who were they to judge this lad?" As if in answer to their silent questions, Jesus smiled slightly and again opened the foliage of paradise, then stepped onto the golden streets.

"Trust Me." He said softly. "Trust Me."

It had been a real privilege to spend these precious moments with Jesus. The time had simply flown by. The group hesitated a moment. Reading their thoughts, the Master invited them to join Him on one more tour. "Would you like to see another Home I have finished?" He asked. They needed no second invitation. The whole group chorused in unison, "Yes Master. We would like nothing better short of having all of your children gathered safely home here with You."

"Where are we going now Jesus?" questioned Faithfulness. This particular elder had been just that. He had been faithful unto death and great had been his reward in heaven.

"We are going to the Palace of Joy." was the Savior's reply.

"Is it a place similar to Trust's?" inquired another.

"No. It is very different from his," responded Jesus.

Soon the group arrived at the entrance to thousands of beautiful homes in the eastern portion of the city. They paused a moment to look up at the glory of the sight before them. A golden street wound up to an archway made of transparent jasper. The colors of the archway were deep reds and oranges with dashes of golden, yellow. At the top of the arch were inscribed the words "HOLINESS TO THE

LORD". Above the archway, stretching miles into the sky, were the beautiful homes of the Saints on this side of the city. The view took away their breath. They stood staring at it for a long, long time. These palaces were higher than any mountain on earth and more glorious then ten of our suns. Jesus had planted beautiful gardens all over and filled them with millions of colorful flowers. Among the gardens brilliant birds swung from trailing vines loaded with grapes and fruit of rarest beauty. Their unceasing songs ascended to God with unquenchable joy. Other plants of varying shades of green and gold were interspersed among the flowers. At that moment there was a flash of red and green. A brilliant parrot glided through the air and came to rest on the shoulder of Jesus.

The parrot spoke into the ear of Christ. "This is wonderful Jesus, won-der-ful."

"And beautiful." responded Victory.

"Yes, beautiful." replied the parrot. "Very beau-te-ful, Jesus." The group smiled as they heard the parrot expressing his praise for his Maker.

As if in a dreamland the group headed up the golden streets into the mansions above. Higher and higher they went. The view changed from every angle. Wide verandas curved into spiraling stairs and winding hallways. Gold and silver archways framed the entrances to intersecting terraces and spacious courtyards. Glistening stairways opened into living gardens with flowing waterfalls and vibrant, green lawns. Speaking out loud created a hundred echoes bouncing off the polished pillars and crystal walls. Thousands of tempting fruits spread their beauty before any who wished to eat them. Plum, peach, apricots, and apples of gold and silver beaconed to the hungry traveler; "Partake and be filled." The buzzing of bees blended with the beating wings of the ruby throated hummingbird. A little sparrow sang from his perch on the flowering branches of the cardinal shrub. Gems of rarity and beauty sparkled from every nook and cranny. At last, they were at Joy's Palace.

Jesus opened the door very slowly. Those closest to Him were amazed at their first glimpse of this wonder of the Creator.

"This," He said, "is the Palace of Joy." The walls were of mirrored gold fashioned from meekness and goodness. Two pillars of sacrifice and selflessness supported the ceiling. As they looked at their reflection coming from the beautiful walls, they remembered the reflection of Jesus shining back from the silver door of the House of Trust.

"If Jesus was the door, what did these walls symbolize?" Jesus directed their attention to a living sofa of self-sacrifice. It was transported from a planet far away. As Jesus visited the people there, He thought of Joy when He saw this work, and had it delivered to her home in the Holy City. It was just her size, but being a living sofa, would grow as she grew. The legs seemed planted in the marble floor and branched outward and upward holding 2 cushions of thoughtfulness. Lavender flowers of grace and joy bloomed from their branches. It was a most exquisite work of art. In front of it on the polished, marble floor was a beautiful throw rug of humility.

From the living room they entered the dining area. A beautiful table of contentment stood in the center of the room. On it were laden many of the same fruit of righteousness that were seen in the House of Trust.

Victory now asked Jesus a question. "Why do you call this a table of contentment? Though this is one of the simpler homes you have built, anyone would be content with it. If Joy is not content with this how could she be content with anything else?"

Jesus smiled back an answer. "Joy will be content with her home here. You see, Joy was born both blind and crippled. Yet she never complained. If she could be content with what earth handed her, she will be even the more content with heaven and what it gives her. Here she will be able to see and run like other children." The group paused to think on that for a while. How cruel Lucifer was to those humans under his control. Each longed for the day when sin and its originator would be no more. He had held the earth captive in his deadly vices long enough.

From the dining area they entered a guest room. It was lavishly furnished with exotic keepsakes from all over the universe. There were many simple things in that room. Little gifts of kindness and friendship, larger items of praise and glory to God. There were musical instruments of many varieties.

"Joy loved music." spoke Jesus. On dark, long, lonely, painful nights her sweet, little voice was often lifted to Me in praise. She loved people but was so deformed people did not love her back or want to be her friend. There was only one person who chose to befriend her. She was forsaken even by her parents. Wherever she travels in heaven and the universe, she will make friends. These friends will give her many little gifts. She will cherish each one as a most treasured possession. I have seen few so simple and yet so loving and content. She will be the happiest little person in all of heaven when these glories are hers forever."

Triumph now asked Jesus another question. "You speak of Joy in the past tense while you speak of Trust in the future tense. Why?"

"Trust is living now," replied Jesus. "Joy rests in her grave and will be resurrected to meet Me when I come in the clouds of heaven. On the way to this celestial city, the two will meet and become best of friends. Death will have no power over them then. They will be Mine when I come to make up My jewels."

The group exited the beautiful palace by way of the veranda. As they left, they caught a glimpse of Joy's robe of Christ's Righteousness, resting on a gold hanger under the shelf holding her crown. She also had a stone, only hers had a new name on it. One of the elders asked why. "Charaeshera, meaning joy and blessing, was christened to her shortly after her death." replied the Master. "On earth when a person dies, and their name comes up in the judgment, I judge them and give them their new name. Their name is based on their character. Trust has not been judged yet because he is still alive. When he is judged, I will engrave his new name on his stone."

With that they were out of the door. They passed a beautiful waterfall and were soon again on the streets of gold. There they said their salutations and headed for various parts of the city, each deep in thought from the things they had seen. "So that was the Palace of Joy and the beautiful home before it, the House of Trust, was it? They must be two very special children to Jesus."

I wonder today, reader. What kind of a home is Jesus building for you? What materials are you giving Him to work with? Will He have the fruit of the Spirit to adorn your table? Will He be able to hang the whole armor of God from your wall? Will your mansion be as wonderful as the House of Trust or as beautiful as the Palace of Joy? Do you have a room where you can kneel and partake of the treasures of heaven? If you do, go there often, and partake of the glorious land. Jesus freely offers you the keys to His kingdom. Prayer is the key in the hand of faith to unlock all the treasures of heaven. Pray often. Use only the best materials in life for your heavenly home. Nothing that defiles will be allowed to enter that glorious land. Jesus holds out the robe of His spotless righteousness now. Let Him clothe you with it. Let Him clothe you now. So be it.

"We are workers together for God. And you are like a farm that belongs to God: You are a house that belongs to Him. Like an expert builder I built the foundation of that house. I used the gift that God gave me to do this. Others are building on that foundation. But everyone should be careful how he builds. The foundation has already been built. No one can build any other foundation. The foundation that has already been laid is Jesus Christ. Anyone can build on that foundation, using gold, silver, jewels, wood, grass, or straw. But the work that each person does will be clearly seen, because the day will make it plain. That Day will appear with fire, and the fire will test every man's work. If the building that a man puts on the foundation still stands after the fire, he will get his reward. But if his building is burned up, he will suffer loss." (1 Corinthians 3:9-14)

CHAPTER 1
THE SILVER TABLE

A cool breeze blew across the Sea of Glass in Paradise. Stately palms swayed gently from side to side, glistening as if covered with a million tiny jewels. Beautiful flowers of brilliant hues waved proudly, lifting their heads in adoration to the King of Kings. There was a flutter of wings. A graceful parrot glided to one of the nearby branches and spoke to a couple of children.

"Joy, Trust, are you happy? Are you happy Joy and Trust?" The children smiled as they watched the bird moved its head from side to side. "Joy, Trust, are you happy?"

"Yes, we are happy, very happy and what might your name be Mr. Parrot?" "Name, Name?" questioned the parrot. "What is a name?" The children laughed and walked on. They were just at the edge of that massive, crystal sea. A long, shiny table made of transparent silver, was spread out for miles. On it set the most exquisite vessels the children had ever seen. They were covered with beautiful gems of all colors. Little relief carvings of excellent workmanship crowned each one. The vessels themselves were made of pure gold and reflected the brilliant light shining from the Throne of God. A group of white robed beings brought fruit of rarest beauty and filled each of the lovely bowls.

The children looked on with wonder. The parrot flew over.

"Joy and trust, are you happy, are you happy with your name?"

How could they be anything but happy? Ever since Jesus had come, they had known nothing but happiness. The wonders of Heaven never ceased to amaze them. As they thought back on many magnificent things that had happened to them in the last week a quiet joy and trust filled them to overflowing. How appropriate that the parrot should choose to call them "Joy" and "Trust".

"What is this long table for, Celestania?" asked the child the Parrot had called "Trust."

"This is the banquet table Little One," was the reply. "Today is the coronation day of His Majesty, Jesus." The angel bowed his head slightly as he mentioned that lovely name. "Jesus is inviting all of Heaven to a Marriage Supper. Each one present will be given their reward. You, Little One and Joy", the angel smiled as he mentioned that name, "will be given a new name. Jesus Himself has chosen it. You will be given something else too, but you will have to wait and see what it is. I am not allowed to give out any more details."

"How can I wait?" cried Joy, "I am just bubbling over with expectations! Will everyone receive this special something, Celestania?"

"Yes, Joy. Everyone will receive a very special gift from Jesus at this supper," the angel replied.

"Isn't Jesus wonderful?" commented Trust.

"Yes, He is wonderful Little One. There is no one like Him in all the Universe," replied Celestania." The angel continued placing the fruit he was carrying on the table and looked back at the children.

Sherry, called Joy by the parrot, had been Celestania's special assignment on earth. He looked at her now so happy in this new world where sin and its fearful consequences were totally erased. She had been such a joy to attend to. He had been assigned to other charges from different generations but this little one was a favorite. One had to like her. She was beautiful as only Jesus could make her. She had been beautiful on earth too, but only a few had recognized it there. It was a beauty of purpose, an inner glow that reached out and touched a person in a special way. Even this mighty angel had been touched by the love this child of the King had developed through severe trials. Life on earth had been hard for her but she had been so very grateful for even the little she had.

The children moved along the table for a while, then felt like an adventure was in order.

"Why don't we go skydiving?"

"Skydiving? What is that?"

"Have you flown much lately?" Trust asked.

"Yes, earlier today I flew over to that beautiful mountain and picked some of those star shaped flowers that grow on top. I made a wreath of them for my hair."

"When you sky dive, you fly as high as you can then just act as if you were diving," answered Trust. "I usually go above the river and zoom down until I am about to plunge in then straighten out and body surf on its shimmering waters. It is really fun."

"Oh, let's do it!" cried Joy. "That sounds absolutely marvelous! I'll race you there, Trust!" With that she was in and air, soaring higher and higher. The children made a couple of circles around the beautiful rainbow that spanned the center of the great city, then started their dive. It was good to feel the wind stream through their hair and go gliding over their nimble bodies. As they neared the river, they turned their necks a little and went gliding over the cool, crystal water. It splashed over and around them. Two trails of sparkling white bubbles stretched out behind them for several feet as they skimmed along. It was truly invigorating to be a part of this lovely place. Soon they were in the air again rising higher and higher. A Bible text came to Trust as he rode the air waves. "but those who hope in the Lord will renew their strength. They will soar on wings like eagles; they will run and not grow weary; they will walk and not be faint." (Isaiah 40:31.) Trust felt his strong wings, wings like the eagle. The Lord was good beyond measure.

Meanwhile, back at the table, the preparations were just about finished. King David and Jonathon were walking together beneath those same stately palms.

"A King, a King," cried the parrot.

"Yes, he is a king Mr. Parrot," replied Jonathon. "One of the mightiest kings ever."

"No Jonathon," replied King David. "I am but a poor shepherd boy. He is the King of Kings."

Jesus was walking with a group of people and came over to King David.

"You were a good King, 'Shepherd Boy'." As He mentioned the name "Shepherd Boy" a lovely smile crossed the face of the matchless, Son of God.

"You will guide my people well, David." He placed His hand on the shoulder of the king and drew him close. His mighty arms surrounded the person He had called. "A man after My own heart." Turning, He gave Jonathon a warm embrace also.

"You were one of my most faithful, Jonathon, and David's most loyal friend. Behold everything around you! This is the city you helped build by your faithfulness."

"How wonderful it is to have Jesus with us Jonathon," David commented as the Savior moved on. "If I had anything, I could give Him I would gladly sacrifice all, but He has need of nothing. Everything I have is His. When I saw the vision of His crucifixion, every nail driven into Him pierced my soul. I would have taken His place in a minute if I could. I owe Him everything and yet can give Him nothing. Never in a million years can I repay my debt to Him."

"I know David. I feel the same way. I too owe Him everything," was Jonathon's reply. "To think He left all of this beauty to come down to our world. I will never be able to understand it."

Jonathon looked off toward the great, golden, water fountains. He took in the evergreen hills seen clearly through the open gateways of the city. Beyond the hills he saw the mountains where Joy had plucked the flowers for her hair. He saw the River of Life flowing through the valley as it passed out of the city, winding its way through the trees and flowers planted there for his enjoyment. He looked at the gates of pearl with their rainbow colors reflecting the surpassing glory of the wonders all around them. He looked down at the golden streets, transparent like glass, and saw the reflection of the great rainbow round God's throne. Then he knelt and looked deep into those glorious streets and saw a reflection there in the polished finish. A perfect mirrored likeness of himself looked back at him and there looking over his shoulder was King David. Could he ask for more than this? With a soft voice, nearly like a whisper, he continued speaking.

"Here Jesus is adored by everyone. Even the angels bow in reverence when He draws near. There He was nothing. He was hated by so many. Now I understand clearly what His plan was. My only regret is I did not do more to promote this Kingdom of His to those around me while on earth. If I were able to go back and live my life over again that is what I would change first, my response to His love for me."

"I too would change things were I to live a life down there again," responded King David. "By His grace, I would change a lot of things."

Just then a mighty trumpet blew. As the crystal-clear sounds pierced the air an echo returned from a million glittering spirals. It was as if all the bells of heaven were ringing, each giving their own lovely sound. Could these be wedding bells? A great hush fell over the vast assembly gathered near the glittering table. Jesus was about to speak.

BIBLE TEXTS

"Be cautious. Don't think these little children are worth nothing. I tell you that they have angels who are always with my Father in heaven."
Matthew 18:10

"I tell you this: I will not drink of this fruit of the vine again until the day I drink it new with you in my Father's kingdom."

Matthew 26:29

"Many citizens will come from the east and west. They will sit and eat with Abraham, Isaac, and Jacob in the kingdom of heaven."

Matthew 8:11

"Come, My Father has given you his blessing. Arise and receive the kingdom God has prepared for you since the world was created."

Matthew 25:34

CHAPTER 2
COME TO SUPPER

At the sound of the trumpet all eyes were fastened on Jesus. A brilliant crown adorned His head. His face was all glorious. His eyes were clear and so full of love they could contain the whole Universe and still have room for each one present. He smiled as He looked over the vast assembly. Joy saw that look of love and knelt in reverence as His gaze reached her. She could not pull away from Him. In that gaze of love she felt as if her very soul was laid out before Him. His love awakened a responding love in her own heart. She felt she must take in that love or forever lose something. Trust too felt that love and bowed in humility before his Maker. The entire company was bowing. Each realized how unworthy they were of such love yet how much they were worth to this Kindly King.

"Rise up My children." As the voice of Jesus rang out the lovely songs of millions of angels broke the stillness. The music ascended higher and higher and the entire company was lost in the sound of that rapturous melody. Joy unspeakable throbbed in the heart of each one present and they found themselves singing along with the accompanying angels.

"Worthy, Worthy is the Lamb. Worthy, Worthy is the Lamb." Jesus was speaking again now. His voice was music personified.

"Come, My people, you have come out of great tribulation, and done My will; suffered for Me; come to supper, for I will gird Myself, and serve you." The complete company responded in one voice "ALLELUIA! GLORY!" (Early Writings p. 19.)

Trust looked at the table now with wonder in his eyes. It was laden with all kinds of fruit. There were pomegranates, grapes, almonds, apples, pears, figs, and oranges so large that it would take two hands to hold them. Each fruit appeared translucent as the brilliant light of that Holy Place fell upon it. There was a pure white substance on that table that reflected the colors of the rainbow shining over God's throne.

"What is this white fruit Celestania," Trust asked?

"That is not fruit Trust," the angel responded. "It is Manna."

"Manna," questioned Trust? "Isn't that what the children of Israel ate in the wilderness?"

"Yes, Little One. The very same food from Heaven."

"It must be very delicious," replied Trust.

"It is, Little One. This Manna is especially good. You will see." With that the angel bid the child sit down. Joy was sitting across the table from Trust. She glanced at him shyly and beamed one of her more radiant smiles. It was a smile so beautiful it seemed as if it had the power to make even the flowers bloom. He returned it with a smile of his own. At that moment there was a flash of brilliant red and green. The parrot glided to Trust's shoulder.

"Trust me, Trust me," cried the bird and settled down to combing Trust's hair with his beak.

Celestania left momentarily. Jesus was making His way to the table. In His hands he carried a large crystal tray covered with a golden fruit such as none but our first parents had ever seen. He came to the side of the stately Adam. A solemn stillness came over everyone as the father of our race looked deep into the eyes of his Savior. As he saw the wounded hand that held out the fruit to him a tear moistened that noble cheek. Jesus lovingly took a towel and wiped it away then embraced that benevolent being.

"Enter into the joy of your Lord Adam. You have fought a good fight. You have finished your work. Enter into My rest." Everyone there responded with "ALLELUIA! AMEN!", as Adam took the fruit and placed it on his plate. The King of Kings lowered the tray and put a brilliant crown on Adam's head. The name "ADAM" stood out in dazzling letters. There was a luminous, star-shaped stone of a deep ruby red color in the center. Beneath it were engraved the words "SAVED BY THE BLOOD OF THE LAMB". Adam took off his crown and placed it at the nail-pierced feet of the Lamb, then bowed to the ground.

"I am not worthy of such a gift Master. You must take it and give it to someone else, someone who is more worthy." Jesus knelt and gently picked up the father of our race, restored the crown to his head, then turned to Eve. A beautiful expression was upon her face. The whole assembly noticed it and read the love that animated from her being. Her long hair glistened with a thousand colors as it reflected the pure atmosphere of that glorious place. Of all the woman in heaven, none were as beautiful as Eve. She was a masterpiece. As she looked into the eyes of her Redeemer, she too felt His love flooding through her.

"Eve. Here is the fruit of the tree of life. Those who eat of this fruit will never die. Eat, Eve. Partake of the fruit of this land that your joy may be full." He placed a glorious crown upon her head bearing her name. She too cast it at His feet and threw herself on the ground. Jesus stooped and quietly lifted the mother of our race, then bid her look on the company gathered at the table.

"Behold your children, Eve. Behold your children." Placing one arm around Adam and the other around Eve He spoke in a voice that filled all heaven with its sweet assurance. "These Adam have accepted the invitation to My Marriage Supper. These are your children. Never again will they say 'I hunger, I thirst' for I will feed them from My table. I will give them to drink from the well of water that springs up into Everlasting Life. No thorn will pierce them, no wicked one offend. None will say I am sick, neither will they die, for I will comfort them. I will sustain them. I will lead them by the gentle ways, for they are Mine forever. I made them and I have purchased them back from Satan. They are twice Mine."

As Jesus finished speaking the angels could contain their joy no longer. A quiet rapturous melody broke forth from their lips. Gabriel struck a note higher and all voices responded in praising God. Louder and louder grew the anthem until the whole of Heaven swelled with that matchless song. "Worthy, Worthy is the Lamb."

Jesus embraced our first parents for a long time then turned and motioned for them to look off to His right. A huge curtain of light covered something, concealing it from the millions of redeemed seated at the silver table. The air was charged with expectancy as the King of Kings lifted one of his nail pierced hands and drew the curtain aside. For a few moments it rolled on and on, opening wider and still wider. There in front of everyone stood The Garden of Eden. Brilliant streams of light flashed from the sky and passed over the surpassing loveliness of the place like gigantic spotlights pointing out the marvelous wonders contained therein.

Gold and silver trunked trees towered upward, spreading their bows outward, forming a canopy of living green. Vineyards with their weighty fruit of red and violet dotted the restful meadows. Gardens with thousands of delicate flowers shone brilliantly as the streams of light illuminated them. Great rivers and crystal waterfalls graced the rolling hills while tall, stately mountains towered heavenward. The palm swayed gently from side to side as its branches, loaded with dates, hung down. There was the citrus grove Adam and Eve had planted. It was mature now with its golden, yellow, and orange fruit in reach of all who would partake and eat. Adam looked at the dwelling his own hands had fashioned. There was the climbing rose he had trained with his own fingers. It towered up and framed a building of breathtaking beauty. It was the same home he had built with Michael the Archangel and his beautiful wife, Eve, at his side. Dark sweet cherries hung from the very trees he had planted and trained. He looked in the silver trimmed window and saw his home just as he had left it that fearful day six thousand years earlier. He saw the door and remembered leaving it for the last time. Beside it, a bed of pineapple grew, filling the air with their sweet, tantalizing fragrance. Off to the left of the golden, stone walk, a large banana plant pointed upward, bearing its load of golden fruit. Apples of red and gold tempted him to enter and partake.

As Adam saw it all, a flood of memories swept over him and He thought of the many happy hours he and Eve had enjoyed in this place of their innocence. He saw the very first animals he had befriended and named. They came to the edge of the garden and looked at him with an inviting twinkle in their eyes. He strolled over to a doe and her mate and stroked them behind the ears. A small rabbit bounded up, twitching its nose as it looked up at him. A great lion with his mate came and lay down at his feet then started purring like a big, contented kitten. From behind the home, his dog came running out, wagging its tail. It was carrying an onyx stone in its mouth. Adam remembered the hours he had spent roaming the garden with this pet by his side. He reached down and took the stone from the dog's mouth and threw it far into one of the meadows. It bounded away to retrieve the gem, grateful for the return of its master.

Eve joined him now and the two took a short walk over the plush green carpet interspersed with millions of colorful flowers. These where the very flowers Eve had planted with her own hands. Tears streamed freely down her cheeks as she took in the surpassing loveliness of it all. They were not tears of sadness. No, no, a thousand times no. Her tears were tears of joy and happiness. She remembered taking those same bulbs from another place in the garden and transplanting them in this very spot. As the realization dawned on them this truly was their garden home, restored more lovely than ever, they returned to the side of the Matchless, Son of God and cast themselves at His feet once more.

"We are not worthy of this Master," they cried. "We

forfeited our right to this place when we disobeyed You. You keep it. It is yours and yours alone. How can we ever dwell in it again, realizing what it cost you to reclaim it from the earth our sins destroyed." Once again Jesus reached down and lifted the two saintly beings to their feet.

"Behold your garden Adam and Eve. It is before you. Go in and take possession of it. I will never take it from you. It is for you and these your children to enjoy forever. Its fruit is your fruit. Its vineyards are your vineyards. The flowers are your flowers. Eternal life is yours forever. All this is yours forever and ever." Jesus raised His hand and made a motion that took in all of Heaven. Come and take possession. Come to Supper!"

Oh, priceless moment, when we are gathered at the feet of Jesus to partake of the "Marriage Supper of the Lamb." The table is even now being stretched out. He is placing the name tags at each setting. Come to Supper, Reader. Place your name on the line and determine that you will be in that company of the redeemed. I _____ _____ will, by the grace of God, be at that Supper in Heaven with Jesus and eat the fruit of The Tree of Life.

BIBLE TEXTS

"Now the Lord God had planted a garden east, in Eden; and there He put Adam whom he had formed."

Genesis 2:8

"And the Lord God said, 'Adam has now become like one of us, knowing good and evil. He must not be allowed to reach out his hand and eat fruit from the tree of life and live forever.' So, the Lord God banished him from the Garden of Eden, to work the ground from which he had been formed."

Genesis 3:22, 23

"For if, by the transgression of Adam, death reigned through that one man, how much more will those who receive God's abundant provision of grace and of the gift of righteousness reign in life through the second Adam, one man, Jesus Christ."

Romans 5:17

"I believe that our present distresses are not worth comparing with the glory that will be revealed in us. The creation waits in eager expectation for the sons of God to be revealed. For the world was exposed to adversity, not by its own choice, but by the will of the one who enslaved it. Now we hope and long for nature itself to be liberated from its bondage and decay and brought into the glorious freedom of the children of God."

Romans 8:18-21

"Blessed are those who receive an invitation to the marriage supper of the Lamb."

Revelation 19:9

"It will be profitable for those servants whose master finds them watching when he comes. I tell you the truth, he will dress himself and serve them. He will have them lounge at the table and will come and wait on them."

Luke 12:37

"These are the people who have come out of the great tribulation; they have washed their robes and made them white in the blood of the Lamb. Because of this, 'they are before the throne of God and serve Him day and night in His sanctuary; and He who sits on the throne will spread His shelter over them. Never again will they hunger; never again will they thirst. The sun will not beat upon them, there will be no scorching heat. For the Lamb at the center of the throne will be their Shepherd; He will lead them to springs of living water. And God will wipe away all tears from their eyes.'"

Revelation 7:14-17

CHAPTER 3
A NEW NAME AND CROWN

I suppose in terms of earth's time the Marriage Supper of Jesus would have lasted for weeks. To the happy throng gathered around that great, silver table however, time was forgotten. Jesus made His way down the line, giving each a golden fruit and a crown of life bearing their new name. Excitement was at a maximum. Joy inexpressible marked the faces of each one present. It was a celebration such as none on earth have ever experienced.

Some of the crowns were heavy with stars and gems of rarest beauty, others were simple with few stars but not one crown was entirely void of stars. All seemed perfectly happy with their crown and new name. The widow who had given two mites received a crown so covered with gems that one could barely see the crown itself. Truly she had laid up for herself treasure in heaven. Little Hattie Wiatt was there. When Jesus came to her, she was given a glorious crown filled with hundreds of glittering jewels. He gently placed it on her head, raised her in His arms, and bid the angels sing a special anthem for her. I'll tell you about her story.

Hattie decided to go to church one day, so with the love of Jesus animating from her heart she set off. She bounded up the steps and opened the large church door. A deacon frowned down at her.

"What do you want," he asked?

"I have come to go to church today, mister," was her smiling reply. "May I come in? I want to meet Jesus."

"Jesus isn't here," replied the deacon gruffly, "and the church is too full for the likes of you. Go on home now." You see, Hattie was very poor. She had put on her very best, ragged dress to meet with Jesus, but it was not good enough for the deacon. Sadly, with tears streaming down her cheeks she went out the door. All heaven was saddened at the sight of this precious little one weeping. Jesus marked each tear that fall from those crying eyes. Though there was no room found for her in the heart of the deacon, the pastor heard her sobs and went out to see what the crying was all about. When he heard she had been turned away, it upset him greatly. "No room in his church? There would always be room in his church for anyone who wanted to come and worship Jesus," he spoke quietly to himself. He picked little Hattie up and set her down beside him in the front. That day while delivering his message he received a vision of a great work to be done in the poorer sections of his city. Like this pastor, the King of Kings and Lord of Lords also made a special place for Hattie in Heaven. He looked down the years to the Marriage Supper and decided then and there that Hattie would have her reward when He came to make up His jewels. Something went out of Hattie that day. Her little heart was broken. Her desire to live waned. A couple of years passed, and the pastor of this same church was called to conduct the funeral of this little girl. After the service, her parents presented him with a small, red purse. In it he found this note. "For the Pastor, to help him build a bigger church, so that everyone can come and worship Jesus." That little purse contained fifty-seven pennies. Somehow, she had managed to save them one by one, week by week, until she could save no more.

What about those pennies? Were they worth anything to Jesus? Yes, yes, a thousand times yes. No price can be put on those pennies gathered one by one for such a long time. When her story came out, over a quarter of a million dollars flowed into the treasury and today on that same location, a large, beautiful church stands as a tribute to Hattie's sacrifice. Above the door is a sign that reads "WELCOME, EVERYONE." Yes, Hattie will be at that Supper with Jesus and she will be given a very special reward. Many thousands of people will be there that had no place on earth. People who were despised, rejected, tormented, and tried for the sake of Jesus. Paul tells us in Hebrews that the world was not worthy of these faithful ones, but Jesus found them worthy and they will be there at that supper table with Him. For the ceaseless ages of eternity, they will enjoy fellowship with the One whom they loved so dearly.

But now, I must get back to our story. As Jesus approached nearer and nearer to Joy her excitement mounted to its highest peak. Would He give her a crown of her very own? Finally, it was her turn. She looked up, up, up, and there He stood smiling down at her. She smiled back. Then Jesus knelt behind her and handed her one of the golden fruits from the tray. She took it in her trembling hands and looked at it with interest. It was nearly transparent. Inside she could see some strands of radiant, red, and gold that gave it a depth of color unlike anything she had ever seen.

"This is beautiful Jesus," she exclaimed! "How did you make it so beautiful? It is too pretty to eat. Must I eat it Jesus, or can I keep it as a special present from you?"

"You may keep it if you like CHAR-A-ES-HER-A." replied Jesus. "Char-a-es-her-a," exclaimed Joy! "Is that my very own new name?"

"Yes, Sherry that is your very own, new name," smiled Jesus.

"It is a wonderful name Jesus, what does it mean?"

"It means Joy and blessings," came the soft answer.

"I will always cherish it Jesus," responded Joy shyly. "Thank you so much for this beautiful fruit and the wonderful name. I love you Jesus."

"And I love you Char-a-es-her-a. Here is a crown and a stone with your new name engraved in it."

With that, Jesus removed the flowers from Joy's hair and wove them neatly in and out among the jewels of her crown, then placed it on her head. He lifted her gently in His arms so all could see.

"Meet Charaeshera!" announced Jesus. "She is one of my special little ones. She has brought Me much joy and blessing." As Joy looked out over the group of people setting around that table, she saw millions and millions of smiling faces looking back at her. So much love radiated from them she felt like each one was her choicest friend. A thousand welcomes came from the happy throng. Some of the people were waving at her. She waved back, then looked deep into the eyes of Jesus. For the moment nothing else mattered. She rested her curly head on His soft cheek.

"I want to be with you always Jesus. "May I always be with you?"

"Yes, you may Charaeshera. You can be with me whenever you like." He then gently placed her on the sea of glass and pulled the chair back for her to again be seated.

As Joy looked at the robe of Jesus, she was surprised at how tall He was. She came a little above His knees. From a distance He looked only a little taller than the rest of the men at the table but now He towered above most of them. Only Adam came close to Him in stature. How, she wondered, will I ever grow up to His size? It seemed like an impossibility now. She took off her crown and looked at it. Jesus bent down again and with a loving smile on His face, gave her another fruit.

"You will need to eat one of these fruits if you ever expect to grow up, Charaeshera." He then went on to the next person at the table.

Charaeshera's crown had five stars on it. There was a large violet one in the middle, surrounded by a white pearly substance that radiated a stream of sparkling lines. The lines were first blue, then green, then yellow, then red, then orange. Every color imaginable was represented. It depended on which way she turned the crown. The other gems were of four different colors. Each were surrounded with a shiny transparent, mirrored finish that reflected the glories all around her. In looking at these mirror-like gems, it appeared her crown had hundreds of jewels. She sat there in admiration at the wonder of it all then picked up the second fruit Jesus had given her. She compared it with the first fruit. The two looked nearly the same. She put it up to her nose and smelled it. A sweet perfume came from the area around where it had been attached to the Tree of Life. She squeezed it a bit and a tiny drop of nectar came to the surface. Slowly she extended her tongue until it touched the tiny drop. It was the sweetest taste ever to enter her mouth. There was something in it that was alive and vitalizing. A current of life began at her tongue and made its way into her body, filling each cell with new life and vigor. She took a bite and slowly dissolved the sweet flavor thoughtfully. The fruit was not like an apple. It was more of a thick jelly substance, a solidified nectar that enlivened her whole being. She wondered greatly.

Thinking of all the things that had transpired over the last several hours, there was something she pondered. Most of the people gathered at the table were in family groups. There were mothers and fathers with children. In some instances, there was a single parent with one or several children. She looked at the people around her. They spoke to her and included her as a part of Heaven, but none acted like a parent to her. Trust had met her shortly after Celestania lifted her heavenward from the dreadful earth in all its devastation. He had acted like a brother to her. She had no brothers or sisters. In the seven days they were ascending to Heaven, she had been so awed by the events around her, she had neglected to ask her guardian angel about her family. She determined to do that soon. There must be someone who knew all about them.

She thought back a moment on the Sabbath the great throng had spent on a beautiful planet. She could still see the three moons that surrounded it, and the reddish sun that gave the whole atmosphere a tinted appearance. She remembered the people there, the flowers, the birds, and the many strange animals. There were animals unlike any on earth. She was so limited in knowledge and there was so much to take in, how could she ever wait for the next moment to unfold? Life was one joyful experience after another. She again thought of Jesus and the comfort she had experienced while in His mighty arms. He loved her. Jesus loved Charaeshera. So few people had loved her on earth, she felt she couldn't get enough of the love that permeated this perfect place.

Now she turned her attention to the basket of fruit in front of her. She reached out and selected a choice, red grape and held it in both of her little hands. It was delicious! She took some manna and dissolved it slowly in her mouth. Trust talked about the people in the wilderness who were given manna to eat. He told her the taste of it was like "wafers made with honey." Trust knew so much and she so little. Who was he? Why had he selected her out from among so many? She looked over at him. He was talking to his father and was that his sister? She would have to ask him. Did he have a mother in Heaven? There were so many questions that required answering. But she had forever to find out all the answers, forever, and ever, and ever, and ever! Eternal life! This was the greatest gift of all. She, Charaeshera, would live forever?! She would never be alone no matter what. Had not Jesus said she could be with Him whenever she liked? That was enough for her. To be with Jesus forever was enough indeed!

BIBLE TEXTS

"Now there is in store a crown of righteousness, which Jesus, the righteous Judge, will award to me on that day and not only to me, but also to all who have longed for his coming."

2 Timothy 4:8

"They will see His face. His name will be engraved on their foreheads."

Revelation 22:4

"Blessed is the man who endures trial, because when he has stood the test, he will receive the crown of life that God has promised to those who love Him."

James 1:12

"The nations will see your righteousness, and the monarchs your glory; you will be called by a new name that Jesus will give you. You will be a crown of beauty in the Lord's hand, a royal jewel in the palm of your God."

Isaiah 62:2, 3

"To him who is victorious, I will give some of the concealed manna. I will also give him a white stone with a new name written on it, a name that is known only to the one who receives it."

Revelation 2:17

"I am coming quickly. Hang on to what you have been given, so that no one will steal your crown."

Revelation 3:11

CHAPTER 4
AMANELOHIYM

Before she knew it, the happy celebration was over and many of the Saintly beings rose from the table to move off to different parts of the great city. The glory of the place was dazzling. Beauty beyond description lay before them as they moved freely from place to place. Joy wanted to go to the Tree of Life and see if she could locate where the fruit had been picked from the branches. She looked up and Trust was smiling down at her.

"Hello Char-a-es-her-a," welcomed Trust with a brilliant smile that showed his sparkling white teeth. "What a lovely name you have. I like it very much."

"Do you really like it Trust, do you?"

"Yes Joy. It is a very beautiful name."

"I like it too," replied the girl. "I like your name also." She looked up at the crown Trust was wearing and stared in wonder and amazement. Unlike her crown, his was made with white gold. The gold went from a denser look at the base to nearly transparent at the top. She noticed that his crown was also trimmed with a ruby red band where it fit on his head. The most startling thing about it was the number of starry gems it contained. They were nearly numberless. In the center of the crown were carved the letters "AMANELOHIYM." "Am-an-e-lo-hiym?" questioned Joy. "Whatever does your name mean?"

"It means Trust in Jehovah," replied her friend. "When I was on earth," and a bit of a sadness crossed his face as he mentioned earth, "I had no faith in God. One evening I picked up my Bible and God spoke to me. I knew a lot of what the Bible taught. My father was a minister. He instructed my sister and I in the Word, but I chose not to believe it until I heard His voice." A faraway look came into the eyes of Trust and he gazed off at the distant mountains shimmering in the glories of the silver, blue sky. "His voice was clear like it was at the Supper. I did not go as He bid. Over the next several weeks, His voice came again and again like it did to Samuel, only each time it was a little softer and more distant."

"Then I heard it no more, only an echo. That echo changed my life. He told me to go into the city and preach. I was a child. I never felt I could preach. Preaching was for older people like my father. My father had been imprisoned for preaching. I saw them beat him and wanted no part in that. As I think back it seemed there weren't many adult preachers left. When I went, it was with reluctance like Jonah. But I went. I went." As Trust mentioned the sentence "I went," a smile graced his face and a spark of life entered his eyes as he cried louder, "I went, and that has made all the difference. They killed me several nights after I started speaking. The next thing I knew, Jesus was looking down at me from that glorious cloud. His face Joy was so loving after seeing all those angry faces around me, I thought I was dreaming. I pinched myself and started talking out loud to see if I could really speak again. You see, a bullet went through my voice box. I could not even cry out. Then it was all black until I saw Him. Oh, Joy. I would do it all over if I were on earth and He called again. Only this time I would go at the first call and not wait for the echo. As I was speaking, I saw a young man begin to cry and run off. I don't even know what I said now to make him cry. It was like another voice, another person speaking through me. It was my voice, but it was not me."

"We were forbidden to speak of God in the city. Hundreds of people were imprisoned and tortured. Satan had taken his throne on earth. At first people everywhere believed he was Jesus. He looked like him. When people asked him for a sign-like they asked Jesus when He was on earth-Satan would look up to the sky, stretch out his hands and bolts of jagged lightening would streak down and burn up whatever he wanted. Then the thunder would come, and the earth would shake. Sometimes the lightening would come down and strike people dead. None dared oppose him except the believers in the true Jesus. As I looked out over the crowd gathered beneath me in that city, I saw hundreds of angry faces looking back at me. It was like facing a thousand angry demons. Among the people though, were others who listened and cried. I learned to trust God those few nights and that is why He gave me this name. I only wished I had learned to trust Him sooner. Once I did turn my life over to His control, there was no going back. I gave Him everything I had, and He gave me everything I needed in return, even the words I was to speak."

The children had been walking toward the Tree of Life as Trust was telling his story. It was before them now in all its splendor. Beneath its two trunks, flowed a crystal river. The river ran through what appeared to be a canal of transparent gold. It was the main street of the New Jerusalem. The river of life flowed down the middle of the street. Joy bent down and dipped her hands in the cool refreshing waters. Beautiful gems, forming intricate patterns, were embedded in the sides of the canal. There were figures of grapes, vines, leaves and patterns of extraordinary beauty and color. Everything was lustrous in appearance and had a polished look that reflected the glory coming from Jesus. The trunks of the Tree of Life were made of transparent gold mixed with silver. Joy noticed the fruit hanging from the graceful branches. It was not the same as she carried in her hand. She would not be able to see where her fruit had been picked from. A new fruit grew that was a deep golden, red; rayed with silver streaks. The shape was that of a pear only perfect in symmetry. It brought an exclamation of amazement from her voice as she reached out to touch it. The leaves of the tree were a golden green and appeared translucent. She plucked a leaf and handed it to Trust. He took it and chewed on it slowly. The flavor of the leaf was like a sweet mint and a fragrance rushed upon the air, adding to the beauty of the moment. Joy then took a leaf and nibbled on it also.

"This leaf taste wonderful," Trust spoke at last. "It has a satisfying feeling about it that enters my being. I feel real peace. Nothing on earth is comparable to this. It makes me feel as if even the worst trials there were but nothing. I suppose I had many trials, but they seem so insignificant. I only wished I had been able to reach more people. I have all these gems in my crown, and I don't know why, or who they represent." At this time, a young man came up to Trust and smiled down at him with great satisfaction animating from his eyes.

"Thank you Am-an-e-lo-hiym for telling me about Jesus. If you had not come into the city night after night and spoke, I would not be here now enjoying this lovely place. Your messages touched me, and I went away broken like Peter. I had rejected God but when you spoke, and I later saw them kill you, I vowed to make your story live. I went away and spoke to others about Jesus and His coming. Thank you for sharing God's love with me. I owe my presence here entirely to you."

As Trust looked into the eyes of the young man, he thought he recognized him. Then he remembered. "It was not my doing La-son-aph. The Spirit of God entered me shortly after I turned my steps toward the city, and Jesus did the rest. Give Glory to Jesus."

"I do give Him glory and honor. He is the only reason why any of us are here," replied Lasonaph. "But thank you for being His instrument. Thank you so much!" Lasonaph extended his hand to Trust then drew him into a loving embrace. "Thanks again," he whispered. "I have brought along some friends who want to meet you. These are the people who heard the story of Jesus from my lips after I heard it from yours." The lad pointed to a large company of people at his side then continued speaking. "We are touring

Heaven to find everyone who is here because of what you said. We have over five hundred in this group alone and there may be many more. You told me along with several more people. We told others and they told even more. As a result, we are all here because of you. God used you in a way He could use no one else. We all owe our presence here to the words you gave us from Jesus, and His sacrifice of love."

Joy looked at the group with wide eyed wonderment. Hundreds perhaps even thousands of people were in Heaven because of her friend, Trust. No wonder his crown was covered with so many jewels. All these people were there because he listened to that voice, that echo, and obeyed. How often she had heard that still small voice speaking to her own soul. She remembered listening to it and obeying its prompting. She remembered other times when she had not listened and felt the guilt. Perhaps, if she had obeyed the prompting of that voice at those other times, there would be people in Heaven because of her. She would be so happy to meet these people. She would have a real family then. She would have a mother, a father, grandparents and perhaps even sisters and brothers like Trust. It would be so wonderful! But she knew that there was no one in Heaven because of her. How could there be? She had never told anyone about Jesus.

Lasonaph was introducing each person to Trust. He was amazed as they kept coming one after another. The parrot was also amazed at the popularity of his chosen friend. He whirred through the air and landed on the boy's head.

"Trust him, trust him," cried the bird as each person came near.

"We did trust him, Mr. Parrot, and that made all the difference." The group moved on along the winding streets and terraced gardens while the parrot fluttered from shoulder to shoulder. Others joined the company and still others. The mighty angels that attended these dear people, went throughout the entire realm of Heaven, and gathered all the people together that had been touched by the messages of Trust those cold nights when he faced the world alone. There were hundreds and hundreds of them.

The reunion lasted for several hours as numberless praises ascended to the throne of God. Joy stood in awe at it all. She still could not figure out why He had selected her as his special friend while traveling to this beautiful place. If he had so many friends, why had he come to her? While she was meditating on this theme, the lad walked over and placed his arm around her small frame.

"I would like you to meet my adopted sister."

"Joy, Joy!" cried the parrot.

"She is a joy to know, friends," responded Trust at the parrot's remark. "Shortly after Jesus came, my little friend smiled at me and I couldn't resist her. She charmed me through and through with that smile. I adopted her as my little sister right then. We had a wonderful time traveling together to this glorious place. She is part of the family too." Joy was introduced to everyone in the group and made many friends there beneath the swaying palms of that better land that waits for you and me. The family of God is all inclusive. No one will be left out, in Heaven. No one will ever be lonely again. There will be no heartaches in this land of plenty beyond the blue. We will all be one, big, happy family with Jesus as King of all. Slowly the group dispersed until only Lasonaph remained with Amanelohiym and Charaeshera. The two lads talked on for a long time.

BIBLE TEXTS

"If you are faithful even unto death, I will give you a crown of life."

Revelation 2:10

"I give you praise Father, Lord of heaven and earth, because you have hidden these things from the wise and educated and shown them to little children."

Matthew 11:25

"Then the angel showed me the river, with the water of life, clear as crystal, flowing from the throne of God and of the Lamb through the middle of the large street in the city. On each side of the river stood the Tree of Life yielding its fruit every month. And the leaves of the tree are for healing the nations...They will not need the light of the sun, for Jesus will be The Light. And they will live for ever and ever."

Revelation 22:1-5

"Blessed are those who keep his commandments, for they will have access to the tree of life and will enter into the city through its gates."

Revelation 22:14

"Jesus answered, 'Everyone who drinks of this water will thirst again, but whoever drinks of the water I provide will never thirst. Indeed, the water I give him will become in him a spring of water bubbling up into eternal life.'"

John 4:13, 14

"The Spirit and the Bride say 'Come!' And let him who hears, come! Whoever is thirsty, let him come; and whoever wishes may take the free gift of the water of life."

Revelation 22:17

"The Lord is not slow in keeping His promise, as some

understand slowness. He is patient with you, not wanting anyone to be lost, but everyone to come to repentance. But the day of the Lord will come like a thief. The heavens will disappear with a roar; the elements will be destroyed by fire. The earth and everything in it will be laid bare. Since everything will be destroyed, what kind of people ought you to be? You ought to live holy and godly lives as you look forward to the day of God, speeding its coming. That day will bring about the destruction of the heavens and earth by fire, and the elements will melt in the heat. But in keeping with His promise, we are looking forward to a new heaven and a new earth, the home of righteousness. So then, dear friends, since you are looking forward to this, make every effort to be found without fault, blameless and at peace with Him."

2 Peter 3:9-14

CHAPTER 5
THE THRONE

Joy smiled her lovely smile as she watched the two talk. When there was a break in the conversation, she told them she wanted to go to her home in the city and put her fruit away. Trust nodded and she left.

"I'll catch up with you soon, Joy," he called after her. She came to the river. With a graceful leap, and a little help from her wings, she easily cleared the canal and landed on the other side. She looked backward and upward to God's Throne then knelt and looked at it again. There was a deep fountain at its base. This was the source of the River of Life. The throne rested on what appeared to be a sea of ice or glass, clear as crystal. The sea stretched away from the base of the throne for miles. Her eyes traveled up, and there, high above the city, was the actual throne. It was framed by two massive pillars that extended up forever it seemed. The tops of the pillars were surrounded by a triple rainbow, a rainbow, within a rainbow, within a rainbow. The throne itself was of a burnished, pearly white substance all glorious and all brilliant. In and around it were some beautiful, living creatures that unceasingly cried "HOLY, HOLY, HOLY. HOLY IS THE LORD."

A light mist surrounded the throne. She could see The Father seated there in all His Splendor and Majesty. Prophets descriptions portrayed Him as the "Ancient of Days". (Daniel 7:13) His eyes were as flaming fire and He looked back and forth over the city. Many angels were ministering to Him, flying to various locations in the shimmering metropolis. Sweet music came from somewhere behind the throne and went out all over heaven. The birds of Paradise sang along as the anthem swelled and lowered in tone. The top of this great throne had been on the cloud when it came to earth to gather the elect. It had led the way back to the beautiful city. And now it rested in its central location within the New Jerusalem.

While looking with awe on all this splendor, Jesus came to Joy and picked her up in His mighty arms.

"I am taking you to meet My Father," He spoke softly. "To Him who overcomes I will grant to sit with Me on My throne!" The melodious words thrilled Joy through and through as she was born higher and higher into the air. Jesus was going to let her sit with Him on His throne? She couldn't believe it. Soon she was by the Father. He smiled at her and spoke her name lovingly.

"Charaeshera! My Son has spoken of you often and your joyful nature has been an inspiration to many. When you were born blind and crippled, most of the people around you did not understand why We allowed such a thing to happen. You were never bitter about your condition. You always looked on the bright side of life even though you could see nothing. We gave you an inquisitive nature and yet you could experience so little of life. This is your reward Charaeshera. You will dwell in Our House, forever. Your eyes are clear now. Your feet do your bidding. All Heaven is before you to explore and roam as you desire. ENTER INTO OUR JOY! ENTER INTO OUR REST!"

Jesus Sat down on His throne next to the Father and placed Joy on His lap. She looked at The Father then at Jesus. The two were very much alike. She studied their faces for a long time then reached up and embraced Jesus in a childish hug.

"Thank you, Jesus, and Thank you Father. I will try to be worthy of everything, but I am not sure I can be. You are so great and majestic and I so small, I wonder that you should even have noticed me." She now turned her attention to the city stretching out below her. It was laid out in a perfect square. The streets crisscrossed each other forming twelve divisions. God's throne, and the Tree of Life

47

were at the center of the city. In four other central locations there were great golden fountains shooting streams of misty spray into the air. As the glorious light hit these fountains, brilliant rainbows arched over each one, amplifying all the gloriously colors in varying hues. Beneath these fountains' sea animals basked in the foamy spray, playing humorous games. Off to the south she saw a group of spiraling, crystal, towers that reached heavenward. They ascended into the heavens almost as high as the throne itself.

"Where is my Home, Jesus?" she asked suddenly. "Which one of those places is to be mine?" Jesus pointed out a very high window looking down on one of the beautiful fountains.

"That is it there, Joy. It is the one to the side of that long staircase above the fountain." Next to the fountain a fashionable garden was laid out with hundreds of flowers and fruit trees. In the center of it many animals roamed freely. The stately giraffe, with its head in the treetops, nibbled on the evergreen leaves. The cheetah and his mate rested in an open area by a crystal waterfall. There were monkeys hopping from branch to branch and birds singing from the swaying palm trees. Joy noticed a little black-haired girl with a tiny crown on her head stroking a huge lion. A red boarder lined the base of her shimmering garment.

"What does that red trim represent Jesus? My friend Trust also has one on his garment."

"That red trim is given to those who died for Me. They did not count their life dearer to themselves then My life. They freely spoke of Me even though it meant their death. That little girl you see was taken with her family to an arena in Rome. Listen to what she is saying."

Joy turned one ear toward the little girl and listened. Her words came faintly but clearly across the expanse of miles.

"You aren't such a bad creature are you, Mr. Lion? I

told Mamma that you looked like a grown kitten the day they took us to that big place. You did not look like you would hurt us at first. I think I was right. You did not mean to hurt us. Jesus did not make you that way. Satan did. He did not like us because we loved Jesus. He got really mad and, in the Bible, he stalked around like a roaring lion seeking to de, de-vour us. I forgive you, Mr. Lion. I can't remember much of what happened but the next thing I remember Jesus came in the clouds and rescued us. I will call you Larry, Larry the Lion." With that she curled up next to the large beast and began picking some of the many flowers that grew beneath her. The large cat seemed to enjoy the special attention she had given him and began to purr contentedly, like a huge kitten.

Joy now looked off toward the Garden of Eden that Jesus had unveiled just hours before. Adam and Eve were there with many of their family members, wondering at all the beautiful things they saw. Eve was rocking a small baby in her arms.

"Who is that baby in Eve's arms?" questioned Joy.

"It is one of her daughters. She lost it several years after Seth was born. It is safely in her arms now. It will grow up in a bright new world without sin." Adam came over and took the tiny one in his arms and held it up. It giggled and cooed at him, waving its little arms and legs with glee. There was so much love in that garden. Abel hardly left the side of his dear mother. In his arms he carried a small lamb. These creatures of fluffy, white, fur were his special care during his short stay on earth. The three moved off toward the beautiful home nestled among the fruit trees.

"I would like to visit the Garden of Eden soon," spoke Joy reverently. "It is so beautiful. You make such beautiful things, Jesus. I want to be right next to you when you re-create the old world over. May I be next to you when you do it and see how you make all these wonderful things, Jesus?"

"Yes Charaeshera. I will let you stand beside Me when I make all things new," responded the Savior with a look of expectant love animating from his eyes. Her request was not drawn out of a selfish heart but rather from a curiosity about how everything was and how it came to be. She cradled herself closer to the face of Jesus and examined the scars on His brow where the cruel thorns had pierced Him. She passed her fingers over one of them and felt the rough edges. She then gently lifted one of His massive hands, placing her own hand over one of the jagged scars left from the nails. A tiny tear trickled down her cheek as she comprehended that those scars were made for her. Jesus gently wiped it away.

"Why do you still have these scars Jesus," she asked?

"I have them because I choose to, Charaeshera. These scars represent victory and love. They remind everyone that separation from the Father is not without cost. I wear the scars because I love you and all those people you see down there. Sin will not emerge again after I create all things new. Everyone will see these scars and realize that God is love. His love was so great that He was willing to let Me go into your world and accept these scars that you might dwell with Me in this better world forever."

"There was a beautiful angel once who loved this place. I loved him dearly but by and by he began looking at his beauty and begin to think of himself as quite important. He started whispering to some of the other angels about how great he was. I talked to him about it, but he wouldn't listen. Finally, he accused the Father of being a tyrant who ruled Heaven for his own selfish desires. Because the Father had all power, Lucifer accused Him of using His power to keep His created ones enslaved to Him. Because He had all knowledge, Lucifer accused Him of predestining everyone to a life that was all planned out for them. He determined in his heart that he would deliberately go against the Father's plans and prove himself right. There was a great battle and this angel, and his followers were cast to the earth. You know the rest of the story, Little One. He entered the garden you see there and waited in the Tree of Knowledge of Good and Evil for someone to pass nearby. He wanted to spread his story about the Father to Adam and Eve and he succeeded. But that is all past now, forever."

"In the future, when these people and those beings on other worlds see these scars, when they hear the story about what happened to Me, they can never accuse the Father of being a tyrant, seeking His own selfish purpose. They can never say He uses His power to control everyone. He didn't use His power to force Me to go down to earth. I did not have to go and die. I freely choose to go because I loved you more than you can ever know. When others see these scars, they will see God for what He is, a benevolent, loving Father who loves all His children and allows them the free power of choice. When they see these scars, they will never again choose to rebel against Him."

Joy was thoughtful for a long time. Then looking up into the loving eyes of Jesus she asked.

"Why didn't my mother and father choose Heaven, Jesus?" A sad expression crossed the face of the Savior as he looked off toward a large building to the east of the throne.

"Come with Me and I will show you," He bore her gently in His arms to an impressive structure surrounded by sparkling, blue water. In various locations bridges spanned the water to the different entrances. There were twelve doors. Three on each side of the building. On the walls were thousands of roses growing from terraced planters. The roses were made up of an array of colors. A sweet fragrance filled the air. It was a truly beautiful place.

Jesus entered one of the middle doors facing Joy's home in the sky. Inside were many seats. There were strange casings in front of the seats. He took her to a seat and did something to the casing. It began to glow and vibrate. A picture formed and Joy looked into the face of her mother for the first time. She studied that face, memorizing every line and wrinkle. The casings were not like a video. They were more like a hologram. One could see the whole scene in three dimensions. Joy could actually feel the features of her mother's face. After looking she felt that face and as she felt it, she remembered.

BIBLE TEXTS

"Men seek refuge in the shadow of your wings. They are filled with the riches and plenty of your house, and you give them water from the flowing stream of your delight; for the fountain of life is with you, and in your presence, we are bathed in light."

Psalms 36:9

"There in heaven stood a throne, and on the throne sat one who appeared like the gleam of jasper and cornelian; and there was a rainbow around the throne, bright as an emerald. Twenty-four elders were arranged in a circle around the throne, each sitting on a throne, robed in white and wearing crowns of gold. From the throne came flashes of lightning and peals of thunder. Seven flaming torches were burning around the throne, they are the seven spirits of God, and in front of them stretched what seemed a sea of glass, a sheet of ice. In the center, around the throne itself, were four living creatures ... they sang day and night without stopping: 'Holy, holy, holy, is God, the absolute Lord of all, who was, and is, and is to come!'"

Revelation 4:2-8

"Now at last God has his dwelling among men! He will dwell among them and they shall be his people,

and God himself will be with them. He will wipe away every tear from their eyes; there will be an end to death, and to mourning, crying and pain; for the old order has passed away! Then He who sat on the throne said, Look! I am making all things new!... I am Alpha and Omega, the beginning, and the end. A swallow from the water-springs of life will be my free gift to the thirsty. All this will be the heritage of those who are victorious; and I will be their God and they will be my children."

Revelation 21:3-8

"He that overcomes, I will allow to sit with me on my throne, just as I was victorious and sat down with my Father on his throne."

Revelation 3:21A

"And one shall ask him, 'What are these wounds in your hands?' Then he will answer, 'These are the wounds I received while in the house of my friends.'"

Zechariah 13:6

"Set your troubled hearts at rest. Trust in God always; trust also in me. There are many dwelling-places in my Father's house; if it were not so I would have told you; for I am going there to prepare a home for you. And if I go and prepare a home for you, I will come again and secure you to myself, so that where I am you may be also."

John 14:1-3

CHAPTER 6
A MOTHER FOR JOY

Joy found that by moving her hand beneath the picture she could go ahead or backward in time. She moved back to her mother's childhood and entered a few scenes. At times she saw angels at the side of her mother. One angel was bright and shining while the other was dark and evil looking. They struggled over her mother. Joy's mother had been named Joyce. For the most part Joyce was a cooperative girl. She never gave her parents much trouble. She attended church and even studied her Bible at times. Then one winter she had her heart set on a visit to her Grandmother's house. She was fond of Grandmother and loved her very much. She had carefully packed her things and was ready to go when her dad canceled the trip because of a severe cold he came down with. Realizing that his parents were frail, he did not want to spread his cold to them. Joyce never saw her grandmother alive again. She became bitter over the incident and never fully forgave her parents. The good angel spoke to her often, encouraging her to forgive and forget but she held to her bitterness like some sacred treasure.

Joy's angel, Celestania, entered the room quietly, unobserved. He spoke gently now.

"Do you know why your grandfather came down with the cold?"

"No," replied Joy.

"Look at what would have happened had they gone to Grandmothers." The guardian angel made some rapid movements on the casing and Joy saw a speeding truck cross a lane of traffic and hit the car carrying her Mother.

"You see Joy, if they had gone that day, your mother would have died along with her parents. You never would

54

have been born and heaven would be forever at a loss if you were not here." Joy thought about that for a moment and reached up and gave the big angel's hand a squeeze.

"I am so glad I was born and am here in this most beautiful place in all of Jesus' creation." Joy moved ahead in the life of that bitter child. She saw the first time Joyce met her husband to be and for the first time, the little girl looked into the eyes of her father. He was not especially good looking. He had a sharp nose that ended rather abruptly in a mass of whiskers. In time they were married. The newlyweds seemed happy enough. Joyce even lost some of her bitterness. When her parents were together, Joy often noticed two sets of angels struggling over them. One striving to tear down, the other aspiring to build up, pointing the couple toward Heaven. Then a mining accident claimed the life of her father. The evil angel that had been by his side gloated with a terrible grin. Her father died cursing God.

Joy was soon inside a hospital room. She saw a tiny baby in the arms of a nurse. A faint smile crossed the face of Joyce as she looked at her new daughter. She would be comforted now after the loss of her husband. But when the doctor told her that Sherry was blind and deformed, bitterness and anger took the place of the last flicker of happiness. Joy heard her mother cry out to God asking; "Why, why, why? Why me? You are not fair God. All I have had in life is bitterness and pain. If this is how You treat all your creatures, I do not want to have anything to do with You! Go away and leave me alone. I don't want to be bothered by You anymore."

Over the next few years, a certain nurse emerged again and again in the picture. Joy needed to be given special care, and somehow the heart of this nurse went out to the little child. She spoke to her of the love of God and of the beautiful home in Heaven He was preparing. She became eyes for Joy as well as feet. She could transport the little girl on magical journeys to fantastic places, and Joy grew to love her as a mother. She could see her story unfolding now. Her loving nature was due in part to her response to this loving nurse.

What a different story her Mother presented. Instead of being thankful that she had eyes to see and feet that could take her where she wanted to go, she closed herself to everything and everyone. Joyce started drinking heavily and soon craved nothing more. She refused to see her parents and forbade them from interfering in her life. Joy saw much that she wished she hadn't. She was satisfied now that Jesus knew best. She turned off the story and looked up at Celestania.

"So, they were my parents. Couldn't they see that what they experienced was nothing compared to these glories that were coming," the little girl made a circle of her arms all around heaven as she asked?

"No, Joy, responded the angel. "They chose not to look beyond their trouble to a better world where pain and suffering cannot exist. They chose not to look to Jesus and accept His forgiveness. It is a sad story. Hundreds of people down there did the same thing. They never looked to God, but let those evil angels shut out the glories of this place. They could not have been happy here thinking only of themselves. Selfishness cannot exist in this atmosphere. But now there is someone you must meet. Come, come with me."

Celestania took Joy to the outside of the building and walked with her to one of the brilliant terraces that contained the reddest of the roses. There, kneeling by one particularly beautiful flower, was the nurse Joy had seen in the story. Joy recognized her immediately and flew into her surprised arms so quickly the nurse was overtaken by it all. The little child smothered her with a hundred kisses.

"I am so glad you are here, Nancy!" exclaimed the happy child.

"Is that really you, Sherry," cried the nurse?

"It is your Sherry, Nancy," responded Joy. "I did not recognize anyone in Heaven. I thought I was the only one of my family here."

"How could you recognize anyone? You never saw anyone before Jesus came in the clouds of heaven."

"I saw you, Nancy. Celestania let me see you in my mind once. I traced your face with my hands. I memorized every feature, and a picture of you formed inside me. You were beautiful then, but you are even more beautiful now."

"Do you really think so?" Nancy reached down and gave Joy a tender hug.

"Thank you, Joy, for showing me a bit of Heaven. You inspired me like no other person. At times I felt like giving up but when I saw you so happy and loving despite your blindness and crippled legs, I remembered that I had a lot to be thankful for. You are the main reason I am here. When Jesus lifted you up, I waved and called out to you. I wanted to run to you at the supper, but I saw my Grandmother further up the table and went to visit her. I am so glad you found me. We will have a lot of great times together. I just love these flowers. They are the most beautiful in all the city."

"Yes, they are, Nancy. What name did Jesus give you?" questioned Joy. Nancy took off her crown and showed it to Joy.

"Jesus calls me Shan-i-thil-ia. I like the name very much. Oh, I'm so glad to see you. It is very exciting to think that I will have my little girl here in Heaven with me, forever."

"Whenever I see a rose, I will think of you Shanithilia," said Joy.

"These are the most fragrant of all the roses," commented Nancy. "Let's take a couple of bunches back to our rooms."

"Rooms?" questioned the little girl.

"Our rooms are right next to each other, Sherry. Jesus thought of it when He designed the city."

"Are they really," exclaimed Joy? "I haven't been to

my room yet. Let's go quickly, Shanithilia, and see it." With that the two were off toward the crystal towers hand in hand. Joy had found a mother to make her joy complete. In His kindness, Jesus had thought of everything. What would Joy like most? She would like to see and be able to walk. Yes, and she would like a mother of her very own too. So, Jesus had planned it all out and now it had happened.

There will be millions of mothers there, reader. There will be hundreds of children there too. Children who are there because of a praying mother or a praying father. Do you have little ones who you want to walk with you on those streets of gold? They can walk with you there. Perhaps your little ones are grown and have a home of their own with their own little ones. They too can be with you in that wonderland to come. Be a praying mother. The loving Father answers the prayers of praying mothers and from eternity's glorious shores, many will trace their entrance through those pearly gates to a praying mother.

I had a praying mother and a praying father. They were very dear to me and I know they will have their place in Heaven with the other mothers and fathers from all ages. Mom and Dad are resting in Jesus now. Their life here on earth was one of sorrow and pain, but that will be forever gone in that glorious world beyond the blue. They will walk those golden streets and raise their voices with the others in praise to God, because by their side will be their two children. By God's grace, and the prayers of these dear parents, my sister and I will be among those who walk on golden streets. Let us pray.

Our Father in Heaven. As a faint picture of the glories to come form from these simple words, hear our prayer. We see a place where mothers and fathers walk hand in hand with the children You gave to them. We see united families worshiping at the feet of Jesus. As we look, we see the children You have tenderly given, walking with us beneath those stately palms. Our desire is to be with You there. We are homesick for this place You have prepared beyond these cloudy skies that cover us now. By faith we look forward and see the rainbow at the end of the tunnel. Even that brilliant rainbow that surrounds Your throne. Take us as we are and prepare us for that journey with You. May we enter as families, united in the love of Jesus.

For some of us though, this cannot be. If this is our lot, help us to endure. Strengthen us for the trials ahead. Bear us gently in your arms and give us what rest you can in this place, displaced so far from your throne. Though we are in this old, dark world, we need not be part of it. You offer Your righteousness for our rags, Your sinlessness for our sins, Your obedience for our disobedience. We accept that righteousness now. Cover us and crown us with that crown of eternal glory that will never fade away. Give us a glimpse of Your beauty and may it never fade from our eyes. In Jesus name we pray, Amen.

BIBLE TEXTS

*"Look, I am creating new heavens and a new earth-
so wonderful that no one will even think about the
old ones again. Be happy; rejoice forever more in my
creation. Look! I will recreate Jerusalem as a place of
happiness, and her people shall be a joy! I will rejoice
in Jerusalem, and in my people; and the voice of
crying and weeping will not be heard there anymore.
No longer will little babies die when they are only a
few days old; no longer will men be considered old at
the age of 100! Only sinners die that young! In those
days, when a man builds a house, he will keep on
living in it-it will not be destroyed by invading armies
as in the past. My people will plant vineyards and eat
the fruit themselves-their enemies will not confiscate
them. For my people will live as long as trees and will
forever enjoy their hard-won gains. Their harvest*

will not be eaten by their enemies; their children will not be born to be the food of beast. For they are the children of those the Lord has blessed. I will answer them before they even call Me. While they are still talking to me about their needs, I will go ahead and answer their prayers. The wolf and the lamb will feed together, the lion will eat straw as the cow, and poisonous snakes will strike no more! In those days nothing and no one will be hurt or destroyed in all My Holy Mountain, says the Lord."

Isaiah 65:17-25

"For this is what the Lord says: 'I will extend peace to her like a river, and the wealth of nations like a flooding stream; you will nurse and be carried on her arm and sit on her knees. As a mother soothes her child, so will I soothe you; and you will be comforted over Jerusalem."

Isaiah 66:12, 13

"Listen to the father who gave you life, and do not despise your mother when she is old. Buy truth and do not sell it; acquire wisdom, discipline, and understanding. The father of a righteous man has great joy; he whose son is wise is delighted. May your father and mother be glad; may the one who gave you birth rejoice!"

Proverbs 23:22-25

"When Jesus saw his mother there, and the disciple whom he loved standing nearby, he said to his mother, 'Dear woman, there is your son,' and to the disciple, 'Here is your mother.' From then on, this disciple took her into his home."

John 19:26. 27

CHAPTER 7
HOMEWARD BOUND

There were several ways to travel in the Holy City. You could walk, fly, or glide along the surface a little above ground level. You could run without getting tired, or just hop and skip along. Nancy and Joy decided to skip along hand in hand. It was a beautiful sight to see them happy in their new found love. There was plenty of time, so every now and then they would stop and talk to some of the people they passed. This is how they happened to come across the reunion of Adam's family.

Before we get into that portion of our story, however, I want you to grasp a little of the massive size of this city. If you started walking today and kept your average walking pace twenty-four hours a day, it would take you ten days to walk from one side of the city to the other. If you walked around the perimeter without stopping it would take over a month. Therefore, our ability to travel there will be different than it is here on earth.

Much of Heaven was open. Families from all generations met in groups large and small for a reunion that need never end. Sometimes ten or twelve generations met in one group. One such group was the household of Adam and Eve. Able was there, with Seth and all his children. Several other sons and daughters of Adam and Eve were there with their children, and their children's children, and their children's children, and so on. Eve was still carrying her little bundle of love when Nancy and Joy passed by this company of giants and went up to speak to them. Nancy was surprised at the size of this baby. Though it seemed small in the arms of its mother it was huge compared to the little baby she had held when Sherry was born. The baby, in fact, was larger than Joy. Nancy did not even reach the waist of Eve. Joy was even shorter.

Eve gently lowered the little one down for them to see. The baby smiled and took up a bit of Joy's hair in her large, little fingers. Then she laughed the neatest laugh. Joy beamed her one beautiful smile and gave a quick kiss right on a rosy cheek. Eve's baby daughter had large, beautiful eyes. Joy had never seen eyes so clear. They were as blue as the sky above the city, and sparkled with the reflections of its beauty. Nancy and Joy left Eve and began to look around.

The beauties of the garden of Eden were everywhere. The home Adam had built was a model of loveliness. It rose out of the garden like a lovely plant. Vines were interspersed with differing kinds of fruit trees. The living foliage formed the structure of the home itself. You could pluck grapes from the kitchen wall or sample oranges while you rested on living furniture that bloomed with flowers and produced fruit of its own. Nothing had died before Adam and Eve were expelled from the garden so all the materials our first parents had used to create this home was either alive or in the form of a mineral or gem. There was another thing about the garden of Eden noticeable to Joy. A melodious sound pulsed through all of it. Before sin, this musical sound pulsated in the whole earth. The trees and flowers loved it. Some would say it was music from the throne of God. When Adam and Eve sinned, a different song permeated the world. It was a song of sin and death. It had destructive power where the song before sin had living power. Joy could hear the living song now. She could feel it pulsing through her and with it, life eternal.

Joy tasted some of the dark, sweet cherries that grew by the doorway of Adam's home. She peaked in and saw the gold and silver furnishings generously laden with thousands of diamonds. Each diamond reflected the glorious light of heaven and transformed it into a myriad of millions of colorful rainbows. On tables of polished marble, she saw some of the oranges and tangerines Adam had plucked from his grove or perhaps the wall itself. She patted Adam's dog on the head, and he wagged his tail with delight.

Enoch came over to where they were and gave them a warm welcome. He was the oldest, continuously living human in the City, over five thousand years young. This was because the Bible tells us he was translated without seeing death from the earth before the flood. His son Methuselah was there and joined him. Methuselah was the oldest man that ever lived, nine hundred sixty-nine years to be exact. God in His great love chose to honor these two saints with long life. It was really something to see them side by side. They presented quite a contrast. Enoch bore a dark, youthful beard and Methuselah had a long, snowy white one that came well below his waist. A twinkle came to the eyes of the ancient saint as he saw Joy.

"So, you are the privileged one all Heaven is talking about, Charaeshera," He smiled a warm smile as he spoke her name.

"Who is talking about me," asked the surprised little girl?

"I heard several mention your name as you came toward the garden. They saw you with Jesus."

"Yes, I was with Jesus. He showed me many wonders in Heaven today. He came and took me up to His throne. It is so beautiful from up there. I could see everything in the whole city. I even saw Eve and her baby girl. The Father is nice too. He talked to me and told me why I was allowed to come to heaven."

"And why did He allow you to come to heaven," questioned the ancient one?

"He said I was brought to heaven because I helped a lot of people, but I don't remember helping anybody. I only remember hearing of the story of Jesus and realizing how grateful I was for His love. I came to love Jesus because I could feel Him right by me every time I began to hurt or get lonely. I told Him I loved Him often. When other people complained of pain, or hurt like me, I told them Jesus loved them too. Some would ask me how I knew, and I told them I could feel Him near me, loving me. When He took me in His big arms, it was like going home. I felt those arms around me many times when down on that old dark earth. I do love Jesus more than anyone else. But I love everyone else too. I am so happy to be here and be able to see all these beautiful things. Thank you, Jesus, wherever you are now."

"I can see now why Jesus took you to see the Father," responded Enoch. "I came to love Jesus the same as you while on earth. We would go on long walks together. I too felt those big arms around me. Then one day He took me here and I have been with Him ever since, except when He came down to earth to live, and die. I missed Him greatly then. But now we are all here together. It is so wonderful. Jesus really is loving and kind to allow us the pleasure to be in His house forever."

Joy smiled and nodded in agreement, then looked toward one of the flowered meadows. There she saw a large table formed from living vines. An unusual event was taking place. Samson had wandered into the camp of Adam and had challenged him to an arm-wrestling contest. Most of the company looked on with smiling faces. The contest was not a matched one. Adam's arm was nearly twice as long as Samson's, so the strong man had his arm cradled in a coconut half and the contest was on. Adam was gaining fast. His muscles flexed strongly, and Samson's arm went down slowly until it just about touched the marble. Then a very unusual thing began to happen. Slowly but surely Samson pushed the giants arm back into an upright position then back in the other direction until it nearly touched the table. The contest was over.

"Well, Adam, you put out some good strength," commented Samson as he took a cluster of grapes from the vine, table and ate them hungrily. "A few more months of this delicious food, however, and I will have you for sure."

Adam smiled and commended him on his strength. Then with a twinkle in his eye he replied.

"You are a good contender my, friend. It looks like I am going to have to work out if I expect to maintain any kind of a lead around here for long." With that, the two clasped each other's hand in a gripping handshake and parted company.

Three little boys were looking longingly up at Muscle Man, admiring his physique. He knelt and told them to hop on his shoulders. Two of them scrambled on his huge frame, but the third was a bit too short. Samson picked him up, carried him on one arm, then ambled off with his admirers to the "Valley of the Giant Plants," just beyond the winding river. The children called it that and were especially fond of the place. There were huge plants that twisted and arched like some ultra-modern water slides. The youngsters spent hours going from plant to plant and frolicking amidst the assortment created especially for them. Samson was a favorite of these children because he always had an interesting story to tell and took time to listen when the little ones sought him out.

Nancy and Joy left the garden and took to the air now. Soon they were in view of the dazzling mansions. They came down next to one of the giant fountains and strolled around watching the otters play tag with the seals. Joy went over to the water and took a long drink from one of the streams that came spouting out of a golden pool. There was no sound of a pump. The water seemed to defy gravity itself. The clear liquid entered her mouth and slid down her throat, vitalizing her entire being with new vigor. There was something about this water that satisfied. It healed the very soul.

The two were at the entrance of the beautiful homes now. They paused a moment to look up at the glory of the sight before them. A golden street wound up to an archway made of transparent jasper. The colors of the archway were deep reds and oranges with dashes of yellow. At the top of the arch were inscribed the words "HOLINESS TO THE LORD." Above the archway, stretching miles into the sky, were the beautiful homes of the Saints on this side of the city. The view took Joy's breath away. Her eyes, so darkened on earth, seemed starved for each beautiful scene. She had to touch, feel, and smell everything to see if it was real. She stood staring at the beauty before her for a long, long time, then spoke.

"These are the most beautiful homes in all of heaven!" she exclaimed in a whispered, reverent tone.

"They are beautiful," responded her new mother. "And higher than any mountain on earth. They are more glorious than ten of our suns. I never imagined such beauty could exist anywhere! It is amazing how Jesus has planted beautiful gardens all over these homes and filled them with millions of colorful flowers."

Among the gardens, brilliant birds swung from trailing vines loaded with grapes and fruit of rarest beauty. Their unceasing songs ascended to God with joy unquenchable. Other plants of varying shades of green and gold were interspersed among the flowers. At that moment there was a flash of red and green. The parrot glided to rest on Joy's shoulder.

"Are you happy Joy? Are you happy you are going home?"

"Yes, Mr. Parrot, I am so happy I can't hold it in any longer." With that the little girl cried out from the depths of her very soul. "Thank You, Jesus, Thank You, and I Love You, and thank you, Nancy, for telling me about this place and the love Jesus had for a little cripple like me." She turned toward the throne as she spoke and caught a faint twinkle in the eyes of the Father as He looked down at her from His place high above. "This parrot calls me 'Joy'."

"What a nice name," smiled Nancy. "You are a joy to be with. May I call you Joy?"

"You may if you like," responded the girl. "Joy is exactly what my new name means, so I don't think Jesus will mind if you call me that. I am happy too and have lots and lots of joy inside me. It just must come out or I think I would explode. Heaven is so pretty, and everyone is so good to me. How could I be anything else but joyful?"

As if in a dreamland, Joy and Nancy started up the golden street into the mansions above. Higher and higher they went. The view changed from every angle. Wide verandas curved into spiraling stairs and winding hallways. Gold and silver archways framed the entrances to intersecting terraces and spacious courtyards. Glistening stairways opened into living gardens with flowing waterfalls and vibrant, green lawns. When they spoke out loud their voice returned to them, bouncing off the polished pillars and crystal walls. A hundred kinds of fruit spread their beauty before any who wished to eat them. Plums, peaches, apricots, and apples of gold and silver, beaconed to the hungry traveler; "Partake and be filled." The buzzing of bees blended with the beating wings of the ruby throated humming bird. A little sparrow sang from his perch on the flowering branches of the wisteria vine. Gems of rarity and beauty sparkled from every nook and cranny. Joy found herself raising her voice with the singing birds as they went ever higher.

"Thank you, Lord, for saving my soul.
Thank you, Lord, for making me whole.
Thank you, Lord, for giving to me,
Your great Salvation so full and free."

Nancy joined her now and the two went singing upward, ever higher.

"Thank you, Lord, for saving my soul.
Thank you, Lord, for making me whole.
Thank you, Lord, for giving to me,
Your great Salvation so full and free."

They were accompanied by their echoes and distant thoughts. Each remembered singing that song on some of the long dark nights when a certain little girl could not sleep because of the pain in her scrawny legs. But the dark night of sin could not be remembered for long.

They came to a wide veranda with a gold and silver table.

"Let's set down for a moment, Nancy, I want to ask you about my family."

"Ok," responded the nurse. "What do you want to know?"

"Did you ever meet any of my grandparents?"

"Yes, on a couple of occasions I saw your mother's parents. Your Mother did not have much to do with them, but they came to see you at times when you were really little."

"What were they like? Were they nice?"

"Yes, they were very loving. It pained them to be treated so by their daughter. They loved her a great deal and wanted to be a part of her life. They would have gladly helped her bear the burden of your care, but Joyce would not let them even speak to you. Your Grandparents never got to hold you."

"Are they in Heaven, Nancy?" questioned Joy.

"Yes, they are, Joy. I saw them at the Supper. When the meal was over, they tried to find you. Where did you go?"

"First, I was with Trust, responded the girl. "He is my adopted brother. He sort of looked after me on the great white cloud going to Heaven. He is a very good friend. and I love him very much. He is not with me now because they had a reunion of all the people that made up the stars in his crown. He has hundreds of stars. After leaving him with his friend Lasonaph, I was with Jesus. He took me to sit with Him on His throne."

"Jesus took you to His throne Joy?" questioned the surprised Nancy.

"Yes, He took me to meet the Father. It was all very grand and nice. I felt so small, though, next to those two greats, Kings."

"So, that is what you, Methuselah and Enoch were talking about? You must be very special to Jesus if He took you to His throne so soon after the Supper," responded Nancy. "He must love you a great deal."

"He told me He loved me. Even the Father told me I had been an inspiration to many. I don't know what He meant by that, though. Who did I ever inspire, and how could a little blind, cripple girl like me, inspire anyone?"

"Oh, but you inspired me a great deal, Joy. You inspired the doctors and nurses who took all those tests to determine if you could be helped. They all admired your happy, loving nature. You inspired all the sick people that ever roomed with you too."

"Well, I am glad then, that I acted happy. I did not feel happy sometimes, but when I acted happy, it made me happier. I hope I get to meet my grandparents soon. I would like very much to have a Grandmother and Grandfather." The two got up from the table and continued upward. At last, they were at the door of Joy's room. She gently touched it, and it retreated quietly into the wall. She looked inside with amazement. There, sitting on some of the exquisite furnishings, were her grandparents.

"We thought you would come here sometime," spoke up Grandfather. "You sure seem to be a busy little girl for all your short stay in Heaven. You are one little person who is hard to catch up with." Joy stared at the two saintly beings with a raptured expression on her face then burst forth with an excited voice.

"Grandmother! Grandfather! You are here! You are really here in Heaven! Oh, I am so happy I will squeeze you tighter than you can imagine! Just let me get a hold of you and you will see what I mean!" She flew into their outstretched arms and hugged and squeezed and kissed them until she nearly turned blue. Grandmother finally spoke with tears of joy streaming down her rosy cheeks.

"You are just like my little girl come home to me again, more beautiful than ever. You have your mother's eyes, and that smile came from your Father, I know." He smiled like that at times, and I thought it was so beautiful. I must admit, he charmed me like no other man except your grandfather. It is so special to have you here, Sherry. You don't know how much we have missed seeing you. Now you are ours forever. Let me have some more of those hugs and kisses. I can't seem to get enough of you." With that Grandmother picked Sherry up and rested her on her sturdy lap. Joy looked deep into her loving face for a long time. She hugged and kissed her repeatedly then hopped into the arms of her waiting Grandfather. They surrounded her completely, and he kissed her while stroking her lovely curls with his big hands. Had she been tired she could have taken a nap, secure in his arms, but she was not tired. She did not know what the word tired meant since entering Heaven. The once forsaken, blind, crippled girl was at that moment the happiest little girl in all the Universe. She had a Mother, a brother, and two lovely grandparents that cared for her more than words can tell.

After all the hugs and kisses were given, Joy jumped down from her Grandfather's lap and looked around her home. It was beautiful. She reached into her robe, pulled out the fruit from the Tree of Life, and set it on a golden shelf. She also placed her crown there, and the stone Jesus had given her with her new name. Her palace was simply beautiful. There were many exquisite furnishings. She had two windows. She went to one now and looked out. There, not six feet away, was a quiet fountain. Joy loved fountains. Further out, toward the center of the city, she could see the tree of life towering into the air. Behind it was the great white throne. She looked up and saw Jesus had gone. He must be with others somewhere in the city. She got up on the windowsill, and a quick leap took her safely to the refreshing water. She let it spray her in the face, causing her curls to form tight little ringlets. She drank some of this water. It tasted even better than the water from the great fountain. She took the flower out of her hair and replaced it with a brilliant pink one that grew next to the stream. Jesus had created a long water slide. Joy climbed to the top and slid down the slide, thoroughly soaking herself all over. She tried it again, and again and thrilled at the speeds she could attain by the time she reached the base. Joy looked back at the window and was surprised to see her grandparents and Nancy smiling down at her. She picked a grape, slowly ate it, then flew back in through the window. She took a more thorough tour of her palace.

There was a living sofa that produced violet flowers. It was in the living room. The flowers had a sweet fragrance that perfumed the whole dwelling. They smelled like Lilly of the Valley. In the dining area was a table set with all manner of fresh fruit. Some she had never seen before. Her grandmother told her some of the fruit came from other planets.

"You mean there are different kinds of fruit on all the other planets," asked Joy?

"Yes." Replied her Grandfather. "I brought some of these home from just such a planet yesterday."

"We will have to go to another planet and see these wonders." said Joy. The walls of the dining area were covered with various gems. Jesus had collected ones that were brightly colored. He knew Joy's eyes would love to drink in the color. Being blind on earth had given her a very special appreciation for beauty, and Jesus had spared no expense in furnishing her home with resplendent colors. There was a veranda off the dining area. The family went there. It was framed with a golden trellis, covered with delicate vines and beautiful flowers of every color imaginable. A cool breeze blew constantly there, and the mists from the waterfall made it a very refreshing place indeed. In the pools beneath the waterfalls there were colorful fish of several varieties. They swam in circular patterns spreading an iridescent shimmer throughout the whole pool.

Joy looked at the walls. They were made of mirrored gold. She could see her reflection perfectly on all sides. She could also see the reflections of all the little treasures there. To Joy, this was the most beautiful place in heaven. She went into her guest room. There were lots of shelves there. Some had interesting things on them, others were empty. She took the red roses Nancy had picked from the beautiful building and placed them in a crystal vase on one of the shelves. She looked admiringly at them. Truly heaven was the best and most beautiful place anyone ever could imagine, and she was the happiest little girl anyone could picture. Celestania looked quietly in from the open door and smiled as only a guardian angel can smile when he knows that all is well. The joy that animated from his little one's face was reward enough for a thousand angels. The memory of this little girl, so happy now with her new found family, would remain in his mind as one of his most precious moments for all time. Joy was Home at last.

BIBLE TEXTS

"No human being has ever seen, heard or even imagined what wonderful things God has prepared for those who love Him."

2 Corinthians 2:9

"With this news bring cheer to all discouraged ones. Encourage those who are afraid. Tell them this, "Be strong and do not fear, for your own God is coming to destroy your enemies. He is coming to save you." And when He comes, He will open the eyes of the blind, and unstop the ears of the deaf. The crippled man will leap like a deer, and those who cannot speak will shout and sing! Springs will burst forth in the

wilderness, and streams will flow in the desert. The parched ground will become a pool, with springs of water in the thirsty land. Where desert jackals lived, there will be reeds and rushes! And a main road will go through that once-deserted land; it will be named the 'Holy Highway.' No evil-hearted man can walk upon it. God will walk there with you; even the most ignorant cannot possibly miss the way. No lion will lurk along its course, nor will there be any dangers; only the redeemed of the Lord will go home along that road to Zion, singing the songs of everlasting joy. For them, all sorrow and all sighing will be gone forever; only joy and gladness will be there."

Isaiah 35:3-10

"Do not lay up in store for yourselves treasure on earth, where moths and rust will come and destroy it, and where thieves can break in and steal all you have saved, but store up for yourselves treasures in heaven, where moth and rust do not destroy, and where thieves cannot break in and steal it, for where you have stored your treasure, that is where your heart will be also."

Matthew 6:19-21

"How lovely is your dwelling, O Lord Most High! My soul yearns, even faints, for the courts of my God; my heart and my soul cry out for the living God. Even the sparrow has found a home, and the swallow a nest for herself, where she may keep her young-a place near your altar, O Lord Almighty, my King, and my God. Blessed are those who dwell in your house; they will ever praise you."

Psalms 84:2-4

"Blessed are those who place their strength in you, who have set their hearts on this pilgrimage. As they travel through the Valley of Baca, they will make it a place of springs; the autumn rains will also cover it with pools. They will go from strength to strength, till each appears before God in Zion."

Psalm 84:1-7

CHAPTER 8
THE UNIVERSE

After Joy left them, Trust and Lasonaph headed south. They passed the great white throne and came to a large arena. It resembled the super dome in construction but was thousands of times larger and had no roof except the sky above. Inside were billions of seats on varying levels. The structure rose heavenward like a colossal hollow mountain. It had been over six thousand years since all those seats had been full. At that time Lucifer, Son of the Morning, had led the vast host of angels in heavenly melodies. Now much of the place was empty. A few Saints and angels gathered in groups, inventing new ways to give glory to God in song, but other than that there was a strange emptiness around it.

"I wonder what this is used for Trust," questioned Lasonaph?

"It looks like a choir room or meeting hall," responded his friend. "We will have to find out sometime more about it."

The two continued on south toward a massive courtyard, several miles square. There was a sense of excitement in the air, as if something were about to happen. The courtyard was made of the whitest marble they had ever seen. Its surface was polished to perfection. Hundreds of garden beds were interspersed in various locations on the courtyard. Millions of exotic plants and flowers pointed their heads to the sky. The flowers ranged in size from tiny ones that would require a magnifying glass for our eyes to see, to large specimens, big enough to walk into and observe all their working parts. A lovely fragrance permeated the air, and the boys looked around for the source. A group of dainty, golden flowers seemed to give them the answer.

Trust jumped high in the air and did a couple of somersaults then landed gracefully back on his feet.

"It is good to be here!" he shouted. "Thank you, Heavenly Father, for allowing me a place here with you in Heaven." He bowed momentarily as he looked toward the throne and seemed to see the Father smiling down at him.

It was on this courtyard that the great minds of all ages gathered to instruct the happy occupants of this golden city. The Twenty-Four Elders often mingled here when they were not in conference with the Father. From these polished floors the Apostles spoke to the people of their experience with Jesus. The One Hundred and Forty-Four Thousand were also walking this courtyard sharing more of the good news about the Kingdom of God. There were people in Heaven who had never heard the name of Jesus or the Story of Salvation prior to His coming for them. There were others who had been dumb, deaf, or blind like Joy. Here the crippled came leaping, the deformed, perfect now in beauty and symmetry, lifted their voices in praise to God. They sat at the feet of these teachers drinking in the knowledge of the wonders all around them. Though on earth they had been despised and rejected, now they shone brightly like the stars. Where pain and agony had ruled, joy and peace now prevailed.

It was to one of these learned men that Trust and Lasonaph came. They saw him sitting quietly in rapt meditation as he looked toward the throne. They sat down on a golden bench opposite him and waited. He seemed to be praying. His eyes were transfixed on the glorious rainbow that surrounded the throne of God; The boys did not wish to disturb him. There was a large aquarium filled with colorful fish and fascinating water animals of all shapes and sizes. The lads became so involved in the antics of some of these creatures, they were startled when a pleasant voice greeted them.

"What may I do for you two young men?"

"We understand that you know a lot about the

Universe, and we wanted to learn as much as possible about it. Do you have time to answer some of our questions?"

"Time is not a matter of concern here in Heaven," replied the teacher. "There is enough time for many wonderful things to happen yet in this new home. Whatever I have I will share with you gladly, although I know so little about what God has created for our enjoyment and His glory. What would you like to know?"

"How big is the universe," queried Trust? The teacher stroked his long flowing beard for a moment, then replied.

"That, son, is a question that cannot be answered quickly. The universe is limitless as far as our understanding is concerned. If you were to travel at the speed of light, it would take you over thirty billion years to get from one side to the other, yet it is not as it seems. In actuality, the universe is a giant sphere. You will go so far, then end back up where you started from. I am sure you remember the books that were written while you were on earth. If you were to give each man, woman, and child here in Heaven sixty-five thousand volumes, and place one letter of each word in every volume, every mile, you would use up the entire set of volumes and still not reach the nearest galaxy." The boys were silent for a while as they tried to comprehend what they had just heard.

"When we entered Orion on our way to Heaven it was so beautiful," responded Trust, "and so large. Those curtains of light, red, gold, violet, and blue, were of the most brilliant hues I have ever seen. Everyone on the great cloud became silent when they first saw them. What do you know about Orion?" The teacher eyed them approvingly, then continued.

"Orion is one of Jesus' most amazing creations. He planned it especially that way for the time when you and I would first enter Heaven. It is over sixteen trillion, seven hundred forty billion miles in diameter. That is staggering when you compare it to your own solar system. You could place thirty thousand solar systems the size of earth's side by side in the entrance to Orion and still have more room." The teacher looked off for a few moments with a happy smile radiating from his face, and the boys tried to comprehend a little more of what they had heard.

They looked at the kindly teacher with his long, white beard and wavy hair. He was one of the privileged ones who had returned to Heaven at Christ's ascension. What a story his life had told while on earth. He was truly a saint, like Enoch of old and one of the Twenty-Four Elders. What wonders he must know. Perhaps he had traveled to some of the distant reaches of the Universe. They must find out.

"Where is your favorite spot in all the Universe," questioned Lasonaph? "Here in Heaven with Jesus," came a soft reply. "But outside of Heaven there is one place I especially like. It fills me with the magnitude of God's love repeatedly. Would you like to see it?"

"Yes, we would!" responded the boys in unison. "Would you take us?"

"I would be glad to take you there," came the reply. "Come with me." The three rose from the benches and walked toward a set of stairs that wound downward from the courtyard into a sub chamber. The boys were amazed to see that even in this lower room the light of Heaven shone as brightly as if they were in the very presence of God. From it they could look out over the vast universe as if peering through a window but there was no glass. Distant galaxies shone brilliantly with their rich array of colors. Stars and nebulae flamed in the sky, lending praise to God along with the entire creation. It appeared that heaven was a planet but not round like earth. It was just different, wonderful in its makeup but indescribable in human language. All the dimensions of time and space seemed to converge here in a mystery that would take the greatest minds thousands of years to fathom. From His throne the Father must have even a better view of the universe, but this was most marvelous indeed. It was truly an awesome place to be, and to be here with one so wise was even more amazing.

Their host pointed them toward a section of the universe, then singled out a distant galaxy that radiated brightly.

"Our destination is this galaxy. We will be visiting a planet at the farthest end of it. It is quite a distance in earth's measurements, but we will be able to reach it rather quickly with God's means of travel. It is approximately five billion light years away. Just beyond it is one of the quasars men became aware of in the twentieth century from earth. That quasar presents an interesting phenomenon that we will study sometime in the future if you are interested. But before we get there, I want to show you one of the largest suns in the universe. This sun could contain over five hundred million suns the size of the earth's in its massive interior. Our wonderful God is a big, big God. He is big enough to do anything He chooses yet small enough to live within your heart and mine. He is powerful enough to create massive galaxies yet loving enough to leave Heaven, giving His life so one tiny, rebellious planet could find Salvation."

"I saw the cross where they hung Him. I saw His blood covering the rocks beneath it. He shed His blood for me that I might be here with Him forever. There were several of us who were resurrected when He was. For forty days we walked around Jerusalem and the surrounding area telling all we met that He was God's Son, the Messiah, the Promised King! People laughed at us and thought we were crazy. I did not know anyone. The people were not from my time, but something came over me and I spoke freely of things I had not known before. The promises of the Prophets, that had been my study, became clear. I know what it means to have Christ within me. His Spirit, His love, His power entered into me and I had a compelling urge to cry out."

"What time in history did you live," asked Lasonaph?

"I lived in the time of the late kings of Israel," replied the teacher. "It was just before the Babylonian captivity. I was one of Daniel's teachers. He was a brilliant student. I knew from the first time I met him he was called of God for a special work. God revealed much to him. We were close, more like father and son than teacher and student. He was so eager to learn and God rewarded that thirst for truth in a mighty way. He was one of the beloved of God and was shown much about this place as was John the Revelator. My heart was nearly broken when the Babylonians came and took him away. I prayed like I had never prayed before that God would protect him from the evils of that kingdom. I prayed for his captors, and I prayed for the king that captured him. God answered many of my prayers. King Nebuchadnezzar is here. I am sure Daniel's influence had a lot to do with it, but Jesus revealed to me that my prayers also helped intervene in the affairs of that kingdom. But now, you lads did not come to hear me talk on and on about Daniel. You came to learn about the universe. Let's begin our journey." The boys approached their new adventure with greater interest. This man must have been one of the wisest teachers of all time if he was Daniel's teacher. He had been in heaven for well over two thousand years and surely would have learned a lot in that length of time.

BIBLE TEXTS

"But to each one of us grace has been given as Christ distributed it. Therefore, it says: 'When he ascended to heaven, he ushered captives into his caravan- righteous saints from all generations-and gave gifts to men.' What does 'He ascended' mean except that He also descended to the lower, earthly regions? He who descended is the very same one who ascended higher than all the heavens, to fill the whole universe. It was He who gave some to be apostles, some to be prophets, some to be evangelists, and some to be pastors and teachers, to prepare God's people for works of service."

Ephesians 4:7-12

"What is faith? It is the confident assurance that something we want to take place is going to happen. It is the certainty that what we hope for is waiting for us, even though we cannot see it up ahead. Men of God in days of old were well known for their faith. By faith—by believing God—we know that the worlds and the stars—in fact, all things--were made at the command of God; and they were all made from things that can't be seen."

Hebrews 11:1-3

"And those who are wise—the people of God—will shine as brightly as the sun's brilliance, and those who turn many to righteousness will glitter like stars forever."

Daniel 12:3

"This is what the Lord says: 'Only if the heavens above can be measured and the foundations of the earth searched out, will I reject all the descendants of Israel.'"

Jeremiah 31:37

CHAPTER 9
OTHER WONDERS

"How fast would you like to travel," questioned the teacher? The boys looked at each other, and then answered.

"We would like to go quite fast, but slow enough to see some of the special things on the way like the large sun you mentioned."

"Would you like to see another illustration of the size of the Universe," asked the saintly figure? He searched deep in their eyes for an answer.

"Yes, what do you have?"

"Here is Earth." A small dot in the universe began to grow until the viewers could recognize some of the continents, but what a tragic scene met their eyes. As the earth was magnified, the lads saw giant ocean waves of red and brown beating against the jagged rocks and remains of great cities. Hurricanes and tornadoes shrieked from place to place. Volcanoes erupted, and the earth heaved and swelled like a boiling pot. Over the ground were strewn the dead bodies of the wicked. Their eyes had been blasted from their sockets. The whole scene brought a sickening feeling to the watchers. The sky was so filled with smoke and dust that the sun was barely visible. Giant glaciers of a reddish, bloody hue crept over the desolation, covering it with a frozen blanket. Lucifer and his demon hosts were roaming endlessly around, adding their shrieks and howls to the wind. Such was the deadly result of sin.

As Trust looked at the spectacle before him a Bible passage came to mind from Zechariah 14:12 "This is the plague with which the Lord will strike all the nations that fought against Jerusalem; Their flesh will rot while they are still standing on their feet, their eyes will rot in their sockets, and their tongues will rot in their mouths." How dreadful were the "wages of sin" when compared to the free gift of God-Eternal Life. The boys could say nothing in response to that calamitous picture. A deep gratitude came from the depths of their souls toward Jesus as never before. They fully realized for the first-time what Salvation from sin meant. They reflected on these things for several minutes. Even though they were thankful for Salvation, they also realized now, how open were their thoughts and actions to the inhabitants of this holy place. Angels, elders, and even the inhabitants of all the other worlds, could look down at any time, and see everything that was taking place on earth. They wondered how often had they been seen doing things that did not bring glory to Jesus? They shuddered at the thought of some of their sins as the exhibition played out in front of them. Nothing was hidden from the Father. How differently they would act if given another opportunity to dwell in the land of the enemy. They would always act as the friends of Jesus they had professed to be.

The teacher paused only a moment longer on the appalling scene, then made the earth to appear as it had once been, with its continents resting in the deep blue of the oceans.

"While you were watching the water creatures in the court, you may have noticed some very tiny specks swimming about. They were single celled creatures. If the earth you see now was one of these tiny creatures and we were to drop it into an ocean such as the one before you, that would be a good illustration of what earth is compared to the vastness of the Universe. That tiny cell could roam the boundless oceans for millions of years and not begin to see all that they contain. So, it is with God's Universe. Eternity itself will not be long enough to discover all that He has in store for those of us who responded to His call and were rescued from sin."

They were traveling now. Constellations, planets and wonders too delightful for words sped past them as they zeroed in on the giant sun. It loomed before them so massive that it blotted out everything else. Immense red, orange, and yellow streamers shot from its surface as the group came to rest on a gigantic planet of unfathomable size.

"Are there people living on this planet," questioned Lasonaph?

"Yes", was the response. "This is one of billions of inhabited planets. It is a large planet. It is large enough to contain all the created hosts in this galaxy at one time. Jesus will come here soon with the redeemed and meet with His created beings in this sector. The meeting is planned for a Sabbath in the not-too-distant future. You will be His witnesses and tell the countless unfallen beings what Jesus and Salvation from sin mean to you. It will be a happy celebration such as none before. Once a month we will meet here or on like planets across the universe to worship and give glory to God for His love. But let's be off now for the Planet of Twin Suns."

Soon they were there and stood back in wonder at the phenomenon stretching out before them. There were two suns, but how different they were from each other. One glowed brilliantly with a light several times brighter than our sun. The other was a dark violet blue and hardly visible. The boys were about to ask what the dark sun was when a long arm of a brilliant, golden, green began to stretch out from the bright sun. It grew longer by the second and made a circle about the dark sun-then for a few seconds there was a tremendous thundering, like a giant gas burner being ignited. The dark blue sun became as brilliant as the bright one. The bright sun, in turn, faded and turned the color the other sun had been. A few minutes passed and the now bright sun sent out a long arm encircling the dark sun. Again, there was the sound of ignition as the dark sun blazed up, nearly extinguishing the former bright one.

"This spectacular phenomenon occurs every 30 minutes. It is like a giant, universal, cosmic clock ticking out the endless moments of eternity." I have come here often and watched it for hours and marveled at the wonder of it all."

He turned to the boys and bid them sit down, then continued.

"You have grasped a little of the magnitude of God. You have seen some of the vastness of His creation. You understand now how small man is and how large God is. He is so vastly superior to you and me that never in a million years will we be able to comprehend even a small portion of His power. Just as He is infinitely greater than you and me, so was His sacrifice in giving His Son, Jesus-greater than you and I can ever imagine. Jesus was slain from the foundation of the world. God knew it would happen and a plan of Salvation was laid out. At the appointed time He sent His Son. He loved like no other, but they put Him on the cross. The matchless Jesus hung on a cross alone. For a few moments all the safety of the universe hung on the cross with Him. Had He failed to live a perfect life, even in the smallest degree, Satan would have been free to spread the terrible destruction you witnessed on earth to the entire universe. He would not have rested until he pulled down the very throne of God if that were possible."

The suns were exchanging energy again, and the three watched with renewed intensity.

"This phenomenon, of all the illustrations I have seen in the universe, best depicts Gods love to me. When the bright sun reaches out to the dark one, it gives everything it has to insure the life of the other. The Great Father gave everything when He gave Jesus. As the one sun is revived by the other, and as both give all to ensure the life of each other, so Jesus drew His strength from the Father only to give it all for you and me. The boys were silent for a long time as once again an overwhelming love for Jesus flooded over them.

They stayed on this planet for a few hours enjoying some of the many other wonders it contained. In one area there were a several caves filled with hundreds of quartz crystals. Inside the caves, the three could see an even more spectacular display of the brilliant color changes that occurred each time the suns ignited. Another cave contained a green emerald gem that glowed in the dark interior like some phosphorescent wonder. As the boys were coming out of this cave, a large animal came up from the water and looked at them with its deep blue eyes. It stood up on feet like a man and had arms and hands with webbed fingers. There was also a long tail attached to its body. The tail helped guide it in the water. It was a creature unlike any they had ever seen. Even the teacher was surprised at the presence of this stranger. He had been on this planet several times. Whenever commissioned to go to some galaxy remotely near this place, he would stop off and watch the mighty suns at work, but never had he seen any form of animal life here. The main form of vegetation was a green mossy–like plant that clung to the rocks near the bodies of water. Further in on the land masses, however, were jungles teaming with tropical plants and flowers. They approached the creature and looked at it closely. In the days of his innocence Adam had held communion with the animals and plants in his garden home. In their immortal state the three also had these abilities to communicate with the animals.

In its own way the animal wanted to join them in giving glory to the Creator who had made it. A light fog was rising into the air as the two suns began to set.

"You have never seen sunsets so beautiful as the ones on this planet," spoke up the teacher. "Two suns setting give double color in the sky."

He was right. As the suns set it truly was beautiful. Just before they sank into the misty sea, the creature lifted its voice in a series of long, sweet sounds. They went out over the evening landscape and returned with several echoes, converging upon themselves like a great harmonic choir. The animal placed its notes in such an order that their sound mingled with the echoes and created a most soothing, harmonious melody.

"What is the name of this creature," asked Trust?

"I do not know that it has a name son," was his reply. "Why don't you give it a name?" Trust thought for a while then asked Lasonaph to help. After several moments they reached an agreement.

"We will call it 'The Majestic Singing Rhap-so-daun-ta.'"

As the suns took their plunge, colors unlike any earth had ever seen spread across the sky. Gigantic electrical flashes streaked outward and upward forming a firework display unequaled in beauty. The Rhapsodaunta arranged its music in perfect timing with these lightning works. It truly was a beautiful planet, made even more so by these melodic symphonies. When darkness finally spread its blanket over the heavens, the four creatures locked arms and gazed into the starry night until five moons rose out of the east and spread their lunar glow over the misty landscape. Songs of praise and thanksgiving drifted back to the pearly gates from this place so far away. It was strange to see evening again, but kind of nice. The sweet melodious sounds of the Rhapsodaunta grew fainter and fainter as the three winged their way homeward.

BIBLE TEXTS

"Long ago, God spoke in many ways to our fathers through the prophets (in visions, dreams, even face to face), telling them little by little about his plans for the future. But now, in these days, He has spoken to us through Jesus, His Son, to Whom He has given everything, and through Whom He made the world and everything there is. God's Son shines out with God's Glory, and all that God's Son is and does marks Him as God. He regulates the universe by the mighty power of His command. He is the one who died to cleanse us and clear our record of all sin. When he had

done that, he then sat down in highest honor beside the Father in heaven. Thus, He became far greater than the angels, as proved by the fact His name 'Son of God,' which was passed on to Him from His Father, is far greater than the names and titles of the angels."

Hebrews 1:1-4

"Listen to this. . . stop and consider God's wonders. Do you know how he controls the clouds and makes his lightning flash? Do you know how the clouds hang poised; those wonders of him who is perfect in knowledge? . . . can you join him in spreading out the skies, hard as a mirror of cast bronze? Tell us what we should say to him. . . Now no one can look at the sun, bright as it is in the skies after the wind has swept them clean. Out of the north he comes in golden splendor; God comes in awesome majesty.

Job 37:14-22

"The heavens praise your wonders, O Lord, your faithfulness too, in the congregation of your holy ones, for who in the skies above can compare with the Lord? Who is like the Lord among the heavenly beings? In the council of the holy ones God is greatly feared; he is more awesome than all who are around him. O Lord God Almighty, who is like you? You are Mighty, O Lord, and your faithfulness surrounds you. You rule over the surging sea; when its waves mount up, you still them. . . The heavens are yours and yours also the earth; you founded the world and all that is in it."

Psalm 89:5-11

CHAPTER 10
A SABBATH IN HEAVEN

On the way back to the city, the three stopped at a planet filled with thousands of butterflies. The ground was carpeted with a glorious array of deep cupped flowers. These flowers were of many beautiful colors. A sweet fragrance filled the air, and the planet was alive with the sounds of singing birds and humming bees. The teacher picked a deep red flower and showed it to the boys. It was partially filled with a nectar-like substance.

"Pick one of these flowers, Ammon and Lason. Then taste the liquid they contain." The boys each picked a flower and tipped it up until the syrup entered their mouth. They noticed that if the flower was red the syrup was red. If the flower was orange the syrup had an orange tint. The most exciting thing about these flowers was the taste of the syrup. It was absolutely the sweetest taste that had ever entered the boy's mouths. There was a tangy flavor that made them want more. Each color flower had its own flavor.

A large butterfly with a two-foot wing spread landed on the orange flower that Lasonaph was holding. The three gathered around and watched as the giant insect unfolded its long tongue and dipped it into the nectar. Its eyes were an iridescent blue-green, and its wings were light blue with deep blue and orange spots. Each spot was trimmed with a dark–almost black–band. After taking a sip, the butterfly shook its head at the boy and flew away.

"Why did he shake his head at me," questioned the lad?

"It is part of his swallowing process," answered the teacher. "His tongue is like a long straw. He sucks up the nectar into his mouth and then shakes his head a little from side to side to get it down. You will find that the syrup in your orange flower is thicker than the syrup in a yellow or pink flower. It is harder for him to get down, so he must shake his head a little. The red flowers contain the thickest syrup."

"That is why you selected a red flower isn't it, Teacher," questioned Trust?

"Yes, you are right, that is why I selected a red flower. This syrup is not only thicker, but sweeter than all the other syrups." The three sampled the syrup from several flowers and had to agree. It was sweeter and thicker than all the others. They wondered why they had not seen flowers like these in heaven, but there was a lot of heaven yet to see.

They selected a few choice red flowers to take back to the city for their friends, then watched the colorful array of butterflies as they flitted from one group of flowers to another. The size of the butterflies ranged from very small to wing spans as large as six foot. Many of the butterflies were iridescent, with colors that changed with every angle of the sun. It was peaceful on this planet and the boys would have liked to stay longer but the teacher told them of a special meeting back in the city. They were going to meet for a Sabbath in Heaven. So, they lifted gently into the air, taking a fast spin around the planet, then found themselves quickly back in the city.

There was a great excitement in the air. Millions of the Redeemed were making their way to the giant Colosseum by God's throne. At the entrance, Joy met Trust and introduced him to her new found family. Trust introduced his sister and father to her, then with reverent step they passed between the giant columns that marked one of the entrances to this colossal amphitheater in the sky. Each person upon entrance was given a golden harp. Joy looked at the harp and noticed the many red and green gems sparkling from the back and sides of the instrument. She carefully tucked it under her arm and continued holding the hand of her newly found Mother. An angel showed them to their seat. They were twenty sections up, and very close to the Throne of God. The silence and reverence displayed in this place was very noticeable. There had never been a gathering of so many human beings in one building before. Complete quiet and reverence marked the very atmosphere. The stillness was felt, and yet it was not a fearful stillness but an expectant, joyful stillness that might break forth in rapturous music at any moment.

If we could but catch a glimpse of the reverence displayed for God in the Holy City by the angels and those chosen ones who returned there with Him at His ascension, we would be much more reverent as we enter our houses of worship here on earth from Sabbath to Sabbath. When we go to church to meet with God we are going to meet with The King of Kings and Lord of Lords. He is our Creator, our Re-creator, our Savior, and our God. He is Emanuel, The Everlasting One, The Prince of Peace. He is The Alpha and Omega, The First and Last, the One Who Was Forever and Forever Is. He is God Almighty. Bow before Him with humility, for He is All in All. All power and authority are given unto Him. Without Him you are nothing. Worship before Him with a reverent heart, reader. He can read your very soul.

A light mist surrounded The Great White Throne. All eyes were riveted to a central area where a light grew brilliant and more glorious with each passing second. As the mist cleared, the face of Jesus appeared-more glorious than it had ever been before. Everyone present felt as if they were arrayed before the judge of all ages. His eyes were as a flaming fire, and none felt they were worthy to be in His presence. With humility they bowed before Him. Angels, men, woman, and children bowed side by side. A trumpet sounded and signaled all to rise. As the saints rose their hands swept over the strings of their harps with the touch of the most skillful musician. An anthem started at God's throne and made its way around that vast assembly gathered there until the whole amphitheater swelled with the sweetest melody that had ever been played. Each person knew when to play their part.

Joy found herself raising her voice now. Something came from the depths of her being that she had not known existed there before. The song grew louder and then softened. All were silent as the group directly around the throne sang a special song. It was the song of the One Hundred and Forty-Four Thousand. Only they could sing this song, for only they had experienced the same feelings that Jesus experienced during those fearful hours on the cross when He was shut out from His Father's presence because of the burden of the world's sin he carried. For several months, these One Hundred and Forty-Four Thousand had been left without a mediator. They had only their hope in God to preserve them from the fearful temptations all around. Like Jesus, they endured the reproach cast upon them and held on to the only thing they could–Jesus was coming soon. Their song was a song of this experience. Their faces radiated a joy that none of the rest of the great throng could totally enter.   After their song, the Twenty-Four Elders sang of their experience, followed by the song of the Twelve Apostles who were nearest Jesus and were directly next to the Throne. Gabriel then took His position as the leader of that vast gathering and led the company in song after song as a million praises ascended to the Father. It had been several thousand years by earth's time since that Colosseum had been full. Every seat was occupied. The angels who had been in those earlier, happier times looked back and remembered the perfect rapture that had filled all of Heaven before sin: Before Lucifer took a third of heavens angels with him in his rebellion against God. But that rapture could not begin to compare with the present joy that permeated Heaven on this Sabbath. It was good to have a full house again. Jesus looked out over the assembly and was satisfied. Heaven was once again full.

A great hush came over the Redeemed and the Angels as God The Father rose from His Throne. Joy noticed that

Jesus was not wearing a crown. As The Father approached His Son all the company again bowed in reverent humility before Him. They were bidden to rise and watch as The Father placed a new crown of glory on the head of Jesus. Music again swelled and re-swelled–the realms of Paradise, echoing back from a thousand spirals as Jesus was crowned King of Kings, and Lord of Lords. The Father gave the Son a set of Golden Keys and bid Him reign over His kingdom. Again, the company bowed in humility before Him as they realized that here was a king who understood them and had given all, that they might partake of the glories of this wonderful place.

After the crowning of Jesus, other recognition was given. One man was beckoned to the feet of Jesus. On earth he had been unable to speak. He had been told about the love of Jesus at an early age, and, as he grew, a secret longing had come over him to sing praises to God. He composed a song of praise for God and within his mind sang it repeatedly. Now he was given a special gift. Lucifer's voice had been unequaled in perfection and loveliness. In the former years before his fall, he would, on occasion, sing the solo part of some of the many anthems. His voice had been multi-dimensional. He could sing many parts at the same time. But when he fell, that voice fell with him. Gabriel had a good voice, but it could not equal that of Lucifer's. Now this man was given a multi-dimensional voice and was enabled to sing as that mighty angel of the past. He sang a song so lovely that all bowed again in reverence to God as he pointed out how worthy of praise, and honor, and glory, Jesus was. And so, the happy hours of this Sabbath in Heaven passed, and the story of Salvation was told and retold. A thousand testimonies were given and great was the happiness of everyone present. There were gathered there the redeemed of all ages. Let the happy moments of eternity come and go. It was good to be in Heaven. Each one present knew that they would not have been there except for Jesus. He was the one who had stepped down and given up His former

Kingdom with its empty seats so that He might be given this present Kingdom with every seat filled.

The Joy that we experience in that place beyond the blue will be a joy that we cannot now comprehend. One thing will be certain. As we look back on our little stay here on earth, with its sin and troubles, we will know that this heavenly paradise was worth every sacrifice we had to make to attain entrance to its glorious realms. Heaven is cheap enough. It is ours for the taking. Jesus has done everything He can to make it accessible to us. The rest is up to us. Will we reach out and accept this gift that He offers? He has opened the doors for us. By faith we can enter that city and eat of The Tree of Life. Are you homesick for Heaven, Reader?

THE SPIRIT AND THE BRIDE SAY, "COME."
AND LET HIM WHO HEARS SAY, "COME."
WHOEVER IS THIRSTY, LET HIM COME.
AND WHOEVER WISHES, LET HIM TAKE
THE FREE GIFT OF THE WATER OF LIFE.
REVELATION 22:17

Drink deeply, friend, drink deeply. That River of Life is flowing for you now. Drink deeply, and thirst no more. Heaven is cheap enough. Its glories are for you. Jesus is calling you, Mothers and Fathers. Jesus is calling you, Children. Jesus is calling you, Reader. Are you suffering from some lingering illness? Jesus is calling you to a place where sickness cannot exist. Is there trouble in your home—perhaps between you and your spouse? Jesus is calling you to a heavenly family where trouble is not known. Are you facing financial troubles? He has streets of gold and a golden crown for you. Are other troubles surrounding you that seem to shut out the glories of Heaven? Jesus is there beside you and He will lead you out of any difficulty or give you His strength to endure it. You who have been used to seeing with four eyes. He has new eyes that will never grow dim. Your glasses will not be needed in Heaven. Those with false teeth, He has a new pair of teeth for you and will give them to you before you eat of the Tree of Life. Have you lost a loved one in death's grip? By the grace of God, you will see your loved one again in that eternal abode with the saved. Is there a wayward child who seems bent on breaking your heart? The Tender Shepherd is seeking that lost lamb and He will do all in His power to see that son or daughter walk with you in Paradise. To miss Heaven will be to miss everything. The trial that is now pressing you down will be nothing then. What matters most is that you will be with Jesus forever. Eternal Life! Think of it. You will live forever and ever, never to die! That youthful body you had will be with you forever! Those who are dear to you can be with you forever. The Heaven experience can be your experience! It will be your experience! It must be your experience! You have an inheritance waiting for you. Take hold of it now! Jesus Himself has invited you. Join me in prayer now as we approach The Throne of Grace.

Our Father in Heaven. We realize that to be a citizen of Your Kingdom we have but to reach out and accept the gift of Eternal Life that You offer. We want to do that just now. We realize we cannot enter that city if we have anything in us that defiles. Search us just now. Notice each sinful desire, each cherished idol, notice everything that is separating us from You. We give these separating sins to Jesus just now and ask His forgiveness. We cannot remove them from our lives. It is beyond our power, but Jesus can remove them and has already done so. We accept the forgiveness that Jesus made possible by shedding His blood on Calvary. We stand beneath that crimson flood and allow it to wash all our sins away.

Thank You, Jesus, for making this possible. Thank You for loving us so much that You were willing to freely forsake the glories of Heaven to seek out the lost and dying ones like me. We cannot understand why You were willing to do that but with humility we accept Your forgiveness.

Create in us a new heart and a new mind. Let Your mind be in us. Come into our lives and transform us into Your image moment by moment. Make us more like You. Give us Your love for the lost and perishing ones next to us. Send Your Holy Spirit to minister to them through us. Use us to further Your kingdom here on earth, and by making ourselves available for Your service, we realize that You will come for us that much sooner. We thank You for Heaven and the hope of Your soon return. We are waiting and watching for You. Give us a love for Your Word, Your Righteousness, Your Salvation and may we meet with You in that Eternal Home that You have gone to prepare for us. This is our prayer in Jesus Name, Amen.

BIBLE TEXTS

"So, the heavens and the earth, and everything in them were finished. And on the seventh day, God ended his work which he had done, and he rested on the seventh day from all the work he had done. Then God blessed the seventh day and sanctified it, making it holy, because in it he rested from all the work which God had created and made."

Genesis 2:1-3

"Remember the Sabbath day to keep it holy. Six days you shall labor and do all your work, but the seventh day is the Sabbath of the Lord your God. In it you shall do no work: you, nor your son, nor your daughter, nor your manservant, nor your maidservant, nor your cattle, nor the stranger who is within your gates. For in six days the Lord made the heavens and the earth, the sea, and all that is in them, and rested on the seventh day. Therefore, the Lord blessed the Sabbath day and hallowed it."

Exodus 20:8-11

"If you turn away your foot from the Sabbath, from doing your pleasure on my holy day, and call the Sabbath a delight, the holy day of the Lord honorable, and shall honor him, not doing your own ways, nor finding your own pleasure, nor speaking your own words, then you shall delight yourself in the Lord; and I will cause you to ride on the high hills of the earth, and feed you with the heritage of Jacob your father. The mouth of the Lord has spoken it."
Isaiah 58:13, 14

"For as the new heavens and the earth which I will make shall remain before me," says the Lord, "so shall your descendants and your name remain. And it shall come to pass that from one New Moon to another, and from one Sabbath to another, all flesh shall come to worship before Me," says the Lord.
Isaiah 66:22, 23

"The Sabbath was made for man, and not man for the Sabbath. Therefore, the Son of Man is also Lord of the Sabbath day."
Mark 2:27

"Do not think that I came to destroy the law or the Prophets. I did not come to destroy but to fulfill. For assuredly, I say to you, till heaven and earth pass away, not one coma or period will pass from the law, till all is fulfilled."
Matthew 5:17, 18

"Blessed are those who do his commandments, that they may have right to the Tree of Life and may enter through the gates into the city."
Revelation 22:14

CHAPTER 11
THE HOUSE OF TRUST

Trust bid his friend a good day after that Sabbath with Jesus. He also sought leave from his father and sister. He wanted to go to his home and ponder on all the events that had transpired. He wanted to think about all the people who met him and traced their presence in heaven to his message. Upon leaving the amphitheater, he quickly took to the air and was soon at the entrance to his home. His was a more secluded dwelling. It was surrounded by giant trees and beautiful flowers. It looked like many parts of the Garden of Eden–in fact, the Garden of Eden was located behind it. Trust pushed back the foliage of paradise and started up the hematite walkway. The stones were beautiful. Looking beyond the silvery exterior of the stones, the inside was of a reddish color. On earth these stones were known as blood stones. If a small one was placed in a glass of water, the water often became tinted red. Trust knew why Jesus had chosen them. He had participated in the death of a martyr, so blood stones were appropriate for him. He noticed the dainty moss surrounding them and examined the numerous fruit trees that were along the path. He plucked a pear-shaped fruit and took nourishment from it, then ate a few figs.

At the entrance to his home, he paused at the silver, mirrored door. He looked at his profile and saw that he had grown some since leaving earth. In fact, he had grown at the least two inches. He looked at his red–trimmed robe. It still hung the same distance from the ground. It had grown with him. That was one thing about the robes Jesus gave. One was enough. He changed the hue a little from pure white to a golden yellow, then touched the door. It rolled back into the wall.

Trust had not spent much time in his home. He had been so busy. He had paused here only long enough to place his stone on the shelf, then move on. He looked at the royal blue walls before entering. They were beautiful as only Jesus could make them. Inside, he picked up a crystal and drank long from the living water. It was wonderful, so soft it soothed his throat and filled him with vigor unlike he had ever experienced before meeting Jesus. He went over to the wall where the whole armor of God was displayed. As he looked it over, he saw there were battle scars where the enemy had tried to destroy him. He looked at the chandelier and the many jewels it contained. There was one jewel for each person who had responded to his message or the message of the friends of the ones who had heard him. He marveled at the number. He could see them all in his mind and recall all their names. Wherever he went in the city or the universe of God, if he saw one of these, they were instantly recognized, and a special bond of love passed between Trust and them that cannot be fully described.

At last, he entered the prayer room. There, kneeling on that soft, velvety carpet, he sought an audience with The King of Kings. He had many questions. Jesus appeared and the conversation began. Trust first wanted to know why Jesus had created such a beautiful home for him.

"I did so little Jesus, why did you bestow all this on me? This home is the most beautiful one in all of paradise. I never dreamed such a place was possible. You knew exactly what I would like and spared nothing to make it perfect in every way. Why?"

"This is only a small token of My love, Trust. You never will be able to totally comprehend what one person saved in the kingdom of heaven means to Me. When I created Adam, he was part of Me. When he sinned, the separation pained Me deeply. When each child was born part of Me was with them also. When Abel was killed by Cain, part of Me died, but I knew Abel would be here in heaven, so it did not hurt so much. There are billions who died and are not in this place now. When they died, a part of Me died with them. So, when people are rescued from the second death by accepting salvation, it is like being resurrected again, brought back from the dead. Because of your messages in that city on those cold, dark nights, hundreds of people are here in heaven and will dwell with Me for eternity. The worth of even one person is greater than all the treasures of this city combined. They are more valuable than anything I can give to you. You gave them to Me, in a way, by sacrificing your wants and desires to build this kingdom. You built this home piece by piece. It is a small token of thanks for your willingness."

Trust remained silent for a time. He looked at the fruit on the table in the dining room. Outside he saw the pond with the swans and the waterfall. Then, with a heart overflowing in gratitude, much in the same manner as a sweet little girl he knew, he rose from his knees and threw himself in the arms of Jesus. The great King took him upon his lap and held him` close like a mother would clutch her child to her breast.

"I love you, Jesus. You mean more to me then all of this." He let his hand sweep around him at all the beautiful things.

"I love you also, Amanelohiym," responded Jesus. "I have always loved you. Long before you were born, I knew of you and longed for the day when you would be created. I watched you grow and suffer the pain of your parent's separation. I wanted so much to comfort you, but you did not ask Me. I will not visit people unless they ask. You did not ask until just before you stood up to give your messages. Then I came with several angels. We pushed back the forces of Satan and allowed people a chance to hear your story of Me. Many people heard and responded. We needed a voice, and you were that voice. From those meetings, the angels went with everyone who responded, and they were in turn given power over the enemy. When they spoke to their friends and relatives, the message went out with power. I will be eternally grateful for what you did. You started a ripple that grew larger and larger. That is how the Kingdom of Heaven grows. It starts within and keeps getting bigger and bigger until it ends in life eternal." Looking deep into the eyes of Jesus, Trust thanked the great King and love grew. Trust did not think he could love deeper, but after meeting his Lord he realized the love he had was minute compared to what it would become as the ages of eternity rolled by. The two rose and went out by the pool. The swans came up to their Creator and He communicated with them. They gave Him praise for His goodness and thanked Him for their own home. By the waterfall, the King again sat down, and Trust again climbed up in His lap. He had another question.

"Why did You bring Joy into my life?" Jesus smiled as He thought of the little lady. She was one of the meekest residents of heaven. There had been so few thoughts of self while she was on earth. She had been content with even the smallest things. He looked off now and, in His mind, saw her with her new found family high in her palace above. Then He answered.

"As you know now Trust, Joy was born blind as well as crippled. She had a family, but those who were supposed to be closest to her chose to separate themselves from her. When she was resurrected, everything was new. The change she experienced from the darkness to the light was overwhelming. She never saw colors. She had never seen people. She had felt them but was unable to form a picture in her mind. She did not know what round was until Nancy traced a circle in her little hand. She could hear and was so thankful for that blessing. From what little she had; she formed her own pictures of what her world looked like. But when she was resurrected, how different it was from the pictures she had formed. It was difficult for her to put the two worlds together. She had a thousand questions and no one close, other than Nancy, to help her make the transition. Nancy had her own family. There were people she never expected to be there. Her brother was separated from her when she was little. She had a close bond with him and needed to experience the trip to heaven with him. It was not as easy for Nancy to be there for her as it was for you. True, Joy was changed as all were changed at My coming, but still did not have perfect understanding. I knew I could trust you to be her guide. She really liked her angel, but needed a person, and you were again willing. You were her first friend near her own age. She will make hundreds of thousands of friends all over the universe, but her friendship and trust in you throughout eternity will be a blessing that is unfathomable. Outside of our relationship, she will be closer to you then anyone else including your father or sister. In short, she was My gift to you. Not as a wife, for there will be no marriage here or in the earth made new. She will be a very good friend, though, and you will grow to love each other very deeply."

"I am really thankful You did bring her into my life Jesus. It is like you say. I have a love for her that is unlike any other, save the love I have for You. I will treasure her friendship and Your gift of her to me forever. I know we will have an eternity of fun together. It is good to have a soul mate. Thank you, Jesus." With this, Trust leaned back and placed his head on the chest of his Savior. Some of the long locks of Jesus' hair fell gently on his face. Trust had finally learned to trust Jesus completely.

Jesus left, and Trust took one more tour of his beautiful house. He traced his fingers over the gold and silver trim around the windows. He gave some thoughtful attention to each plant in his yard whether large or small. He smiled at the flowers and sensed them smiling back. Then he flew to the tallest tree in the grove behind his home in Eden and looked out over heaven. A heart full of praise ascended higher and higher until he saw the smiling face of the Ancient one seated on His throne. Heaven was beautiful enough. Here was peace, here was love, and here was Joy. He pondered on Joy for a moment. She was such a happy little person. He was glad she had smiled at him on the great white cloud. He realized he loved her deeply, with a bond that could not be broken. His love for her was more like the love a father has for his child. She should have been called the trusting one. She trusted him right from the start and had inspired him in a way no others had. She had been a most precious gift from Jesus.

"Jesus knew just what I needed," declared Trust to himself. The boy turned his attention to the Garden of Eden. It was the most beautiful place in all of heaven. He thought back on the pictures that came to mind before he saw this place. Nothing on earth, not even his imagination, could grasp the beauty. At the center of the garden, a symmetrical hill rose toward the heavens. It was carpeted with a rainbow of colors. There were flowers from the top to the center. From the center on down, it appeared like a topaz, nearly transparent. At the base, surrounding it, were the homes of Adam's decedents. They were crystal mansions and appeared to be carved right out of the mountain. Off to the right was a beautiful lake. Cascading streams flowed into it. Adam's home was the most elaborate of them all.

Trust now turned his attention to the center of the city. He looked at the Tree of Life and the Great White Throne rising high above it. Then he spotted Nancy, Joy, and her grandparents. They were headed toward his home. From another direction he saw his father and sister coming. He would have company soon. He flew down from the tree and met Joy just as she was coming to his hidden path. He jumped out from behind a shrub and scooped her into his arms. Looking deep into her dark, shining eyes, he told her he loved her. Then he planted a sweet kiss on her ruby–red lips.

"I love you too, Trust." responded Joy. "Thank you for being my very best friend." She took his face in her little hands and returned a sweet kiss of her own to his lips. Trust greeted Nancy and Joy's grandparents, then slipped back behind the shrub. As soon as his sister appeared, he jumped out and gave her the same treatment he had given Joy. She displayed more surprised than Joy. He had never been affectionate with her. On earth she had been somewhat of a bother. Now however, a deep love came over him for her. Next to Joy, she was a priceless treasure. He led the little procession toward his silver door. It was time for them to see the house of Trust.

BIBLE TEXTS

"When you pray, you should go into your room and close the door. Then pray to your Father who you cannot see. Your Father can see what is done in secret, and he will reward you openly."

Matthew 6:6

"Now the one who plants the plants and the one who waters them have the same purpose. Each will be rewarded for his own work. We are workers together with God. And you are like a farm that belongs to God. And you are a house that belongs to God. Like an expert builder I built the foundation of that house. I used the gift God gave me to do this. Others are building on the same foundation. But everyone should be careful how he builds. The foundation has already been laid. No one can build any other foundation. The foundation that has already been laid is Jesus Christ. Anyone can build on that foundation, using gold, silver, jewels, wood, grass, or straw. But the work that each person does will be clearly seen, because the Day will make it clear. That Day will appear with fire, and the fire will test every man's work.

1 Corinthians 3:8-13

The wall was made of jasper. The city was made of gold, as pure as glass. The foundation stones of the city walls had every kind of jewel in them. The first stone was jasper, the second was sapphire, the third was chalcedony, the fourth was emerald, the fifth was onyx, the sixth was carnelian, the seventh was chrysolite, the eighth was beryl, the ninth was topaz, the tenth was chrysoprase, the eleventh was jacinth, and the twelfth was amethyst. The 12 gates were 12 pearls. Each gate was made from a single pearl. The street of the city was made of pure gold. The gold was clear as glass.

Revelation 21:18-21

A person who loves innocent thoughts and says kind words will have even the king as a friend.

Proverbs 22:11

CHAPTER 12
PLANET OF SNOW

Time in Heaven is measured on a much different scale. There is no sun and no night. On earth when we refer to a day, we speak in terms of the sixteen or so hours we spend in consciousness. We sleep the other eight or so hours, and that makes up what we call a day. Seven of these days make up a week and thirty or so of these days make up a month. In Heaven there is no sleeping. There is rest though, and for several "weeks" that is what the redeemed did. It was like a long vacation where nothing went wrong. Joy and Trust visited their friends and enjoyed the fellowship of new acquaintances.

Joy especially enjoyed being with her grandparents. They traversed the city together and took in its many wonders. The little girl loved the fountain areas. There were nine intersections where the golden streets crossed each other. The streets were very wide and had a beautiful fountain in the center of each intersection. These fountains were fed by the river of life. Joy and her grandparents spent many hours by them, watching the animals as they played beneath the foaming spray. Joy had never been allowed to swim on earth, so this was a sport that she especially liked. Each fountain was surrounded by a beautiful garden. These gardens contained fruits of every description and gloried in the brilliant light that came from the Throne of God. A million flowers raised their heads proudly toward the King of Kings. Their fragrance permeated the entire atmosphere.

One day when Joy and her newly acquired family were walking in the gardens by one of these fountains, Celestania came by for a visit. The mighty angel asked them how they were enjoying the wonders of Heaven and inquired if they had any desire. As Joy saw him, she opened her arms for him to pick her up. She had been denied love so much as a child, she could not get enough of being cradled in the arms of a mother, grandparent, or even an angel. As he lifted her gently, she remembered when Jesus had taken her in His arms to meet the Father. She looked deep into the eyes of her angel and asked him a question.

"Could you take us to a planet somewhere outside of Heaven?"

"I would be glad to," responded the angel. "What kind of a planet would you like to go to?"

"Take us to a planet with some very tall mountains," responded the child. "I enjoy those mountains outside the city very much. They are so green and the flowers there are so crisp and colorful. I like to see the woods and how the light shines through them. I like the mossy carpet and the little bees and the colorful birds. It is all so wonderful, but I want to go to a place where there is snow. Could you take us to a place where there are tall mountains and lots of snow? On earth I felt snow and they told me it was cold and white. I want to see how white and how cold."

Joy's Grandparents looked at each other with a remembering smile. They had experienced many a winter together on earth. The thought of that place returned to them now. It seemed so cold and dark. Winter was always associated with some of the more bitter experiences they had endured. Winter to Nancy brought an entirely different reaction. She had been raised near a mountain and had spent hours skiing down its slops. She tried to envision how it might be to ski now with her new body. It responded so quickly to the impulses her mind sent. It would be marvelous to stream down slopes of pure white and feel the frosty air enter her lungs again. Yes, to the mountains it must be. The five strolled off to the courtyard and entered one of the subterranean chambers. The angel pointed to a particular galaxy and commented on some of the many features it contained. This galaxy was known from earth as the Spiral Galaxy of Andromeda.

"The galaxy you see here, Joy, is made up of over one hundred billion suns. Each sun in this galaxy is bigger than the sun you had on earth."

"How many is a hundred billion, Celestania," asked the little girl? The angel smiled and looked quietly at the precious bundle in his arms.

"Do you think you could count to two hundred fifty in one minute?"

"Oh, yes," replied Joy. "That would be easy."

"You are going to be in Heaven for one thousand years, then Jesus will take this great city down to the earth and make that His capital kingdom. If you were to start counting now and were able to get two hundred fifty numbers out each minute, you would reach one hundred billion by the end of the thousand years. If you were to visit a sun in this galaxy each minute, it would take you over two hundred fifty thousand years to make the circuit. When you finished it, there would still be hundreds of billions of other galaxies waiting for you to explore." The little company was silent for a long time, trying to grasp the magnitude of what the angel had said.

"Each of these galaxies contain hundreds of millions of suns. Jesus rules all of them. He spoke one sentence and they were billions and billions of them shining in all their splendor, praising Him for his love and goodness. Trillions of inhabitants on these planets all paid homage to Him. They worshiped at his feet and gave Him their devotion. Yet He saw the little planet called earth dying in darkness and gave up everything to go down there so He could bring you here to be with Him.

In this galaxy you will find one of the nicest snow planets in all the universe. There is a company of redeemed leaving for this mountain planet right now. Would you like to join them?"

"Yes," responded the group with one voice. "That would be very nice.

There were about fifty people in the company. Some were skiing enthusiasts; some preferred snowboarding, while others just liked to go where their friends went. One artist wanted to make a larger–than–life, snow carving of giraffe. Then he wanted to slide down that snowy neck just for the fun of it. Another person liked ice caves. At sundown, the ice caves on this particular planet gave a brilliant display of extraordinary color. Trust came up and joined them. With much enthusiasm and excitement, the company set off for the snowy mountains of Lanex.

On the way, they stopped briefly at a tropical paradise. The inhabitants there were generous people and gave a great feast of the rarest fruits and nuts in that part of the Universe. There were some fig shaped fruits that came close to the flavor of the fruit Joy had tasted from the Tree of Life. The color of this fruit could not be described. It was a new color Joy had never seen. The angel explained how the color had been present on earth, but the light penetration had been so subtle, the human eye could not see it. There were some tiny, orange, cherry–like fruit that tasted tangy like the soda pop we are used to drinking on earth. There was also a white fleshy fruit that looked like a pear but had a flavor so unusual it seemed to stay in the taste buds for hours afterward. Joy placed a couple of these fruit in her robe to enjoy later back in heaven. Another fruit was a deep purple color and was comprised of a grouping of twenty-four seeds. Each seed was surrounded with a juicy skin. Trust separated one of the seeds from the cluster and popped it into his mouth. As he bit down, the sweet juices squirted out and pulverized his mouth with a wonderful flavor. He shared this with Joy. She too, took some of the seeds and noticed that each seed had an entirely different flavor. It was so amazing she ate two of this fruit and enjoyed every bite. It was too wonderful for words. Trust flew to the top of a tree and chose two of the largest fruits and brought them back to her. She placed these also in her robe. When she got back to the city, she would plant one of these trees near her waterfall. She cut off a branch from the fruit tree and tucked it away with the other fruit. That would be her new tree. Nancy and grandmother smiled as they watched.

After the meal, the company strolled to one of the giant bodies of water and watched the waves roll in as the people on that planet played sweet melodies on their musical instruments. Some of the group went surfing on the giant waves, others sat down on the thick green carpet of grass and watched the birds of paradise as they winged their way from tree to tree, dipping into the water every now and then for a drink. As the sun set on this tropical paradise, they watched it spread a hundred radiant colors over the waves before disappearing below the surface of the water. The company then took to the air and were off again for the planet of their choice. Soon it loomed before them in all its splendor.

It was a giant white gem reflecting the light of its blue sun. Grandmother and Grandfather expected to be struck with the icy blast as they came in for a landing but were surprised to feel as warm as they had been on the tropical paradise planet. They inquired of Celestania.

"Why are we not freezing cold here? On earth the winters were so bitter we could not bear them–especially when we grew older." The angel smiled.

"When Jesus came to earth to get His people, each one was given a new body, a body of radiant energy. The food you eat is also energy and fuels your whole being when eaten. Your new body is surrounded by a robe of light. Each robe is made up of the glory that comes from the Father. Your robe automatically adjusts to the surrounding temperatures. If we had a thermometer here it would read ten degrees below zero. You do not feel the cold because your robe keeps your immediate surroundings at seventy–four degrees. Your robe also gives you oxygen to breathe while you are traveling through space. It would also sustain your physical need for nourishment if necessary. Another feature of your robe and body of energy is its frictionless nature. We came here at tremendous speeds. Several times faster than the speed of light. Your robe allows for this speed."

"You can also change the color of your robe," continued the angel. "What is your favorite color, Grandfather?"

"I was always fond of blue."

"Turn your robe blue then," the angel suggested.

"How," asked Grandfather?

"Just think that you want it blue, and it will be blue." Grandfather did and was amazed as his robe took on a royal blue hue. He experimented with various shades then settled for one a little darker than the shadows of the mountains. Others in the group experimented with various colors on their robes. Joy chose a pastel yellow with a golden border around her neck and hem. It was amazing to see all the different colored robes against the snowy white background. Trust already knew of the possible change in color and settled on red.

Joy now turned her attention to the mountain looming in front of her. She looked up, up, up, up. Higher and higher her eyes traveled, then she saw the top. It was way up there. She dropped into the snow then started moving her arms and legs to form an angel. She looked up at her angel and smiled.

"I want to feel the cold. How do I feel the cold Celestania?"

"Just wish it." responded the angel. Joy wished it, and felt it growing colder and colder. It was only for a moment though. She remembered how cold, cold was.

"Joy."

"Yes, Mother Nancy."

"Do you want to try skiing down that mountain with me?"

111

"Yes, I do."

"Let's go. Are you coming with us Trust?"

"I sure am, Nancy. You couldn't keep me away."

"How about you, Grandma and Grandpa," asked Joy?

"Not now Dear. Your Grandfather wants to go with Bennidad to the giant ice caves, I think I will go with him," stated Grandmother. "You three fly along now and have some fun, we'll be all right." The group took to the air and were quickly at the top of that gigantic mountain. Nancy had fashioned some skis out of giant icicles at the entrance of one of the ice caves. She had also created some ski poles. Trust did not want to ski. He wanted to snowboard. He cut a board out of a sheet of ice. With their new found powers, they fastened the skis and board to their feet, and started down the seventy-five mile stretch of mountain. It was wonderful to be on skis again. Nancy showed Joy how to bend her knees and take the jumps. By the time five or six minutes had passed, she was skiing like a pro. Trust had no trouble at all learning how to snowboard. He had been somewhat of a skateboard enthusiast in Chicago. The snow sprayed up brushing over their face while behind them three trails of white followed from the top of the mountain.

They tried the mountain from all sides and had a wonderful time, then skied off to see the giant snow sculpture. The giraffe was nearly completed. The sculptor had used ice to support the neck of this mighty structure. The gravitational pull on this planet was several times greater than the pull of earth or Heaven, and the sculpture had to be dense enough to support the weight. That was another amazing feature of the light robe. It adjusted to all types of gravitational pull. The artist flew to the top, and with shouts of glee grasped the neck of the snow beast and slid down. He asked Joy, Nancy, and Trust if they would like to give it a try. All three did, with great delight. How quickly the day flew by. On Lanex a day equaled one hundred twenty hours. As the giant blue sun began to set in the azure sky, the artist,

Joy, Nancy, and Trust headed for the ice caves. The rest of the group had assembled there to watch the changing colors, the sky created in as the sun set. It really was a wonder to see. Celestania led them in a few songs of praise as the last rays of color faded into a star-spangled night.

They were in one of the denser portions of the galaxy and viewed the stars with great wonder. Thousands of them twinkled, displaying every color possible. In one area five suns were so close together, they appeared to be one giant sun. It would be awesome to fly through those giant balls and see them looming all around. They looked at one particularly colorful area. It was a giant nebula composed of the deepest reds one could imagine.

"Let's pass through that nebula on our way home, Celestania," exclaimed the group together. "Then we want to fly by those five suns." And they did just that. As the vivid colors surrounded them, they thought of the crimson blood Jesus shed in their behalf on a cruel cross so far away. His blood had met the requirement "Without the shedding of blood there is no remission from sin." Jesus had paid their price with His blood and had washed them whiter than the snow they had played in that entire day. What wonder! Each passing moment brought on more love for this Creator, Mighty God, and Savior. The name of Jesus was on every lip as the gates of the Holy City came into view.

BIBLE TEXTS

"God thunders marvelously with His voice; He does great things which we cannot comprehend. For He says to the snow, "Be on the earth: likewise, to the gentle rain or the heavy rain, or the rain of his strength."

Job 37:5, 6

"Have you entered into the depository of the snow, or have you seen the treasury of the hail?"

Job 38:22

"Purge me with bitter herbs, and I will be clean; Wash me, and I will be whiter than snow."

Psalm 54:4

"Come now, and let us reason together," says the Lord, "though your sins are dark like scarlet, they shall be as white as snow; though they are red like crimson, they shall be as wool."

Isaiah 1:18

"For my thoughts are not your thoughts, nor are your ways my ways," says the Lord. "For as the heavens are higher than the earth, so are my ways higher than your ways, and my thoughts than your thoughts. For as the rain comes down, and the snow from heaven, and do not return there, but water the earth, and make it bring forth and bud, that it may give seed to the sower and bread to the eater, so shall my word be that goes forth from my mouth; it shall not return to me void, but it shall accomplish what I please. And it shall prosper in the way which I sent it."

Isaiah 55:8-11

"And He was transfigured before them. His clothes became shining, exceedingly white, like snow, such as no launderer on earth can whiten them. And Elijah appeared to him with Moses, and they were talking to Jesus."

Mark 9:2-4

CHAPTER 13
WORKING WITH JESUS

Not all the time in Heaven was spent in worship, leisure, and travel. There was a work appointed to each person gathered on that golden shore. It was not hard work, neither was it the most pleasant. But it was necessary so Lucifer's charges, that God the Father was not fair, could be cleared in everyone's mind. It also made it possible for everyone to understand why some of their loved ones were not with them in Heaven. Joy had gone often to the building where she had first seen the record of her parents' life. Trust had gone there too. In this sacred hall the whole truth about everyone that ever lived was revealed. Joy and Trust were heading for it now when their friend Mr. Parrot joined them.

"Hello Joy. Hello Trust. Are you happy? Are you happy with Heaven?" "Oh yes, Mr. Parrot!" exclaimed the children with one voice. "Heaven is wonderful. It is the grandest place in all the Universe. And what about you; are you happy?"

"Very happy." responded the bird. There was a flutter of wings and a brilliant gold and green female parrot landed on Joy's head. The little girl lifted her hand, and the creature took a quick hop, curling her bright, orange feet around one of Joy's fingers. She was very beautiful. Her feathers were iridescent and changed back and forth from gold to silver in the glorious light that surrounded her. She spoke in a questioning voice more musical than her suitor's.

"Joy? Trust? What a wonder! What a wonder! Hello, children." With that, she jumped into the air and came to rest on Joy's shoulder.

"Why hello, Mrs. Parrot!" exclaimed the children in delight. "You are very beautiful! Why haven't we seen you before?"

"Too many wonders, children," she replied.

"I suppose you are right Mrs. Parrot," responded Trust. "There are so many wonderful things in Heaven, we haven't begun to see even a small portion of them yet."   "Do you like her?" questioned Mr. Parrot. "Isn't she a wonder?"

"Why of course we like her, Mr. Parrot," returned Joy. "She is very beautiful, and just right for you. I think you two make a good pair." The Parrot moved his proud head back and forth, then hopped up in the air and turned around on Trust's shoulder. He looked at the green and gold lady with admiration in his beady, little eyes than spoke again.

"Starlacia is wonderful." The children were quick to pick up the name.

"That is a very beautiful name for a lovely lady," expressed Joy. Then she directly addressed the lady with a question while pointing to the red and green creature combing his feathers on Trust's shoulder.

"What do you call Mr. Parrot, Starlacia?" The little bird moved her head back and forth then up and down as she eyed him.

"Stalandon," she stated quickly.   Trust stopped and grasped the Parrot with both hands, then looked him directly in the eyes.

"Is your name Stalandon?"

"Si, Si," replied the bird.

"Are you talking Spanish or English," probed Joy?

"Spanish," questioned the bird? "What is Spanish?" The children laughed and laughed at the endless wise cracks this wonder of paradise came up with. They were even more surprised to hear both Starlacia, and Stalandon laughing with them. This made quite a spectacle as they crossed one of the great, silver bridges that spanned the water around the large rose covered building.

"How many languages in Heaven do you birds speak," he questioned?

"Heaven's language," came the reply. And so it was the language of Heaven. Trust returned the bird to his shoulder perch as they entered one of the twelve doors. These two little ones had learned a great deal about God's love in the few weeks they had been here. Every day called forth new wonders and new revelations about this love. The Plan of Salvation was so simple, it seemed hard to understand why so many chose to ignore the way of escape Christ had made for all in His victory on the cross. Jesus was in the building as the children entered. He spent a great deal of time here, explaining to the various companies how He had arrived at each decision. He looked down at these two beloved children and smiled. He held out one of His hands and the two birds flew to it quietly.

"Starlacia and Stalandon, it is very good to see you again," He said. His voice was soft and musical. Love was the all-powerful trait of that voice that had spoken worlds into existence. He was so tender and loving one couldn't help but be drawn to Him. Even these creatures now resting on His hand knew He was the Creator and made a slight bow as He addressed them. He gently stroked their heads with His free hand, smoothing out their feathers with a gentle, downward sweep.

"Joy and Trust, Heaven is blessed by your presence. You have helped fill this place with laughter and singing. You have made it more complete and I love you both greatly." He returned the birds to the shoulders of the children, then placed His long arms around them, giving each an affectionate hug as He led them to one of the casings. The children thrilled at His gentle touch. He had a sweet fragrance around Him like a mountain meadow, washed clean after a spring rain. There was a strength about Him that made one feel weak in His presence. There was a peace that penetrated everything when He was near. It was a peace that surpassed human understanding. How often had the millions of the people, whose records and deeds were recorded in this building, gone to this mighty Prince of Peace, and found refuge from the fierce attacks of the enemy. Somehow, in His presence, all was well. This peace now sheltered the children as they went over the actions and lives of the lost in the room.

"We are going to look at your Mothers records today, Trust. She came so close to choosing Heaven." He worked His hands back and forth and the casing began to glow. A picture of a very beautiful lady appeared. She was smiling and running in a field of flowers. In the background, a white-capped mountain raised its head over the golden plains. He did something else to the casing and the children could enter the experience of the woman, even detecting her thoughts and motives. She was praying as she ran. It was a prayer of thanksgiving. Her whole being was directed in giving Glory to God.

"I loved her very much Trust," spoke Jesus very affectionately. "She had a way of talking to Me that made Me love her more than you can understand. She knew Me here and we had great times together. I shared many secrets with her when she was Mine and I was hers." The matchless Son of God paused a few minutes, letting those happy scenes sink into the experience of the little group watching from beyond. At last, He moved ahead in the life of this woman.

When Trust's father received the call to go to a mission in Chicago, it was a sad experience for this lady. She loved her mountain home in the country. A portion of her died when the dirty streets and sidewalks of that metropolis came into view. The living conditions in the mission were not good. The soup kitchen shared its scanty board with the cockroach and carpenter ant. Day after day they brought the alcoholics in off the street and cleaned them up while giving them a hot meal. As this lady washed the residue from the faces and smelt the foul order coming from the mouths of these fallen children, she often thought of her mountain home and longed to run there and hide away. If she were but a honey bee, flirting from daisy to daisy, how much better her life would be. As the pictures flashed before them, there was a steady decrease in prayer. Her tender heart, once melted by the love of Jesus, hardened daily.

One day as she was working on a particularly obnoxious

case, the lady that began to emerge from beneath the filth opened her mouth and spit in the face of Trust's Mother. She had been half conscious, chewing on some tobacco. The wad hit its mark and the red juice trickled down the tired face of the minister's wife. She was so surprised; she struck the lady with the back of her hand before she had time to think. A moment later, she realized what had happened, and left the room crying. From that time on she failed to trust God. The lady was too drunk to give the strike any thought at all. Indeed, the man she lived with dealt much harder blows than that daily. To Trust's mother, though, it was as if she had committed the unpardonable sin. Like Moses in striking the rock that represented Jesus, she had struck the Son of God in the person of this wretched child. She closed her heart to any further prompting of His Spirit and died that day spiritually. As she shut out the presence of her Salvation, she opened herself up to the evil one and allowed him full control in her life.

She took the children and left the mission and her husband. They moved to a small apartment in one of the suburbs, where she passed on her corrosive feelings to Trust and his sister. She was nearly successful in erasing the training her own hands had instilled in them. Only the prayers of a loving father kept the angels of darkness from completely shutting out the light that came down from Heaven. As the closing, destructive events fell like a plague upon the earth, the Holy Spirit made a final, desperate attempt to reach this woman. She nearly responded. The call was so urgent, but probations hour passed while she was in the valley of decision. A tear trickled down the face of Jesus as the children saw Him stand up and make the pronouncement.

"He that is filthy, let him be filthy still," So closed the book on this once child of the King, and there was sorrow in Heaven as the angels of God looked down on the millions who refused to respond to God's last call. So close to Heaven, and yet so far. Three words could have made all the difference in the destiny of this woman. "Lord! Save me!" but Heaven waited in vain for this utterance. Her voice, once lifted in praise and adoration to the Creator, will be silent forever. What a loss eternity suffered in this loved one. It was a terrible loss for Jesus too. She was on His mind when He cried "It is finished," on that cross so long ago. So close and yet so far. Don't let this be your experience, Reader. Don't miss Salvation by three words. Won't you say them with me now? "Lord! Save me!"

Trust leaned back and let his head come to rest on the strong arm of Jesus. He had seen his mother's records before, but never had to pass judgment on her. The Savor looked into his face with compassion and love.

"Are you ready to see what I have decided for her?" Trust nodded, responding.

"You are all knowing, Jesus. I trust your judgment completely. I am ready."

"I took her entire life into account. I considered how different the picture might have been had she stayed in the mountains. Here is the result of her sacrifice in going with your father to the city." Jesus made some pictures emerge on the casing. There were two hundred and forty-three people in Heaven as an indirect result of her work in Chicago. The children saw them dressed in white robes beneath everlasting skies of glory. They were singing a song. Jesus pointed to a woman who had her arms around a couple of children.

"This is the woman your mother struck in her moment of weakness. These are her two children. They are three of several gathered here in Paradise. I considered this when I decided her case." Jesus looked at Trust with a love so deep that everything else lost all significance. Trust knew full well he could leave the results of his mother in the hands of this Kindly King.

"She will suffer only a moment." There was a long pause, then Trust responded.

"You are righteous, O Lord. Your ways are just. You have judged fairly." The strong arms of the Master encircled him once again as the pictures faded from sight.

Trust's Mother missed Heaven by so little. Had her former love for Jesus remained strong with her new surroundings, she would be with them there going over the records. But she, like so many, failed to trust God completely. Lack of trust in God causes the thief to steal, the disobedient child to dishonor his parents, the idolater to worship his gods of stone and metal. It causes the man to look with lust on his neighbor's wife, the murderer to revolt against his victim, and the liar to pour forth his deceptive words. Failing to trust God caused Israel of old to walk in the ways of wickedness. It caused the pious leaders in Jesus day to raise Him up and crucify Him on the cruel cross, there to shed His sacred blood for the wickedness of man. And today it causes us to separate ourselves from our only means of Salvation. Can God be trusted? If He can create a hundred billion galaxies, He surely can solve even the most difficult problem we could ever encounter. He who can hang giant suns, five hundred million times larger than our own feeble one, on nothing, is surely big enough to do what He says He will do. Why are we so slow to trust the One who loved us so much He was willing to give up everything to assure us a place in Heaven with the bright, shining angels? He would have come even if it meant blotting His own name out of the Book of life. He loves us that much. His love was demonstrated by His sacrifice, and His call goes out today,

"Take no thought of what you will eat or drink, or how you will be clothed. I know your needs and will supply them. Trust and obey."

So ended the session with Jesus. The children were silent as they left the building. Even the birds refused to talk as they made their way to the home of our first parents, that beautiful Garden of Eden.

BIBLE TEXTS

"For God so loved the world that he gave His only begotten Son, that whoever believes in him should not perish, but have everlasting life."

John 3:16

"Most assuredly, I say to you, he who hears my word and believes in him who sent me has everlasting life, and shall not come into judgment, but has passed from death into life. Most assuredly, I say to you, the hour is coming, and now is, when the dead will hear the voice of the Son of God; and those who hear will live. For as the Father has life in himself, so he has granted the Son to have life in himself, and has given him authority to execute judgment also, because he is the Son of Man. Do not marvel at this; for the hour is coming in which all who are in the graves will hear his voice and come forth-those who have done good, to the resurrection of life, and those who have done evil, to the resurrection of condemnation. I can of myself do nothing. As I hear, I judge; and my judgment is righteous, because I do not seek my own will but the will of the Father who sent me. I bear witness of myself; my witness is true."

John 5:24-31

"Do you not know that the saints will judge the world? And if the world will be judged by you, are you so unworthy to judge the smallest matters? Do you not know that we will judge angels? How much more, things that pertain to this life?"

1 Corinthians 6:2, 3

CHAPTER 14
A BETTER UNDERSTANDING OF GOD

After the children left, Jesus made His way back to His throne by the Father. It was nearing the time when He was to make a special trip around the universe with several of His redeemed. Since returning to Heaven, several representatives from unnumbered planets had come to the Holy City with invitations for the King of Kings to visit them with a delegation of His chosen ones. They wished to honor Christ and join with Him in a victory celebration. Hundreds of these planets were preparing, and the time had come for Him to make His first journey since finishing this phase of His work on earth.

A bright light enshrouded the throne as the Father and Son held conference together. Soon the brightness lifted, and all eyes were fastened upward. Gabriel was commissioned to blow a mighty trumpet. As the clear, penetrating sounds went out over the city, several of the redeemed recognized in it the call of God and began to make their way toward the great white throne. The group was composed of the champions of truth from all ages, starting with Adam and continuing down to the One Hundred and Forty-Four Thousand. Among the group were Seth, Enoch, Methuselah, Noah, Abraham, Joseph, David, Elijah, Elisha, Daniel, the Apostles, Steven, Paul, and several others like Luther, Huss, Jerome, Miller, White, Livingston, and Andrews. Joy and Trust were not included in this select group, but they like others did not feel left out in the least. One thing was apparent on all the Saints headed toward the throne, each had a crown so laden with starry gems, the crown itself was hardly visible. This select group had, with whole hearted surrender, allowed themselves to be used as instruments of the Holy Spirit. Certain angels had been included in that call also, and many of them joined with the company gathering around Jesus and His Father.

As they drew ever closer and closer to Christ, the Holy Spirit drew them in a circle of brilliant light ten-fold greater than any that had yet graced Heaven. The beautiful mansions and gardens appeared more glorious than ever in this brilliance coming from the company. The light became so great that the heavenly hosts at last lost sight of them. It was Christ's purpose to give these chosen ones a greater understanding of God and the Plan of Salvation. Since the beginning of sin, every detail in the downward spiral of Lucifer and man was faithfully recorded with an accuracy thousands of times more sophisticated than man can begin to conceive of here on earth. The Father had captured every detail of the great drama and placed it in a time capsule. It was possible to go to any point in the drama and see clearly what was happening at every stage. One who was privileged enough to partake in this experience could see with accuracy what was happening in Heaven at the time of the first advent of Christ or the temptation of Eve and the fall of man. They could see what was happening in the satanic realm, as well as be a participant in the experiences of those humans living on earth at that time. They could see all the thoughts of everyone displayed, along with the motives of Satan and his host of evil angels. They could see the activities of heavenly angels as they were each appointed their work in the plans of God. They could behold the drama, as God, with all His knowledge, saw it thousands of years earlier. It was a real privilege to be appointed to this group. If we could but once see the entire picture as these chosen few could see it, sin would hold no more attraction for us. We would gladly give up everything for Christ and the cause of God, and never look back. Our efforts directed toward earthly pursuits would be channeled toward heavenly ones. We would accept Christ's victory over sin and become partakers with Him in His kingdom.

While gathered close to Christ, the group could look in on Heaven before Lucifer started his rebellious course against God. They were able to see the throne as it was then. Around the throne were the Four Spirits of God, or as John the Revelator calls them, the Four Living Creatures. These Four Living Creatures are part of the work of the Holy Spirit. This group was able to watch the activities of the Holy Spirit in each phase of the drama. They were taken to the time when Jesus was about to create the first angel. They entered the experience as He brought the elements together, and with skillful hand weaved the fabric of Lucifer's soul, giving him life. They watched the first look of adoration this mighty prince gave his Creator and saw the love that passed between the two as they roamed the realms of glory. They saw each angel as it came forth from the Creator's hand, praising Him for His excellence and Glory. They saw the perfect order and harmony that existed then and entered the experiences of these angels as they sang their anthems of praise to the King of Kings. The moment He created the first angel, Christ stepped down and became one with them. At this time, He was known as Michael the Archangel. Lucifer, Son of the Morning, was the most exalted of the angels and stood next to Michael. In his innocence not a thought of rebellion marred his noble mind. Michael stood on the right of the great white throne; Lucifer stood on its left.

As the drama continued to unfold, the group saw the very first time this leading angel questioned God. The Father and Michael were about to create the world. Michael was called from His post and shut in by the glory around the throne. Lucifer wondered why he had not been taken into this council, and a bit of doubt about the Father's wisdom entered his mind. Was not he more beautiful than Michael? Why then, was he left out? The group of Saints now gathered around the throne saw why Lucifer was not invited into this council. In His foreknowledge, the Father knew that the world would soon become the one dark spot in the universe and choose a course against God. He knew that Lucifer would be at the forefront of this rebellion. The Father and the Son needed to work out a Plan of Salvation for man should he choose to join in the rebellion. Had this mighty angel been given access to this foreknowledge, he would have been a hundred times more effective in his assaults against Heaven. Even in all his wisdom, the mind of an angel would not then be able to grasp the full nature of the events that were so soon to transpire. He could not have believed and would have been appalled that the thoughts he now harbored could eventually lead him to take the life of the Son of God. Because of this, God chose not to invite him to enter the plans for the creation of man. God could have revealed the nature of sin to him in all its evil and blackness. Indeed, had he seen the ultimate results of his sin; he may have chosen not to enter upon that course of action. God would not do this, however. Before there ever was an angel, there were laws governing the Kingdom of God. His kingdom was built on love and the free power of choice for each of His created beings. This power of choice must remain on the rule books of His government. It could not be changed. Lucifer must choose his own course of action, for God would do nothing that could in any way be construed as forcing anyone to obey Him.

For a long time, Jesus and the Father were shut in by the Glory surrounding the throne, then Christ announced to the angels His intentions to create man. For a time, things returned to normal in Heaven. Lucifer continued his leadership of the heavenly hosts. All seemed well, but the group of saints and angels shut in by the glory of the Father saw darkness beginning to gather in the soul of Prince Lucifer. With every thought he harbored against the government of God, this darkness increased. At times Jesus would council with him in private, pleading with him to turn from his ways before he exhausted the mercy and patience of the Father. Lucifer pivoted back and forth in his decision and for a time seemed content with God's will. Whenever he focused on the position of Michael and compared it with his own, however, the old feelings would return, and he would allow the darkness to penetrate him further. Soon, he was no longer content to keep these things to himself. He went out among the other angels with his questions of doubt. The seeds he sowed found a ready place in the souls of many, and soon the peace and harmony that characterized Heaven at its beginning was broken. The group wept as they beheld with sorrow the fall of Lucifer and his followers.

They watched as the drama continued. The four living creatures left the immediate presence of the Father and with Jesus traveled to a place outside of Heaven. They saw Michael stretch forth His hand and instantly where there had been nothing, billions and billions of independent bodies of matter drifted in a universe around Heaven. Jesus went to one of these bodies of matter and called out in a clear, loud voice.

"LET THERE BE LIGHT." Instantly, the universe took on a new look. The light from around the throne of God went leaping out to these places the instant the words were uttered, and they were enshrouded in glory. On the second day, the Creator spoke again.

"LET THERE BE A VAULT, BETWEEN THE WATERS, TO SEPARATE WATER FROM WATER." The Four Living Creatures moved out from the presence of Christ over the waters and divided the waters on the earth into two parts. A sheet of water now covered the world, and another surrounded it several miles higher in the sky. It was as if someone had encased this little speck of matter in a giant greenhouse. The waters above the earth filtered out the cold. The place became warm like a summers evening. On the third day the Creator spoke, and land rose out of the waters. There were great lakes and rivers. He spoke again and, on this land, trees and flowers appeared with all manner of vegetation.

As this was taking place, the group was able to look in on the activities of Lucifer. He had been cast out of Heaven, and, with his angels, stood watching from afar, Michael's work as He brought the world into being. There was a sort of medium territory midway between earth and what was soon to become the sun where these angels of darkness took their stand. They dwelt there in that limbo land–a dimension outside of earth–quarreling and bickering, each fighting for the highest place next to their mighty leader.

On the fourth day the voice of the Creator called out. "LET THERE BE LIGHTS IN THE VAULT OF HEAVEN TO SEPARATE DAY FROM NIGHT AND LET THEM SERVE AS SIGNS BOTH FOR FESTIVALS AND FOR SEASONS AND YEARS. LET THEM ALSO SHINE IN THE VAULT OF HEAVEN TO GIVE LIGHT ON EARTH." Instantly the sun stood blazing in the sky with all its brilliance. Throughout the universe, trillions of suns shone in all their splendor, and around them independent bodies of matter circled in perfect order and harmony.

The group watched as each passing day brought forth new wonders from the hands of Jesus. They watched with tender regard as Jesus formed Adam from the dust of the ground. As Adam saw himself being created, he fell at the feet of Jesus and was followed by the others gathered near Christ. They could see it all happen so clearly. They were partakers with Christ in everything as He brought order out of nothing. They walked with Him in the Garden of Eden on that first Sabbath day and lifted their voices in praise as "the morning stars sang together, and the sons of God shouted for joy." (Job 38:7.) They saw the tree of life and the other tree–the tree of the knowledge of good and evil. Lucifer too saw the tree and began to realize that here was an opportunity for him to spread his rebellion to this new world. He pondered the thought for a while. He shrunk from the consequences that surely must be his should he dare to lead this new order of beings to separate themselves from God. On one hand, he rather liked the challenge, yet he could not get the picture of Michael creating the world out of his mind. As he saw the power come forth from the hand of this rival, he realized that He was more than an angel, He was indeed God. Finally, his mind was made up. He took a dispatch of his closest angels and returned to Heaven. At the gates of the city, he stopped a passing angel and bid him call for Michael. The Son came and listened as Lucifer confessed his sins–admitting his mistake. He asked Jesus to allow he and his angels back into Heaven. Were he returned to his former position, next to the throne, he vowed he would never again question the wisdom of God but would become his most devoted follower.

Each of the angels with him repeated the scene and begged to be readmitted to their former positions. Tears streamed down the face of Jesus as He listened to Lucifer and his followers. He loved these beings more than words can tell, but they had gone too far, too far! They could never again be accepted into the government of God. Time and time again they had been given a chance to repent and be saved but they all had passed the limits of God's mercy. Jesus had given them many chances. Adam and Eve on the other hand would only be given one chance. If they failed to trust God, the wages of sin called for their death. Their second chance would come but what a price. Their redemption would cost the life of the King of Kings and Lord of Lords. Jesus knew what Lucifer would do with man and that made His sadness even greater. He knew too that Lucifer would never be satisfied if taken back into heaven. With His foreknowledge, He saw Lucifer would never again be satisfied to submit to the rules of heaven after having experienced the complete power that came from leading his own subjects.

As Jesus told him the consequences of his sin were too great to be readmitted to Heaven, hardness boiled up in the heart of this Prince of Darkness, he left the presence of

Jesus, determined more than ever to do all in his power to fight against the will of God. Michael was superior to him in every way and he hated it.

"Why Him? Why Michael? Why couldn't he have been a god? He would be a god." He immediately took his position in the tree next to the Tree of Life. One day as a beautiful serpent flew by, Lucifer convinced him to land. The serpent was among the most beautiful of all the creatures. Attached to his body were wings of gold and silver that dazzled the eyes of the beholder. As this creature flew from place to place, all eyes turned to watch in wonder. This, thought Lucifer, was a fitting symbol of himself. Was not he the most beautiful of angels? So, in time, the serpent was in this tree when Eve approached. The company watched in sad expectation what they knew was soon to happen, but a surprise awaited them that would reveal a lot about God.

BIBLE TEXTS

"How are you fallen from heaven, O Lucifer, son of the morning! How you are cut down to the ground, you who weakened the nations. For you have said in your heart: 'I will ascend into heaven, I will exalt my throne above the stars of God: I will also sit on the mount of the congregation on the farthest side of the north: I will ascend above the heights of the clouds, I will be like the Most High.' Yet you shall be brought down to Sheol, to the lowest depths of the Pit. Those who see you will gaze at you, and consider you, saying: 'Is this the man who made the earth tremble, who shook kingdoms, who made the world as a wilderness and destroyed its cities, who did not open the house of his prisoners? All the kings of the nations, all of them sleep in glory, everyone in his own house; but you are cast out of your grave like an abominable branch, like the garment of those who are

slain, thrust through with a sword, who go down to the stones of the pit, like a corpse trodden underfoot. You will not be joined with them in burial, because you have destroyed your land and slain your people. The brood of evildoers shall never be named."'

Isaiah 14:12-20

"So, the Creator planted a garden called 'Eden,' in the east; and there he put the man whom he had formed. And out of the ground the Lord Made trees that were pleasant to the sight, to grow and produce good fruit. The tree of life was also in the garden at its center, and near it the tree of the knowledge of good and evil. A river flowed through Eden to water the garden, then it divided and became four rivers.

Genesis 2:8-10

CHAPTER 15
THE PLAN OF SALVATION

As the time for Eve's fall approached, Adam drew close to the Savior. The arm of the Mighty King encircled him, and a look of love crossed the face of the Son of God. The throng watched, but at the time when Eve reached out to pluck the fruit, the scene was blotted out. In its place were written the words "FORGIVEN." Adam breathed a sigh of relief as the scenes continued. "FORGIVEN" was written over his part in the drama also. And so, as the saga continued to unfold, each person in the company watched their part in the drama. If they had any sins, that portion of the scene was always blotted out by the blood of the Lamb. As the company saw the mercy of God, a text came to their mind. "As far as the east is from the west so far has, He removed your transgression from you." (Psalms 103:12)

The group was for a time, taken into the council room with the Father and the Son. They saw them discuss the proceedings that must take place now that man had fallen. The Plan of Salvation was made simple enough that none need be lost. Within the soul of each person, Christ would write a basic law of right and wrong. If the individual lived up to what they believed was right, more knowledge was given. In this manner, truth was preserved amid the darkness and progressed toward the total restoration of the man or woman to the image of God. If men and women failed to live up to the basic knowledge of right and wrong planted within them, eventually the knowledge of right was removed, and they were enshrouded in a thick darkness that completely shut out the beams of light that were ever coming from the throne of God. As soon as an individual turned from the right, Satan and his hosts of angels were upon them, leading them ever further down the path of destruction.

Adam and Eve lost a great deal because of sin and gained very little. They did not need a knowledge of evil to make their life more complete. All they needed, and more, was provided for them in the garden. With this knowledge of evil, they lost the right to partake of the tree of life. They were banned from their lovely home. They lost the natural traits of God's righteous character. They exchanged God's holiness for a nature that was attracted to sin. In place of love, peace, and harmony they became partakers of evil, suffering, and sorrow. But saddest of all, these evil traits were passed on to their descendants. Sin has contaminated every succeeding generation from the birth of Cain to our own day.

As soon as there was a sin, however, there was a Savior. Jesus immediately stepped between guilty man and God. Man's condition was hopeless. He needed Salvation from the consequences of his actions. "For the wages of sin is death, but the gift of God is eternal life in Jesus Christ our Lord."(Romans 6:23) Jesus would provide this Salvation by trading places with fallen man. He would accept the death the fallen race had earned that they might have the eternal life they forfeited through sin. He would accomplish two things in this plan. He would restore man to the image of God, then restore him to Eden.

As the company beheld the plans the Father and the Son laid out to redeem man, they were excited and happy. How could anyone be lost? Every provision was made for the sinner to be returned to the favor of God. After seeing the power and goodness of God, even the Prince of Darkness wished to be restored to the favor of Heaven. Why would not everyone want to take advantage of the Salvation so freely offered?

As the drama continued to unfold, they saw why so many would choose not to accept God's grace. In choosing sin, the natural inclinations of the race were not toward God. Another god had stepped between them and the true God of Heaven. Satan and his agents exalted self. Man's nature was now self-orientated rather than God-orientated. In (Romans 8:5-8) Paul sums it up this way. "Those who live according to the sinful nature have their minds set on what that nature desires; but those who live in accordance with the Spirit have their minds set on what the Spirit desires. The mind of sinful man is death, but the mind controlled by the Spirit is life and peace, because the sinful mind is hostile to God. It does not submit to God's law, nor can it do so. Those controlled by the sinful nature cannot please God."

Something needed to happen to change the nature of man from evil to good. In council, the Father and Son long considered this and made every provision for its fulfillment. To once again become a partaker of the divine nature man needed to die to his old sinful ways and be born again into a new life. Jesus, the angels of heaven, the Father, and the Holy Spirit would all go to work on behalf of the sinner who desired this new nature. They would push back the dark forces of Lucifer. The Holy Spirit would even fight the spiritual battles for any who wished to be members of the Kingdom of Heaven. All a person needed to do was ask, then be willing to be led, obey, and they would be led. All heaven was at their disposal to help in every way possible.

The group was transported ahead in the time capsule to the life Christ lived while on earth. They watched it unfold–perfect at every stage. The apostles thrilled as they saw their own response to this King and marveled how they could have been so slow to understand His purposes. From the other side of Heaven, a whole new outlook of His mission presented itself to them. They saw Lucifer and his evil hosts concentrating their greatest efforts to overshadow Christ and shut Him away from His Fathers presence so they could gain control of Him. They saw His constant dependence on the Father. As with Jacob and his ladder that reached to Heaven, they saw the angels of God ascending and descending, aiding Christ in His labors. Some were sent ahead of Him to prepare the way for His work. Several of them followed wrestling with the evil angels to prevent them from destroying the influence of the miracles of Christ. As the work of Jesus progressed, men united with Him in the war against evil. Little by little, Satan was forced to retreat, and there was joy in Heaven as the Kingdom of God advanced on earth. The Kingdom of Heaven started small, in the hearts of the people who responded to Christ. Then, as they used the knowledge gained from Him, more knowledge was given and with that knowledge, greater power over the enemy. The enemy doubled and tripled his efforts to circumvent this Kingdom, but Christ was, and is, stronger than Lucifer. The devil is no match for the Son of God.

Next, the group saw the crucifixion. They walked with Christ to the garden. It was there the Father first started withdrawing His presence from the Son. As the beams from glory grew less and less, the enemy pressed upon the Savior, covering Him with an overpowering darkness. Satan had kept a faithful record of every sin transferred to him in the sacrificial system designed to point to the Lamb of God. Jesus must bear these sins and pay the penalty for them. Sin was repulsive to Him. As Satan transferred these sins on Him, His spotless nature recoiled from the contamination of evil. Each sin took strength from His soul. He was caught in a slow, agonizing death from which their appeared to be no escape. He could not reach out and receive light from the Father to sustain Him. He must bear the penalty alone. As the weight of these sins pressed down upon Him, great drops of blood fell from His brow.

"If it be possible, Father, let this cup pass. Never-the-less not My will but Yours be done." The words were wrung from the dying Savior as the darkness overpowered Him. The group turned from the scenes, unable to endure the pain of their beloved King. At last, Gabriel, unable to bear the sight a moment longer, came to strengthen Him. The burden of sin was, for a time, lifted and He was able to endure the shameful events described in the Gospels.

The group watched everything and were partakers in His suffering. They felt the burden of sin He carried. They walked with Him up the stony path to Calvary and felt the scourge of the Roman whip. The thorns pierced their own brows. They felt the weight of the cross and fell with Jesus on the rocks beneath Him. When the nails were driven into His flesh, they felt the pain. They hung with Him upon the cross and became partakers in His agony as Satan directed the final assault on the Son of God. They marveled that a created being could treat his Creator with such cruelty. At last, the remaining rays of light from the Father were withdrawn. Jesus had become sin and the abhorrence of the Father was upon Him. The sun refused to shine. Darkness enveloped the entire earth. Satan and his demon hosts were given full sway over their Creator. Assault after assault was hurled. Finally, it was enough.

"It is finished! Father into Thy hands I commend my spirit!" The cry rang out through the universe and forever settled the issue of rebellion in the minds of unnumbered observers. Sin was conquered and would never rise again, but it must run its course. Though the observers from other worlds had made their choice, there were millions on earth who had not yet been given the opportunity to decide who they would follow. If they did nothing, they were the property of the Prince of Darkness and would be destroyed. If they wished to become a part of the everlasting Kingdom, the way was opened for them to become sons and daughters of God. The drama must continue until every living person made their choice—either for eternal life or for everlasting destruction.

Jesus now turned to the group around Him. His deep love for each one overpowered them as He looked into their faces.

"I endured all the shame of the cross for you. I offered my death to pay the penalty for your sins. You accepted My gift. You exchanged your sinful life for My spotless one. I took your sins into the tomb with Me and left them there. When I was resurrected, you were resurrected also, to a new life with Me. You were not content to keep the good news of Salvation to yourselves but spread it so many could be here in this place with Me forever. Well done! You have been faithful in little now you will be given much. Since you loved Me above all else, since your greatest desire on earth was to be with Me, you will be with Me, you will be My special messengers throughout the endless ages of Eternity. You will go with Me wherever I go. Millions of unfallen beings will give you honor as we travel to their homes. I am yours and you are Mine forever."

As this blessed assurance came from the lips of the King, the group gathered close around Him, fell at His feet, and gave Him homage. Their position would always be next to Christ. He had chosen them as His own. They would go with Him wherever He went. What a privilege was theirs.

The company continued their travel through time. A picture of the work of Jesus began to form—more and more beautiful with each passing age. Though one with the Father, Jesus had chosen to be represented as an angel as soon as angels were brought into existence. After man's fall, He condescended to become a human. He took on the nature of man after sin had degenerated the race for four thousand years. After gaining the victory over sin in man's behalf, He had returned to the Father—still in His human form—and would forever be kept within the confines of a human body. Gone now was His ability to be present in more than one place at a time. After the resurrection, He became the mediator, the go between man and God. At the appointed time He, as High Priest, entered the Holy of Holies and pleaded the cases of His chosen with the Father. At the end of this time period, He took off His priestly robes and put on His kingly ones then headed for earth to extract from the Prince of Darkness those who had chosen to be His. At that time, the Father had given Him complete control in the affairs of man. He was to reign until every enemy was at last brought to ashes. The last enemy He would conquer would be death.

The company with Jesus were advanced ahead to the time when that great city of God was to be transported to earth. They were shown the closing scenes of the drama. They watched the final destruction of sin and sinners. They saw death and destruction cast into the lake of fire. They were observers as Jesus recreated the world more beautiful than before.

When all was done, and perfect order and harmony once again throbbed throughout the realm of God, Jesus did a very beautiful thing. After His victory over Lucifer on the cross, the Father had given Him a set of golden keys. These were the keys to the Kingdom. His work was to rule until He had conquered everything lost by sin. The assembly remembered that first Sabbath in heaven when Jesus was again given some keys. This was for the benefit of all present. Those gathered in the great arena did not see what Jesus did with those keys for that was something He would do in the future. As the final scenes in the time capsule ended, Jesus approached the throne and handed these keys back to the Father.

"I have finished the work you gave Me to do Father. Here are the keys. Take them, You are ruler now. It is my desire to dwell forever with these I have redeemed from sin." So ended the saga of the lost world. Jesus had done it all. He was God and He was Lord. He was Man and He was the Savior of man. He was Priest and He was King. He was all things to all people. He was All in All.

Where do you stand today reader? Are you directing all your energies toward the Kingdom of Heaven? The way is open to you. You have been given the opportunity to exchange your life with all its woe and misery for the perfect, spotless life of Jesus. He loves you. He took the death your sin requires upon Himself so you may receive everlasting life with Him and the Father. He loves you so much, He would have gladly forfeited His right to the glories of Heaven so you or I might have the opportunity to be there. Such a sacrifice was not necessary. He did not have to come and save us. His love for us was so great though, He couldn't help Himself. He came and He conquered. In doing this He did not forfeit His right to Heaven but is alive and will be with us throughout the endless ages to come. You can have the assurance of being with Him forever.

Pray with Me. Dear Jesus: I accept your gift of Eternal life. Take my fallen nature and restore me to Your image. I want to die to sin and self so I may be reborn into Your Kingdom. Take me for I cannot even give myself. You must do it all Jesus. Do it now! In Jesus name I pray. Amen.

BIBLE TEXTS

"These are they which follow the Lamb wherever he goes. These were the ones redeemed from among men, being the first fruits unto God and to the Lamb."

Rev.14.4

"For now, we see through a glass, darkly; but then face to face: now I know in part; but then I shall know even as I am also known."

1 Corinthiens 13.12

"And men will come from east and west, north, and south, and sit in the kingdom of God. Many who are last will be first. Likewise, those who are now first, may be last."

Luke 13:29, 30

"And when they were come to the place, which is called Calvary, there they crucified him, and the malefactors, one on the right hand, and the other on the left. Then said Jesus, 'Father, forgive them; for they do not know what they do.' And they parted his raiment and cast lots. And the people stood looking on. And there were rulers also with them who derided him, saying, "He saved others; let him save himself, if he be Christ, the chosen of God let him now come down form the cross." And the soldiers also mocked him, coming to him, and offering him vinegar, And saying, If thou be the king of the Jews, save thyself. And a superscription also was written over him in letters of Greek, and Latin, and Hebrew, THIS IS THE KING OF THE JEWS. And one of the malefactors which were hanged railed on him, saying, If you are the Christ, save yourself and us. But the other answered and rebuked him, saying, "Do you not fear God, seeing you are also condemned? And we indeed deserve to die; for we will receive the proper reward of our deeds: but this man hasn't done anything amiss." And he said unto Jesus, "Lord, remember me when you come into your kingdom." And Jesus said unto him, Verily I say unto you today, you shall be with me in paradise. And it was about the sixth hour, and there was darkness over all the earth until the ninth hour. And the sun became dark, and the veil of the temple was torn in the midst. And when Jesus had cried with a loud voice, he said, Father, into your hands I commend my spirit: and having said this, he died. Now when the centurion saw what was done, he glorified God, saying, Certainly this was a righteous man."

Luke 23:33-47

"For, behold, I create new heavens and a new earth: and the former shall not be remembered, nor come into mind."

Isa. 65:17

"For as in Adam all die, even so in Christ shall all be made alive. But every man in his own order: Christ the first fruits; afterward, they that are Christ's at his coming. Then the end will come, when he shall deliver the kingdom back to God, even the Father: He will do this when he has put down all rulers and all authority and power. For he must reign, until he has put all his enemies under his feet. The last enemy that shall be destroyed is death. For he will put all things under his feet. But when he says all things are put under him, it means he will omit nothing but will put all things under him. And when all things shall be subdued by him, then Son also will be subject unto him that put all things under him, that God the Father may be all in all."

1 Cor. 15:22-28.

CHAPTER 16
JESUS ANSWERS WHY.

After coming out of the time capsule, the special group dispersed for a while. As one walked throughout the glories of that better world, they would see them here and there in different places of the city. Most of them were silent and reflective as they contemplated the experience they had just encountered. None felt worthy of the great gift Jesus had given them. There was no quarreling for the highest place of honor. Only the sincerest humility existed in that group. As they saw the entire drama of sin unfold and play out its course, they had a near complete understanding of why things had happened as they did. Every question for them was answered. Many in heaven still had questions though. The record room had answered the most immediate and personal questions, but there were some general ones that needed to be addressed. For this reason, another meeting was called in the great amphitheater. By the tens of thousands, the heavenly throngs began making their way to their appointed places. Jesus would show portions of the same drama to the entire population of heaven so all questions about the why of sin would be forever settled.

Joy, Nancy, Grandmother and Grandfather made their way quickly to their seats. Trust and his family were also moving to their places. From all over the city, people left their celestial activities to attend this meeting. Throngs and throngs who had left heaven for all parts of the universe, returned with their angel guides. At last, the place was full. Everyone was seated. Once again, a mist or fog enshrouded the throne of God. Slowly at first, then brighter and brighter came a light. It burnt away the mist and high above the assembly stood the great white throne. It was a triple throne. In the center sat the Ancient of Days–God the Father. On His right stood Jesus–God the Son. On the left one could see the mighty Gabriel. At the base of the throne were four beautiful creatures. They were like the description given by John in the book of Revelation but much more sophisticated. These were the embodiment of the Holy Spirit. John represented them as four beings, yet they were one. They were omnipresent yet there, at the base of the throne. As the throne appeared with the Father and Son, all those present at the assembly, including the angels, bowed to the ground. Not a sound was heard in that colossal amphitheater. Every head was bowed, every eye closed. Soon Jesus bid the group arise and the voices of millions and millions of angels rocked the foundations of the New Jerusalem. The redeemed joined them in giving praise and exultation to the King of King and Lord of Lords. One pulse of harmony throbbed throughout the whole of the kingdom as the Father and Son were exulted repeatedly.

At last Jesus and Gabriel sat down. This was the signal for all the people to be seated. Jesus looked over the entire throng. The redeemed and angels all felt His gaze upon them. Love everlasting radiated from Him, and in that look, each knew how much He loved them. Each knew He was acquainted with their entire life. They also knew He could read their thoughts. Joy wondered how Jesus could answer the questions of millions and millions of people all at once. Would they ask Him one at a time? If so, they would be there forever. But even as she thought of this question, the answer came quickly to some central part of her mind. Then she knew she only had to think of the question and Jesus would answer it. She had a one-on-one audience with her Lord and Savior. She asked why Nancy had never married and Jesus answered that the man she had been engaged to, had left town with Nancy's best friend two days before the wedding. The event had so hurt her, she never again trusted men. From that point on she threw herself into her work. Not far away Nancy had just asked Jesus about this same thing.

"Jesus."

"Yes Shanithilia," He responded.

"How could Henry appear to be so kind and loving to me and seem so dedicated to You when inside he was a totally different person? How could you let go of him or anyone for that matter, and have them not be here in heaven?" Jesus allowed Nancy to look deep into His eyes. His love surrounded her, and she felt a deep compassion coming from her Lord and Savior. Then He answered her questions.

"Henry was raised in a Christian home. He was expected to do everything right. For years that is how he lived. He took his parents beliefs and lived them. After he got out on his own, Satan came at him full force. Because he had never developed his own belief system, but took that of his parents, he was an easy victim. He felt freedom for the first time from the restraints that had been imposed on him. He knew how to act the part of a true believer because he had spent a lifetime doing it. He was engaged to you to please his mother. She took a fancy to you and told him you were the one for him. He led on that he loved you. You fell in love with him. You had no reason not to. Outwardly he appeared the perfect man for you. You fell in love with what you thought he was. Had he gone through with the marriage however, you would have had heartache after heartache, as you discovered his sincerity was only an act. He would have gone from one woman to another, even as he did before and after his marriage to your friend. In the end you would have lost your trust in Me and ultimately eternal life. There were many such people on earth who are not here in heaven. Outwardly they looked like the best of saints but inside they were entirely different. My first gift to Henry was life. What he did with that life was supposed to be his gift back to Me. His heart was so full of thoughts of self that there was no room for Me, you, or anyone else. He thought the life he had was his and he could do with it whatever he liked, but there were consequences to his actions."

"You asked how I could allow him or anyone to die, and lose out on eternal life? They chose it. They chose not to be here. They chose not to accept My second gift of eternal life. I made every effort to show Henry My love for him. I invited him to look away from his earthly life to the eternal one I had in store for him. He refused to do that. He did nothing with the measure of faith I gave him. Remember the parable of the talents I told while on earth? Henry did nothing with the talents he was given. They were given to be a blessing to others. He used them to indulge his own selfishness. Without a supply source to continue to draw from, soon the talents were all used up and his soul bankrupt. At last, he allowed Satan full sway in his life, and while indulging in the most awful sins, Satan came and claimed his own. I was nearby ready to reach out My hand and draw him back from the death grasp of the enemy, but he looked Me in the face and told Me to leave him and never bother him again. With pleading eyes, I tried to show him there was hope. I called again and again but Henry closed his mind to Me. He cursed Me and I turned away and wept. It was hard to let him go but it was his choice. My gift to people is first life and then life eternal. Their gift to Me is what they do with what I gave them. If they willingly gave the life, I gave them back to Me, I gave Eternal Life back to them in an even exchange. If they did not give their life to Me or did so unwillingly, then how could I give them anything more? Self was so big, there was no room for anything else in their life. If they did not want Me in their life on earth, it would have been like a hell to put them in My presence for eternity. When I came to them on earth, they looked at Me as a tyrant, robbing them of what they called freedom. They thought I caused them to be guilty about how they were living. They did not want Me around then, so I had no choice but to leave them to the decisions they made."

"Everyone who is not here chose not to be here. That

is how a kingdom of love must operate. That is why I gave the power of choice to all My created beings. The Father and I built this kingdom on that principle. It is an eternal law that can never be changed. If people really love Me, they will want to please Me and do what I ask. In doing that they will find the truest happiness because that is how I created them. I created them to love Me, to be friends and companions of Mine. I created them to be My sons and daughters, a royal household. When they follow Me, they find their truest joy and happiness because that is how they are made. They are designed to look beyond themselves. That is the only way a kingdom of love can exist successfully."

After hearing the words of Jesus, Nancy was overwhelmed. He had made it so clear. For years she had blamed herself for Henry's weaknesses. She had wondered if perhaps she had done differently, he would have been here with her, but now she saw he clearly chose to forsake the gifts of Jesus. He chose not to be in the family of God. At that point, an overwhelming love came over her for Jesus and the Father. They really did know how people would be the happiest. When she had buried her own wants and desires in service to Joy and others, she had been truly happy. As she gave love, love was given back to her. The more she helped others the more willing they were to help her. What she had sown on earth, she was reaping now in a heavenly, bountiful harvest. It was a universal law she would study for eternity. She had given and given of herself but now she realized, she could never out give her Lord. Eternity would prove that a kingdom of love was the best possible kingdom to have.

Trust's father had a question that had bothered him ever since he moved to the mission in Chicago. He wondered why thousands of innocent children had been abused, murdered, and destroyed by Satan? He looked back to a time when going to the door of some wretched soul, he was sickened as he saw where an eight, or nine-year-old boy had over dosed on the steps. No sooner had he thought this question, but the answer came softly, directly from the heart of Jesus.

"The enemy hated children, Tom. He couldn't break the love that so many of them had for their parents and those who mistreated them. I placed that love in their hearts. I saw it all too. I cried with the children and hurt with them as they experienced every painful thing. I wanted to go to the aid of each suffering victim, and I did rescue some from the clutches of the enemy. There were thousands who would have died had the angels not intervened. If someone, anyone prayed for these little ones, I usually did intervene. I sent the angels to surround and protect them. But for many the experience of losing that child, or seeing the love even when facing death, eventually brought repentance to the hardened heart of the tormentor. That love I gave these little ones softened the lives of many of their persecutors and they are here in this throng today."

"Tom. If you were to add up all the deaths, all the injustice, all the pain and all the bad things that happened just as they did, and count the number of souls saved here in the kingdom today, you would find that despite all the evil, all things worked together for good for those who loved Me. Why? Because out of all these bitter experiences, the largest number of people possible are here in the kingdom today having their questions answered just as yours are. Let's take the experience of that nine-year-old you remembered. I know the end from the beginning. Had Satan not succeeded in killing him with those drugs, he would have grown up to be a murderer. But before he murdered his first victim, he would have pushed drugs to another fifty young people and destroyed their lives while doing it. Of those fifty young people, eighteen are here because his death kept him from being an instrument of their destruction."

"Do you remember that little girl who disappeared from the department store Tom?"

"Yes Jesus," Tom replied. "I remember they found her

two weeks later."

"She is here today rejoicing with her parents. After her death they had such an overwhelming desire to see her again, they turned to Me and now they, with twenty-five others, are in this assembly. Through this tragedy twenty-eight people are here who never would have had the opportunity to come to Me. Had she lived; she would have brought heartaches unnumbered to her parents. The worst one would have been her marriage to a man who did not love her. Had that happened, three children would have been brought into the world who would have been a curse to society. With the loss of that girl, hearts were softened and made ready for the working of the Holy Spirit.

"Do you see that man and woman over there, Tom?"

"Yes Master," came the reply.

"On their wedding day the woman was killed. She had just said, 'I do,' and they were kissing when a sniper, aiming for the man, missed, and hit the woman. The man almost died from the loss, but had they stayed together, financial pressures would have destroyed the home they were about to create. He married later and through that relationship found salvation. Today both the women and the man are here in the kingdom, but after it happened, many doubted I was a God of love. They asked why but now they know that all things worked out for the best. They know the answer, and they will never question My workings again. I will soon wipe all these painful memories away Tom. There will be a memory of the dark night of sin, but it will seem so small compared to the joys of eternal life, that all will never again think of the sorrow and loss they experienced on earth. The leaves from the Tree of Life are a healing balm to all the suffering ones. Their joy is now complete. In My presence is fullness of joy and eternal blessings are flowing out to all who chose to forsake the world of sin for this better, glorious one. I love each one of these dear people more than any can know. I love them so much, My death on the cross was a small price to pay for all the happiness you see. I love you, Tom. Do you have any more questions?"

"Yes Jesus. I have one about my wife. When I encountered her, she was the most humble and sincere person I had ever met. At the college I attended they made me a Chaplin after two years. I talked with hundreds of students. She was the most spiritual of them all. Her trust in You was unwavering. When we dated, we prayed together, and most of our conversation centered around You. We felt You were leading us and never doubted our union. How could a person who was once converted–who had unlimited faith in You–turn and lose out completely? Was there anything I could have done to keep her in touch with You?"

As Tom asked these questions from the bottom of his heart, he was able to see the face of Jesus as He responded. A deep sadness came over that blessed continence. The body of his Lord seemed to quiver and sway with sorrow. Tom could clearly see the love Jesus had for his lost wife.

"I would like to let you in on a little secret Tom. When a young man such as yourself entered the ministry at our colleges, Satan personally selected two of his most skillful angels to attend the student. These angels worked night and day to attempt to divert the mind of the ministerial student from Christ. They probed every weakness that was in man's nature. If they found one cherished sin, one aspect where the person had a chance of turning from God, they worked on that weakness without restraint. Many of the students had several weaknesses. These fell easily. Others took more time. It takes time for a person to fall from morality. But little by little as they open the mind to the working of Satan, he takes a firmer hold. Kathy was one of My beloved when she was on My side. She had a way of talking to Me that was very personal. She came to Me as she would a trusting father. I loved her with an everlasting love. She had one weakness which is a strength. That was humility. Humility is a virtue. It is a gift I give to people. But humility and self-degradation are very close. She was unable to discern between the two. Satan's angels found this weakness in her and were always hammering away at it. In putting herself down, she thought she was doing the humble thing. Since the angels could not weaken you, they turned to her. She failed to realize I came into the world to lift people up. I did not condemn the woman taken in adultery. I did not condemn the woman at the well. I did not condemn Peter. Peter condemned himself. I built him up. The enemy is the accuser of the brethren. I am their Savior. When that woman spit in her face, Kathy condemned herself as a failure. She felt had she not struck the woman but been more Christlike, she would have represented Me better. That is what happened to Kathy. Even before this woman, she began to look more and more to herself. She looked at her weaknesses and dwelt on them. The enemy noticing this, gave her more opportunity to dwell on her own faults. At last, by beholding, by criticizing her own life, she became changed. It was gradual and almost imperceptible. She chose the course she perused. After criticizing herself for so long the next downward step was to criticize others. Your children were victims of this criticism. In the short years that followed your separation, she almost undid all the spiritual training she had given earlier."

"In answering the second question, was there anything you could have done? Yes. You felt she was strong, that her relationship with Me was deeper than your own. You failed to believe that she could have any weakness. You saw her as so united with Me, she had no need of encouragement. Had you built her up more, had you continued your daily prayer sessions with her after you went to Chicago, the three of us would have been more than a match for the enemy. Where two or three are gathered in My name, I am with them, and if they ask anything, I will give it to them. Satan kept you so busy doing good, you neglected to recognize the needs of your own wife. But don't get Me wrong now. Though you did not meet fully her needs, you must not blame yourself for her loss of heaven. She made a conscious choice. Not once but over, and over, and over again. Finally, after rejecting the prompting of the Spirit long enough, He could no longer speak to her. Your son also had this weakness. He almost followed his mother's example. He listened however, where she did not. He learned to trust Me."

"You are love Jesus." responded Tom. "And I love You more than anyone. Thank You for giving me eternal life. I don't deserve it, but You gave it to me anyway."

"You do deserve eternal life," replied Jesus. "Everyone who is here deserves eternal life. That is why I gave it to them. Each were tested. Each proved I could trust them with this gift of salvation."

Joy's Grandfather asked the question "Why did you let my wife die when I needed her most?" To this the tender words of Jesus came back.

"If you blame Me for her death John, then I must also be blamed for her birth? Had she not been born; she would not have died. I was not responsible for her birth. Her parents chose to bring her into the world. If you say I am responsible for her birth, then you must blame Me for all the births that were not planned. The rape victims, the accidental child that came because of someone else's choice. Am I to be blamed for these? No. I am not responsible for these. Though I knew of them, I did not make the choice of bringing them into existence. So, if I am not to blame for her birth, then why do you blame Me for her death? Death is a result of the work of sin and the enemy of all, Satan. If you say I am responsible for the births and deaths, you are in effect saying I am responsible for sin. I am not responsible for sin. I did not cause it. I created beings with the power to choose good over evil, but many chose evil. By choosing evil they opened the door for Satan to come and take control. I did not make that choice for them. The choice was theirs. Even though I was not responsible for sin, I took the blame for it. When Adam and Eve sinned, I was hurt more than you can know. I knew what I must do to rescue them from the clutches of Satan. I knew I would have to come down to earth and pay the penalty for sin, and sinner. There was great sorrow in heaven when I announced I must go become a man, suffer, and be destroyed by the devil. Thousands of angels prostrated themselves at My feet and begged Me to send them. But the life of an angel could not pay the penalty for sin. Only I could go and make a way for them to have eternal life. On the cross the price was paid, John, and eternal life was freely offered to all who would choose it. Your wife is with you now. During those long months after her death, I was beside you, bringing comfort through your sorrow. Earth was not worthy of her. She chose life eternal and as she closed her eyes in sleep, her last words were a prayer for you, John. She prayed that you would remain strong and not falter but continue to trust in Me and I answered that prayer. Through all those long, lonely days, during all those long, cold nights, I was with you. We got through it didn't we? Now eternal life is yours. Never again will you have to leave her side. 'O death where is your sting? O grave where is your victory? I am the Resurrection, I am Life.' That life is life eternal."

After every question was forever answered in the minds of each one gathered in that vast throng, the drama of the ages again unfolded in the sky high above the throne of God. This time all the evil was gone, and the vast company saw only the working of God in a world held captive by Satan. They saw the Holy Spirit in action. They saw the Creator and even God the Father's part in the drama. Every question was fully answered. Jesus had reached into the mind of each one and given them a deeper experience in the way of salvation. The subjects of the kingdom were made up. The righteous rejoiced over and over again. Counting the cost, each realized heaven was cheap enough. It was free! Jesus rose and as He did, His image filled the entire area. He seemed to grow larger and larger until His form encompassed everyone. He was exulted and glorified, and once again all the company gathered there, fell down and worshiped Him.

BIBLE TEXTS

"And we know that all things work together for good to them that love God, to them who are the called according to his purpose."
Romans 8:28

"Therefore, I say unto you, Take no thought for your life, what you shall eat, or what you shall drink; neither for your body, what you shall put on. Is not the life more than meat, and the body than clothing? Behold the birds of the air: they sow not, neither do they reap, nor gather into barns; yet your heavenly Father feeds them. Are you not much better than they?"
Matthew 6:25, 26

"But my God will supply all of your need according to his wealth in glory through Jesus Christ."
Philippians 4:19

"And whatever you shall ask for in my name, I will do, that the Father may be glorified in the Son. If you ask anything in my name, I will do it. If you love me, keep my commandments."
John.14:13-15

"The meek he will guide in judgment: and the meek he will teach his way."
Psalms 25:9

"You are constantly with me: you have held me by my right hand. You shall guide me with your counsel, and afterward receive me to glory. Who do I have in heaven but you? There is none upon earth that I desire beside you."

Psalms 73:23-26

"Come unto me, all you who labor and are heavy laden, and I will give you rest. Take my yoke upon you and learn of me; for I am mild and lowly in heart: and you shall find rest unto your souls. For my yoke is easy, my burden lite."

Matthew 11:28-30

CHAPTER 17
FLASHBACK

After learning why things had happened on earth the way they did, the entire populace of heaven was silent. Some were weeping as they recalled the last few memories of their friends and loved ones. Others expressed deep love and gratitude for the grace Jesus had displayed in granting them eternal life. Still others seemed saddened by the facts they had been told when the secret sins of their beloved were revealed to them. After hearing the words of Jesus, many suffered pain and sorrow as well as peace and understanding. Then Jesus did a very wonderful thing. He made the understanding so complete in each person's mind, they could no longer be sad or sorrowful. In each case they recognized mercy had been used and Jesus was just in judging the way He had. They realized had that friend or loved one been there with them, they would have eventually chosen a course toward rebellion again, even as their earthly decision revealed. Had that happened, the eternal happiness of heaven would have again been shattered. It was then gladness replaced the sorrow. Happiness overcame sadness, peace took the place of turmoil. Charaeshera remembered a Bible text. "And God will wipe away every tear from their eyes and there shall be no more death, nor sorrow, nor crying; and there shall be no more pain, for the former things have passed away." (Revelation 21:4) And so they were. Joy could no longer remember all the pain she had suffered. Well, she could remember if she wanted to, but what was the use now? Why would she choose to remember those things? In comparison to the bless of this heavenly place, all her earthly trials and troubles vanished into insignificance. Yea, there would be some sorrow yet.

There would be some hurting. Healing still needed to take place, but in a perfect atmosphere of love and peace, healing could take place. Jesus would not wipe all the tears away yet. That would come after He created the new heaven and a new earth.

With such an all-pervading happiness, the angels of God could keep silent no longer, neither could the redeemed. Gabriel opened with a musical note that swelled through the courts of heaven. Then he was joined by billions of voices as the music resounded through all of heaven, but it did not stop there. The occupants of countless worlds caught the echoes of the song as it rolled throughout the entire universe of God. The anthem swelled and swelled until with one voice, all sang. The name of Jesus was glorified, exulted, and lifted above every other name. He was finally All in All to all His creation. He was the great I Am simply because He was. Only one world was not singing. That was the shell of a planet once called earth where Lucifer and his fellow angels were imprisoned. They alone were screaming in rage and rebellion against the Great I Am.

After the music stopped, the vast assembly filed out of the various exits. They were preparing for a journey with Jesus. He was taking the New Jerusalem to one of the larger planets in the universe. Jesus was calling an assembly of the other created worlds. Delegates from all His creation in one sector of the universe would be there and the redeemed of the earth would be the key witnesses. They would tell the story of salvation from the standpoint of sin and rebellion, to redemption through Jesus. This trip would be a new experience for the occupants of heaven. The New Jerusalem had been traveling toward one of these giant planets all the time. Heaven was designed that way. In terms of modern understanding, it could be viewed as a giant star ship, propelled by the power of God, traveling where He willed. During the last six thousand years, heaven had hoovered not far from earth. It was in close contact. Never had it been closer then when Jesus had condescended to earth as a baby, lived among His lost children, and died to grant them a place in His everlasting kingdom. Trust remembered reading in Ezekiel how God's throne traveled throughout the providence of Israel back in Bible times. Now all of heaven was moving throughout the endless universe of God.

Amanelohiym went to one of the transparent walls. It was thick yet he could clearly see through it. There was only a little distortion of the area surrounding the outside wall. He summoned Charaeshera to his side. They could not see any movement whatsoever. They took to the air and circled high in the sky, far above the city. They still could not see any movement. The Glory of God shown so brightly it formed a barrier nothing could penetrate. No one could see in, neither could anyone see out until they got a long way away from the city. The two children went still further into the heavens. Finally, they broke through the glorious barrier. Then and only then could they see heaven moving. The view was inspiring. Up ahead they were traveling toward a gigantic galaxy. It was a spiral galaxy like the one earth was part of. They could clearly see the center swirling around what appeared to be a large sun. The sun had apparently exploded sometime back and formed a beautiful gaseous cloud. There were colors beyond color. In places the cloud extended into different groups of stars. In other places it receded, leaving dark spots amidst the color.

Trust found he had an imagination that was simply fantastic. By taking mental pictures and moving the colors of the gaseous cloud back, then doing it again and again he could create an animated view of the explosion of that sun from its birth to its state sometime in the future. He must have taken hundreds of mental photos and set them up one by one. When he went back and played the scenes recorded in his mind, he could clearly see the whole drama unfold before his astonishing eyes. He shared his discovery with Joy. She too, after a little practice, could do the same and marveled at what she imagined had happened. Trust thought back and remembered the trip from earth to heaven. It was hard for him to go too far back. He only went as far back as the pain that pierced his throat when the bullet passed through it. He remembered the streaks of jagged light that pulsated through his mind as his body functions became separated from the impulses of his brain. He remembered not being able to breath. He once again felt the strangulating effects of death and watched as everything faded into darkness. Then Jesus had called him. At one moment he was and then he wasn't. Things went blank and then He heard the voice of Jesus. He felt the pain, then the healing and the power that surged through him, the new life, the new creation. Time stopped and then started again as quickly as it had stopped. He never knew a year and one half had passed between. He remembered the closing scenes of earths final drama. Because he had been killed during the final presentation of the three angels' messages, he had been resurrected a few days before the second coming of Jesus in the special resurrection. Jesus had called several people from death at that same time. There were the very solders who had struck Jesus while he stood in the court waiting for the sentence from Pilate. The ones who drove the nails through his hands were brought back to life. Also resurrected at that time were the spiritual leaders of Jesus day, who were foremost in working against Him during His three-and-one-half years of ministry. Many of the worst offenders of God throughout the ages past were brought back to life at the command of the Creator. Pharaoh, who refused time and time again to let the Israelites go was resurrected along with others. They roamed around the rocking and reeling earth in fear and turmoil, trying to find a reason why they had been called from their dusty graves. No one could tell them.

All eyes were focused on the heavens. A small dark cloud was advancing steadily toward the earth. It commanded everyone's attention. The scientists who were yet alive, pointed their telescopes toward it. The large dishes set up to catch the sounds of the distant stars were trained on it. Statesmen and slave alike were riveted to this thing of awful mystery. It seemed to the wicked, an evil omen spelling out their destruction. There were the living saints standing in little groups. Their faces were suddenly changed. They lit up brighter than the noon day sun. If they passed near an unsaved person, that person fell back, unable to bare the glory of God as reflected in His chosen. A mighty earthquake rocked the world. Jagged flashes of lightning, larger and more powerful than any ever before, flashed across the heavens. It was truly fearful. A bright rainbow formed an arch across the entire heaven. The skies were dark and gathered blackness. The wicked looked on the scene with fearful doom.

Trust came back out of his daze. His flashback had been so real it was almost as if he had re-experienced the whole thing all over again. He shook himself and looked around for Joy. She had just completed her version of the star expanding when he again talked to her.

"Joy?"

"Yes Trust."

"What do you remember about your death?" It was a most unusual question for Trust to ask. Especially now when there was so much to see.

"Not much, Trust," was the little girls reply. "During the last few days, I was drugged so heavily I really did not know much of what happened. All I remember was feeling very tired. The people around kept telling me to hold on, to not go to sleep, to stay awake. They were pleading with me. They made all kinds of noise. They tried to get me to drink something. All I wanted to do was sleep and that is what I finally did. I just closed my eyes and went to sleep and the next thing I remember was Jesus waking me up and I was all healed. The hard part for me to understand at first was going to sleep in the hospital and waking up in the cemetery. Had not Celestania–my guarding angel–been there to explain everything to me, I would have been very confused indeed. Then I looked up on the cloud and saw Jesus smiling down at me and I loved Him even more than ever because now I could see Him. I could see! I could see! I could see everything! But mostly all I wanted to see was Jesus. He was so beautiful. I could walk too, and run! I was no longer crippled. It was all so very, very wonderful! The trip to heaven was just super and when I met you, and became your friend, I had everything a girl could wish for. I had Jesus as my best friend. I had Celestania, my angel friend, and I had you as my human friend. Thank you so much for talking to me."

"You're sure welcome Joy. You are such a special friend to have. Had you lived on earth longer, you would have been old enough to be my mother. You slept deaths sleep for about thirty-four years before Jesus came. That would have made you about 22 when I was born. My resurrection was different Joy." Trust explained.

"Jesus woke me up at a different time then you. He woke me up so I could see all the final things that happened on earth. I found out just a little while ago I am to speak to the people of the new world. I am to tell the story of how Jesus rescued us from the clutches of Satan. I will be glad to tell what I know but why would people want to hear the story of sin?"

"They are probably curious Trust. They have never been enslaved to that tyrant called the devil. They were born free, and to see who Jesus left heaven for will help them to love Him in ways they never experienced before. It will all work out ok, Trust. You will see."

"Yes Joy," was his reply. "I know they need to hear the story of Salvation from our lips but why would Jesus choose me to tell part of it? I did nothing special. I only listened to the voice in my mind and obeyed it. What else could I do?" The two were silent for a long time after that. They both thought back and remembered the trip to heaven. It was truly awesome. One moment their feet seemed planted on the ground then they went up as gravity fell away. The earth started to move away from them. It was so huge. It did not seem like they were moving up. The earth seemed to be moving down. There were millions and millions who were leaving earth behind. The law of gravity had no effect on them. They remembered the first glimpse they had of the face of Jesus. For Joy it was when He had called her from her grave. For Trust, when his eyes had first caught a glimpse of Him on that small dark cloud. By the time he was able to see Jesus though, the cloud had become very bright. Thousands had fallen all around him, but he had stood with eyes transfixed, and then he had seen Jesus. That was all that mattered. Jesus had come to take him home. He would never feel the pain of sin again. The New Jerusalem would be his home forever.

Trust again remembered the change that came over his body. At one point he was trapped in the tight grip of a darkened form, the next it was changed to all brightness and light. Life surged through him like a current through the wire. Every cell of his body came alive with a vitality never experienced. He felt the freedom that came from separation from his old body and the expansion of the new one. He never imagined how good he could feel. Then he remembered seeing his father. He appeared out of nowhere. Two strong arms reached out to him and he buried his face in his father's robe and cried for joy. He remembered looking for his mother and was saddened a bit when she was not there. He looked into his father's eyes with questions and just saw a head shaking. Father knew the question and gave the answer before it was ever asked. Then his little sister came up and he got out of his father's grip and took the little girl up in his arms and kissed her rosy cheeks. She was beautiful. Only Joy came close to her beauty. Trust had found Joy shortly after leaving the earth and she reminded him so much of his little sister he had stopped to talk to her. From then on, the friendship had grown until now he considered her fully his sister. He was so used to having her around, he could not imagine heaven and Jesus without her.

The seven days it took for that great procession to get from earth to heaven passed very quickly. When they finally did catch their first glimpse of the great city, it was but a star in the distance. Then more rapidly than what seemed possible, it grew larger and brighter with each passing moment. A group of majestic angels had made their way quickly to the front of the procession. The city was very close now towering miles into the sky. It dwarfed any earthly mountain. Trust remembered the brightness and splendor of it all as if it had happened yesterday. There were walls of transparent Jasper. The Father entered first with the throne. It went over the top of the wall and took its place at the center of the city high above everything else. With the throne inside the city, a dazzling, glorious light shone out and everyone cried "hallelujah." The angels that advanced ahead had positioned themselves on the top of the great wall facing the throng. They concentrated themselves above the giant gates of pearl, dazzling in their brightness. The entire company of saints stopped. The angels at the front of the crowd now cried out with one mighty voice,

"Lift up your heads, O ye gates, and be ye lifted up ye everlasting doors so the King of Glory may come in." From the top of the wall above the gates, the angels answered,

"Who is this King of Glory?" The angels on the cloud answered back,

"The Lord strong and mighty. The Lord mighty in battle. He is this King of Glory. Lift up your heads O ye gates and be ye lifted up ye everlasting doors so the King of Glory may come in." Then the response came again from the top of the wall only this time it was much louder.

"Who is this King of Glory?"

"The Lord strong and mighty. He is this King of Glory.

Then something wonderful happened to the gates. From the time Trust had first seen them, they had been closed. Now they were moving open. They receded into the transparent walls. As they opened, brilliant streams of bright glory pierced the cloud they were on and the angels begin to separate all the people into 12 equal groups. All the groups were arranged into long rectangles. They spiraled out from the city like spokes on a bicycle. Soon Trust walked through the gate. What met his eyes was literally out of this world.

There in front of him were mansions of indescribable beauty. They towered into the heavens. Crystal spirals graced every corner. There was a brilliant, triple rainbow–more beautiful than any earthly one–surrounding the throne of God. From His throne high above the Father watched the mighty procession of saints entering through all twelve gates. Jesus stood in the middle beneath the throne by the Tree of Life. All the streets from all the gates ended there on what John the Revelator described as the sea of glass. The Tree of Life was the tallest and largest of all the trees in the city. Its dual trunks were crafted of gold and silver. On all sides of the sea of glass, palm trees stretched up heavenward. They were gigantic. Some reached nearly to the top of the walls. Birds of paradise filled the azure skies. Twelve flocks of snow, white doves flew in formation over the groups of people assembling around Jesus. The formation of the birds spelled out the words VICTORY, GLORY BE TO THE FATHER AND TO THE SON AND TO THE HOLY SPIRIT. Off to the sides of the broad streets of gold were fields of beautiful flowers. Giant animals grazed peacefully in the evergreen meadows. The atmosphere was charged with a living current that vitalized everything with vibrant, vitality akin to nothing on earth. Yes, Trust remembered it all very plainly. The beauty and splendor were beyond imagination. He was home in a place more glorious than words could ever portray, and he would be there for ever and ever. He would live with his Lord and Savior, Jesus Christ for eternity.

Then the angels had sung songs, songs so sweet all present seemed to melt into one melody.

The children looked up ahead now. They had entered the galaxy. Multiple suns with their orbiting planets were streaking past them at incomprehensible speeds. They were all different colors. Some were large, some small. Some had many planets others had none. There were some planets with many moons, others did not have any. Joy looked off to her left and saw a group of three hundred comets all heading the same direction they were traveling. As they moved past them, some of the comets seemed to advance and recede among each other. It almost appeared to look like a school of dolphins swimming alongside of an ocean liner. It was very beautiful. Then the procession began to slow. They passed a mighty sun. Great streamers of red, orange, and yellow flames shot out from its surface. The children could peer far into it and see at the center a ball of fire, white and so hot it was transparent. It reminded trust of a plane ride he had taken on earth as a boy. He had been amazed at the clouds, how they seemed to form soft cushions of foam. He had envisioned jumping out of the plane and bounding from cloud to cloud, twirling, turning somersaults, and landing on the soft foamy surfaces all around him. Now as he looked into this mighty sun, he felt he could do the same, but the sun was on a much larger scale. It was massive. Proverbs 4:18 came to mind. "The path of the just is like the shining sun, that shines brighter and more glorious unto that perfect day." Truly it was a shining path. Trust could clearly see how the Lord had led him up that path. And it had become more glorious and brighter every day, but now back to the journey. The heavenly city with its occupants had nearly stopped all together. Up ahead loomed a huge, huge planet. Its proportions were astounding. The whole of the heaven was covered, and it still went on and on, out further and further until it began to curve around and tower up forever. The entire populace of heaven could easily get lost on that giant. It would hardly be noticed. It was a very large planet indeed. It was large enough for the entire population of that portion of the universe to come and worship God. After all of them came, there would still be more room. The Creator was truly an awesome God. His ways were past finding out. His glory and majesty untouchable. It was truly awesome to think that God was bigger than this. But God was and He is, and He is bigger than His entire universe combined for He Created it. He created everything.

BIBLE TEXTS

"For the living know that they shall die but the dead do not know anything, neither have they any more a reward; for the memory of them is forgotten. Also, their love, hatred, and envy, has now perished; neither have they any more a portion forever in anything that is done on earth."

Ecclesiastes 9:5, 6

"But I would not have you to be ignorant, brethren, concerning them which are asleep, that you should not sorrow, even as others which have no hope. For if we believe that Jesus died and rose again, even so God will bring with him those who sleep. For this we say unto you by the word of the Lord, that we who are alive and remain unto the coming of the Lord shall not preclude them which are asleep. For the Lord himself shall descend from heaven with a shout, with the voice of the archangel, and with the trumpet of God: and the dead in Christ shall rise first: Then we which are alive and remain shall be caught up together with them in the clouds, to meet the Lord in the air: and so, shall we ever be with the Lord. Wherefore comfort one another with these words."

1 Thess 4:13-18

"Behold, he cometh with clouds; and every eye shall see him, and they also which pierced him: and all nations of the earth shall wail because of him."

Revelation 1:7

"Lift up your heads, O ye gates; and be ye lifted up, ye everlasting doors; and the King of glory shall come in. Who is this King of glory? The LORD strong and mighty, the LORD mighty in battle. Lift your heads, O ye gates; even lift them up, ye everlasting doors; and the King of glory shall come in. Who is this King of glory? The LORD of hosts, he is the King of glory."

Psalms 24:7-10

"And Enoch also, the seventh from Adam, prophesied of these, saying, Behold, the Lord cometh with ten thousand of his saints, to execute judgment upon all, and to convince all that are evil among them of all their wicked deeds."

Jude 1:14

"After the resurrection, there will be no marriage. Men and woman will not be married to each other. They will be like the angels in heaven."

Matthew 22:30

CHAPTER 18
A DIFFERENT WORLD

The planet–heaven, or if you wish to call it New Jerusalem, came to a halt several miles above the giant world. To the occupants on that massive sphere, it appeared like a dazzling star, ten times brighter than their bright blue sun. Their eyes were perceptive. They could see many of the saints circling the sparkling gem. They could hear the voice of Jesus as He called the redeemed to order. They were about to exit the city. Jesus assembled them in the same manner as they had entered. In the Holy City, New Jerusalem, there are 12 gates. Each gate has the name of one of the sons of Jacob. Each son of Jacob had a particular type of character. The entire population of heaven had entered with the group most like them in personality. Likewise, the 12 apostles had matching personalities with the sons of Jacob. They headed up each procession with the original sons of the ancient patriarch. Behind them were the countless hosts of heaven. At the command of Jesus, they all left the city, each through their individual gates. They headed toward the giant planet in one vast body. The group formed a perfect square. Jesus was at the center. Around Him were His closest associates and around them the 144,000. They landed on a large plain of long, beautiful grass.

Joy was amazed as she looked around this beautiful place. Heaven was spectacular but this place was dazzling. As she looked above her, there were what appeared to be giant people. They were all nearly the size of the handsome Adam. Then the assembly fell on their faces as the occupants bowed in worship at the presence of their Maker and King. The angels had also come and they–with the occupants–bowed in humble acknowledgment as Jesus lifted His nail pierced hands in blessing. Then He bid them rise as His mighty voice rolled over the miles and miles of assembled throngs.

"I have come and with Me are those I left heaven to redeem. They are here all-around Me. They have chosen to stay with Me throughout the endless ages of eternity. They will always have access to My presence. I have chosen to dwell with them. You have watched the drama unfold. You have followed each fearful and glorious movement. You have seen the triumphs and the victories. And you have seen the tragedies and the heartaches. You watched as I shed My blood for these very ones around Me and you were surprised that Lucifer, one of the most privileged angels in the universe, could take away My life under the cruelest circumstances. Now these have come to tell you how salvation from that fearful world has changed their lives. They have lived in slavery to a most cruel master. He put each of them through dreadful and trying circumstances. He robbed them of health, happiness, and joy. He chained them with habits of sin. He murdered them one by one, but they looked for a better world, a more perfect one, a brighter city whose builder and maker is God, and they prevailed. Now they are here with the life they have chosen. I present them to you, saved through My blood, redeemed through My salvation, restored completely to the My image. I present to you the occupants of planet earth. Listen to their story."

As Jesus finished speaking once again the entire throng gathered on that giant planet bowed in worship and admiration to their Creator. Then the music began again, and the strains echoed and re-echoed through the realms of that beautiful place.

After the testimonies and singing, Joy was able to leave the assembly. She had met a girl about her own age on this planet. There was a great difference in size though. The girl of this world was over six foot tall. She was larger than most men Joy had known. She was only seven years old. The planet hosting this gathering spun at a faster rate than earth, but because its size did not make as many rotations. Gentalacia, the girls name, would have been only six years old had she been born on earth. Joy was eight. The two were an instant match. Both loved beautiful things. Joy's love of beauty came from her former blindness but Gentalacia's came from an inner love for beauty. They walked off toward one of the many homes. In time the bigger girl picked Joy up and set her on her shoulders. The little girl could see better then. The tall grass made walking more difficult, for her legs were very short. From her higher position she was amazed at the shape of the dwellings coming up. There was a type of plant that grew on that planet that was of a most amazing shape. It would have been considered a tree on earth, but no tree there grew so tall as these trees. There were thousands of them. They towered miles and miles into the sky. They had a strong, sturdy trunk with roots that went deep under the ground. As the trees towered up, they grew wider and wider. Three quarters of the way up some flared out to the left, then to the right. Others, more to the right than the left. Others seemed to be perfect in symmetry. After flaring out quickly, they towered up still further, then came back in a rounded top, who's uppermost point was exactly above the point where the trunk emerges from the ground. One of these massive trees was right above the girls.

"This is my home," spoke up Gentle. "I live up near the top. Would you like to come and see my room Joy?"

"Oh! Please, Please let's do," responded the little girl. "How do you get up there? Can you fly?"

"Oh yes. All the inhabitants of our planet can fly. But we usually allow the plant to elevate us to our homes. Come along with me and see." Gentle had set her down on the ground again. Joy followed as the tall girl approached the trunk. She looked above her and saw the underside of the huge branches. The tree did not have leaves per say but long, mossy like strands of rope. They waved beautifully with the gentle breeze that constantly blew on this globe of splendor.

At a strange opening, Gentle paused a moment. There was a transparent film–like glass–closing the opening from the outside. The girl went up to it and walked through quickly. Joy approached the entrance cautiously. She reached out and touched the glass then quickly pulled her hand back. It was like touching a slimy liquid. It felt cold and eerie to her hand. She could see Gentle inside motioning for her to enter.

"Don't be afraid Joy. It will not get you all wet. Just walk through it and you will see." Joy took a deep breath and closed her eyes. She stepped back and took a flying jump, then she was through. Inside she ran her hands over her robe. It was not wet at all. Inside though she noticed a change in climate. Outside was warm and humid, inside cool, and dry. She thought it would be dark but was surprised to see that the trunk, if that is what it was, was translucent. Brilliant yellow light came through it from the large sun high in the sky. Gentle remarked at how bright it was. Then the girls remembered the New Jerusalem hanging like a sparkling sun itself, in the sky high above. There would be no night on that planet for several days. If Jesus were here with the golden city, the skies would be bright. Though heaven was not as large as the planets sun, it was far brighter.

The girls entered another chamber and again joy saw the fluid, the slimy substance that had challenged her dignity earlier, only this time it was like a river. Without a moment's hesitation, Gentle plunged into it and was submersed. She appeared to be breathing normally.

"How could this be," questioned the little girl as she wrapped her arms tightly about herself? Any other fluid she had experienced cut off the breathing portion of her anatomy. Though her light robe sustained her under water, her lungs ceased to function. She thought of the river of life in the city and remembered plunging into it with Trust. After seeing her friends' room and spending time with her, she would take Gentle to her own beautiful one in the sky. But now a decision faced her. Should she dive in or just walk through? She knew so little of dread. On earth she had experienced discomfort and did not relish the thought of how uncomfortable the slime might feel. Then her friend reached out of the fluid with her giant hands and drew the little girl in like a mother would clutch up her little child. Joy was powerless to stop her. She was outside then in, cool then cooler, but that was all. There was no discomfort. The slime did not even seem to touch her robe or body. There was a small layer of air preventing it from reaching her. In a flash they were whisked high into the tree. Soon they were in a large hall that appeared like purest gold. The walls sparkled, even as the walls of her own room in the golden city. There were windows, even as there were windows in the New Jerusalem. But the windows in the tree did not look out over the city, they looked out on other branches, other hallways, other rooms. You could not look up and see the sky. You could not look out and see the giant plain. All you could see were other branches and those long, green ropes of mossy substance. Joy reached out one of the windows. Each window was covered with the liquid slime. She saw a strange red fruit. Was it a fruit? Dare she pick one? She looked to Gentle. Gentle nodded and told her it was good to eat. There were several types of fruit. They were all sizes and shapes, similar to the Tree of Life in heaven that bore a new type of fruit every few time cycles. Joy picked one and put it to her mouth. The large girl took hold of her hand. She removed the fruit and pushed a pinkish spot on the end. It popped open in the form of an umbrella. There were orange, fleshy strings filled with juice. The large girl took one, bit off the end, and sucked the golden liquid from the tube. She plucked one and gave it to Joy. Joy followed the example of her taller friend and marveled at the flavor. It was unlike anything she had ever tasted before. She had tasted many different flavors in the last few months–if we can say heaven has months–but this flavor was entirely new and tingled like a gentle soda. Joy was at once addicted and sucked on string after string.

Gentle entered another chamber of slimy fluid. Joy followed this time without hesitation. It was fun to be propelled through tubes at unforgettable speeds. Then they were in a very long hallway. Gentle quickly made her way down it. Joy had to run to keep up with her. Her legs were just too short. But at last, they came to a large room. It was Gentle's home. She entered again through a slime door and inside flopped down on one of the giant sofas. I suppose you could call it a sofa. It was more like a foamy sponge. As Gentle sat down, she nearly sunk to the floor if the room had a floor. It was hard to tell. It was also translucent and appeared to be very thin. Joy marveled that it held the weight of her gargantuan friend.

"This is home," commented the big girl as she pulled another strand of flesh from the fruit she was holding in her hand. "This is where I was born and raised. I have three brothers and a sister. We each have our own room. Whenever another child is born, another room grows out from our house. Our tree grows larger with each birth. To other planets we are known as the tree people. We grow to be taller than some of our neighbors. Our solar system supports two planets that have life. I have been to the other planet five times. We go there once each year. We go there for an agape, love feast. They come mostly at harvest time. We trade with the other planet. They like the fruit and sponges from our trees, and we like the liquids from their mountain fountains." Joy was listening to the story in its entirety. It was simply fascinating.

"When we heard Jesus was coming to our planet, we were so happy," the big girl continued. "We have been watching the drama of sin on earth ever since its beginning. I have not because I am just a little girl, but my grandmother is over five thousand of your earth years old. She was born about the time of your great flood. She could not understand how the water destroyed all that beautiful world. Our liquid is different as you have experienced. You can't drown in it. Beyond the plains there are bodies of it. We can walk in it and breath, even as we do here in this room. Under the fluid, at the bottom of what you call lakes, we grow our vegetables. I will take you there soon. We have something like your watermelons growing there but yours are so small and ours so large there is a massive difference."

"How do you know so much about our world," Joy questioned as she shifted her position on the spongy sofa?

"We have been there, Joy," responded Gentle with a note of certainty in her voice. "It is in the time dimension used by the angels. We can see you, but you cannot see us. I personally have never been to your world, but my parents have. They went during what you called, World War One. The sights were so terrible they hurried back and never wished to return. The ancient patriarch of our planet, the equivalent of your Adam, has been their numerous times. He and his wife are the oldest and wisest on our planet. Their tree stands the tallest. It is far taller than ours and much bigger around. They have kept us informed of the history of your world. How could you stand to live in slavery to that evil angel?"

Joy was astonished. She never realized she had been an actor in the drama of the ages. She had not known earth was the theater of the universe, observed by countless worlds and invisible beings. Angels, yes, Nancy had told her about the angels, but she had not known about other beings from unfallen worlds. Joy answered the question.

"I never knew anything else Gentle. It was not slavery to me at all. It was life. We knew we would have pain and sorrow. We did not know anything else. When happiness came, we were happy. When sorrowful things happened, we were sad. But when Jesus came and gave me back my sight, that was the happiest time of my life. He gave me back my legs too. I could see and I could walk, I could run and even fly. I loved Him very much then, but I never knew how much I really loved Him until He took me in His giant arms and let me set with Him on His throne with the Father. Then Jesus became my very, very, very best friend and that is what He always will be. He even said I could be near Him when He re-creates our old ugly world and makes it brand new again."

Now it was Gentle's time to be astonished. She just sat and stared at the little girl with her mouth wide open. She was speechless for what seemed like hours. She tried to say something, but the words would not come. Finally, she squeaked out this question.

"You, You were actually in the arm, arms of Jesus, and got to see the Fa, Father?" The big girl lowered her head in great reverence as she spoke the Father's name. Now it was Joy's time to be surprised again. She had not begun to realize how special it would be for someone to have been in the arms of Jesus. As the thought of her unworthiness came over her, she too lowered her head in reverence. Then with a soft voice continued.

"Yes, Jesus came and talked to me personally, first at the table at the great supper. He gave me a beautiful fruit from the Tree of Life. I still have it in my room. Then He gave me this exquisite crown with its colorful gems. After that He served a lot of other people. I have a boy friend named Trust who has a bigger crown. His has thousands of gems in it. After he left me with a friend, I went to the noble Tree of Life in the center of the city. I wanted to see if my fruit from Jesus matched the fruit growing there. It didn't. Our tree grows different fruit every month although since there is no sun in heaven, there are no months or days. I was peering up at the magnificent white throne of God, when Jesus came and scooped me up in His mighty arms. He carried me high above the city to the Father. I put my tiny fingers in the nail prints of His hands and laid my curly hair on His massive chest. I would have gone to sleep there but I was not tired. He told me all about the city and took me to my good friend, and earthly nurse, Nancy. I was so happy. I had not seen Nancy on the cloud going to heaven. Then Nancy took me to meet my very own Grandmother and Grandfather. I am just the happiest little girl in the whole universe, I think. Jesus loves me and so do all of these wonderful people."

"I love you too." acknowledged the bigger girl. You are so little and loveable. You are almost like a little sister to me and I have just met you." With that Gentle threw her big arms around Joy and gave her a kiss on her forehead.

"You are so fortunate to be so loved by Jesus. I probably will never get that chance to be in His arms. I know He loves me but how could He ever love me like He loves you?"

"You spoke of your Grandmother and Grandfather. You did not mention anything about your Mother and Father. Where are they? Why were you all alone when I saw you?" Joy lowered her head. It was hard for her to tell her new friend she had no Mother or Father now. Sin really hurt sometime. Finally, she got the courage to speak.

"My Mother and Father choose not to accept the gift of salvation Jesus so freely offered. They actually shook their fist in His face and cursed His name. It hurt Him beyond words to love them so much and be scorned by them so much. He tried to tell them about His love for them repeatedly, but they refused to listen to His voice. Finally, He just bowed His head and let them go with the choices they were making. They are in the grave down on our shattered planet. There will be a time soon when Jesus will call them from sleep. When He called me, I was happy to see His smiling face. When He calls them, they will be terrified of Him and will hide their faces from His presence. They never loved Him. They will hate Him for bringing them back to life. They will probably curse Him again for judging them. They will blame Him for all their troubles. But that is not the way Jesus really is. He is love and anyone on our world who responded to His love, went to heaven with Him. My parents never really knew the depth of how much Jesus loved them. They never will understand anything that you and I know. It is better they sleep now. They will never know what they missed by choosing not to accept Him into their lives."

Gentle was again silent. Try as she might she could never comprehend how anyone could refuse to accept the gift of eternal life through Jesus. She never could experience the happiness the little girl before her felt in the presence of Jesus, for neither angels nor unfallen beings can comprehend the joy that our salvation brings. It will be the study of the ages, themes we will contemplate for all eternity.

Joy went into Gentle's room. It was spacious. It had windows that did open out over the plains. It was on the outermost edge of the branches. Joy looked out the window and thrust her hand through the slimy glaze. She could feel the warmer air. Way off to the north, if that planet has a north, was a large body of water, if one can call it water. Joy pointed toward it.

"Is that where the giant watermelons grow," asked Joy?

"Yes," replied the girl. "We will go there soon but first let me show you the rest of my room. Sit down on my bed." Joy let her entire weight fall on the giant sponge like mattress. It swallowed her up almost entirely. It was so soft. In her room at the city Joy did not need a bed. She did not need to sleep. Though she had a body, it was unlike her earthly one. I am not just talking about the crippling effect of sin. Her heavenly body was a glorified one, more like the body of angels. The food she ate was pure energy. She could touch, taste, and feel everything around her but the body she now had was different than any of the planetary people. Where theirs needed rest, hers did not. Jesus made that clear when He said, "you shall be as the angels," and when John the Revelator said, "there will be no night there for the Lamb is the Light," He meant just that. It was hard to explain. It cannot be explained in terms of our earthly language. Words are not adequate to characterize it but we will have to experience it someday when we go to be with Jesus in that eternal city of youth. Though her body type was more like the angels, Joy was still small. She would still have to grow up to the full stature God planned in the beginning.

"Could I take one of these giant sponges back to my room in the glorious city," asked Joy as she put her feet on the floor again?

"Yes, you can," returned Gentle. "They grow softest near the center of our tree. I will give you a set of matching ones if you can accommodate them in your room. I have been growing two of them in the shape of fish."

"Fish," questioned Joy, her small nose wrinkled a bit as she asked? "Do you have fish on your planet?"

"Oh yes," she responded with excitement! "We have lots of them. They take care of our aquatic gardens for us." Gentle showed Joy more of her room. There were little treasures and things the girl had collected from different places on the planet. She had little cups and saucers of dissimilar colors. They grew them also. They took different plants and programed their genetic make-up to change and produce distinct shapes and many useful items. These they traded with other cultures. The girl was quite a collector. She had somehow captured the image of her family on some agates. Joy saw the girl's Mother's face, perfectly reproduced within the stone. She was a very beautiful woman. Gentle's Father was as handsome as any she had ever seen. The brothers were also very nice looking. One had long, golden hair that appeared to crown his deep blue eyes. It was truly amazing! The girl turned the stone in her hand a little, then faster and faster. The image captured there moved like a living person. It was uncanny to say the least. Joy could almost hear them talking as they moved within the stone. This was some advanced form of photography. Gentle told her several hours of real, live footage were stored within the stone. Each stone was equipped with a mini sound system. There were unquestionably some amazing things Joy saw there in the girl's room. Then Gentle took a little stone from one of the smaller sponges and gave it to the girl. As Joy investigated its center, she saw her new found friend.

"I want you to have this if you like. It is my image captured within. Whenever you think of me in the future as you are traveling from place to place with Jesus, all you need to do to remember me is look into the stone and I will be there looking back at you."

"O thank you Gentle! This is really the best gift anyone has ever given me. I will cherish it as my most treasured present wherever I travel." With that the girls left the room. This time they did not use the fluid motion system of the tree. They stepped through the window and flew quickly to the large body of liquid in the center of the large tableland.

When the girls sat down on the shoreline, they could investigate the liquid and see the vegetables growing deep within. Gentalacia took a step into the fluid. She began to walk out and beaconed Charaeshera to follow. The smaller girl's head was quickly submersed. She was a lot shorter than her companion. She found she could breathe easily under the fluid. They advanced toward a large patch of melons. Joy thought large, when Gentle had mentioned the size, but she was unprepared for the massive expanse of the largest of these melons. They were humongous. One towered high above the girl's heads. Gentle explained that a melon of this size could provide a meal for the population of an entire tree. They would take the melons and fly them to the center of the plant, then lower them to the master dining room. On special Sabbath's these melons were a favorite. The wonderful part of it all was if the people just wanted a little taste of the melon, they could cut a small hole in the rind and reach in and pull out some of the sweet, juicy interior, then feast to their hearts content. Gentalacia did that and placed some of the ripe, red fruit in a pocket of her vestment. She took Joy to visit some of the other vegetables. The wonders the little girl saw were genuinely astonishing! They stayed in the liquid gardens for hours going from one wonder to another. From time to time they would advance to the surface and taste some of the vegetables that appeared of special interest to Joy. On one trip up, Joy was startled by the movement of some huge organism. She saw the fish Gentle had mentioned.

"Are these the fish that help to care for your gardens," asked Joy? "Yes," responded Gentle. "They keep the ground around the plants stirred up so the roots can grow and absorb the nutrients necessary for their massive growth. Our planet is so large, and the gravity so strong, a melon such as I showed you would burst open if it were not grown in the aquatic gardens. Its sheer weight would crush it. The liquid displaces a portion of the weight of the melon so the vegetables can grow to such tremendous sizes. The gravity also accounts for the soft sponges we use for our couches and beds. We really need them because the downward pull on our bodies is very powerful. Had not adjustments been made for your weight before you came, and had your body been like it was on earth once you laid down you would probably not have had the strength necessary to get up from the surface of our world. But that was all taken care of. Our light robes compensate for a lot of things. They are part of the all-sustaining power of Jesus. Without them we would not survive in many places."

About that time the great mealtime bell tolled throughout the vast recesses of this unusual orb. It echoed from tree to tree, hillside to hillside. A great banquet had been prepared. The host planet had spared no expense to supply the guest with the very largest and best fruits from their harvest. It was a tithe to God. They were happy to return to Jesus a portion of what He had blessed them with. The people came from all directions. Each of the planets represented were sectioned off in perfect squares. There were billions of them. They spread out over the great plain like the sands of the sea. It would take months to get around to all of them. Accommodations had been made decades in advance. Jesus had communicated with this planet many times over the last several years. He had blessed them with a most bountiful crop of food. Everything had produced a hundredfold that year. The fruit was larger and sweeter.

The vegetables were so abundant they grew on top of each other. What a meal that first one was. There were exotic foods from all the planets.

Trust had never seen such a variety before. There was everything imaginable and unimaginable. He had not heard of the giant melons until several of them were brought from the aquatic gardens and opened for serving. He had missed Joy. She had slipped away from the group shortly after his speech. Now that his part of the introduction was through, he began looking for her. He chanced to run into Celestania and asked where he might find Joy in that vast assembly. The angel directed him to the two girls who really happened to only be just a few yards away.

"Joy," Trust called out. "Where have you been all this time? I have been looking all over for you. I even flew back to the city to see if you were there, but the city was nearly empty."

"Hi Trust," replied Joy. "Have I been gone that long? It seems like only moments since I heard your testimony. I met Gentle and she took me on a tour of her planet. There are wonders here you would not believe."

"Like the gigantic melons," questioned Trust as he pointed to one at the center of a large group of people.

"Yes. The melons and a thousand other wonderful things. I made the best friend I could ever hope to meet. This is Gentalacia, Trust. She is a native of this planet and lives in that giant tree, right over there. Her room is the most wonderful place you could ever hope to visit. It is beautiful. She asked if I could spend the next several days with her. It is ok with her parents; I just need to find Grandmother and Grandfather and tell them where I will be staying. I will probably stay with her for a few days then she can come up to my room in the city. We will have so much fun. Would you like to visit her tree after the meal Trust?"

"Yes," replied the young man. "I have been eying those trees for the last couple of hours, hoping someone would invite me over to one of them." Just then one of Gentalacia's brothers came up to her. He was a little taller than his sister. He seemed mildly curious with Joy. She was such a little, pretty person. He had not ever seen any miniature people before the congregation arrived from heaven. Gentle did not hesitate to introduce both Joy and Trust to him. After getting his curiosity satisfied with Joy, he turned his attention to Trust. He had heard him speak at the meeting and assumed he was someone so special, he probably would never get a chance to speak with him alone, but here he was talking to him. It was an awesome thing. Just as the girls were the same age, so were the boys. They struck it off great, right from the start. Though they were the same age, the difference in height was very apparent. Willing–Gentle's brother–was about eight foot, two inches tall. Trust was under five feet. The kids presented an apparent contrast as they walked side by side. They headed over to where Joy had last seen her Grandparents. They had not moved far. They too had made friends with some of the planet people. It was not a coincidence that the very people who befriended Joy's Grandparents were the parents of Gentle and Willing. They would be their hosts while on the giant world. Many a happy hour would be spent in their spacious tree house. After all the introductions were made, they sat down to the meal. Joy was also amazed that Gentle's oldest brother was the same age as Nancy. Now that was very interesting indeed. His name was Meekalo. He towered some sixteen feet into the air and was nearly three times as tall as Joy's adopted Mother. Of course, Nancy did not have a problem with that. She had always favored tall men, but this guy was beyond her wildest expectations, ever! How often does a sixteen-foot gentleman take an interest in a six-foot woman?

The meal was delightful indeed. Jesus gave the blessing. He opened His nail scarred hands and pronounced the invocation. Then all were seated and begin to eat. It was a time to be remembered for ages to come. Millions and millions of unfallen beings mingling with the redeemed from the earth-the very people Jesus left the eternal glories of the universe to rescue from sin. Everlasting life yet stretched ahead of them for ceaseless ages to come. Wonder of wonders and glory be to Father, the Son and Holy Spirit for evermore. Someday reader, someday you too may travel to worlds of wonder, unknown to you though they are now, and mingle with the inhabitants of strange, exotic places. All it takes is Faith in the words of Jesus, and belief in Him. Eternal life everlasting will be yours for eternity. Plan to be a part of this new epoch now. Do not wait a moment longer. The time is just about here when Jesus will come and take us to wonders never imagined. "Even so come Lord Jesus." Amen and Amen.

BIBLE TEXTS

"In the past God spoke to our ancestors many times and in many ways through the prophets, but in these last days he has spoken to us through his Son. He is the one through whom God created the universe, the one whom God has chosen to possess all things at the end. He shines with the brightness of God's glory; he is the exact likeness of God's own being and sustains the universe with his powerful word. After he made men clean from their sins, he sat down in heaven at the right side of God, the Supreme Power. The Son was made greater than the angels, just as the name that God gave him is greater than theirs. For God never said to any of his angels, "You are my Son; today I have become your Father." Nor did God say to any angel, "I will be his Father, and he shall be my Son." When God was about to send his first-born Son into the world, he also said, "All of God's angels must worship him." This is what God said about the angels; "God makes his angels winds, and he makes his servants flames of fire." About the Son, however, God said: "Your throne, O God, will last for ever and ever!

With justice you rule over your kingdom. You love the right and hate the wrong, that is why God, your God, chose you and gave you the joy of an honor far greater than he gave to your companions." He also said; "You, Lord, in the beginning created the earth, and with your own hands you made the heavens. They will all disappear, but you will remain. They will grow old like clothes; you will fold them up like a coat, and they will be changed like clothes. But you are the same, and you will never grow old." God never did say to any of his angels: "Sit here at my right side, until I put your enemies as a footstool under your feet." What are the angels then? They are all spirits who serve God and are sent by him to help those who are to receive salvation."

Hebrews 1:1-14

"Through faith we understand that the worlds were designed by the word of God, so that things which are seen were not made of things which do appear."

Hebrews 11:3

"He made the stars also."

Genesis 1:16

CHAPTER 19
THEATER OF THE UNIVERSE

After the meal, great excitement pervaded the air. It was about time to see the story of salvation from start to finish. Least any in God's universe harbored the idea that happiness could come from being apart from the Creator, they must see exactly what happened when others had earlier made that decision. The tables were cleared of the food and eating utensils. The vast throng, unnumberable as the sands of the sea, leaned back in their foamy cushions and turned their attention to the heavens. It was a drama that would never be forgotten. Lifted high above the planet, they could see the throne of the Father and the Son. Jesus, the Creator, raised His nail scarred hands so all could clearly see the marks of shame.

"This," He cried, "is the story of Salvation." It was the time capsule of Lucifer's rebellion and the reign of sin. Now the entire congregation seated there on that massive globe could see for themselves what the privileged few had seen earlier in heaven, only this time there would be live speakers to testify that what was recorded was indeed true.

At the start of the drama, the skies grew black, and the darkness permeated everything. Soon a small speck of light appeared and grew ever brighter and more glorious. Before time there was God, eternal, all powerful, all knowing, omni-present. But even God can get lonely so there were three, God the Father, God the Son and God the Holy Spirit, three but one. God the Father was the Ancient of Days, wise, and understanding. He was the head or leader of the One. God the Son was His exact likeness. He would be closest to the subjects. He was the Creative force of the One. God the Holy Spirit was the unifying solvent between the Father, the Son and all the created subjects. So, the One decided to create subjects, ministering spirits who would minister to all of creation. They would be called angels. Since the Son was the creative force of the One, He was given the leading role in this creation. So early one morning the Son looked out a window to the universe. Far away in the distance there was a cloud of white. The universe was eternal in size even as the One was eternal. The Son walked along the white and gathered handfuls of stardust then with His own two hands formed the very first angel. He would be called Lucifer, Son of the Morning for that was when he was created. So, the Son created a masterpiece of a being. He was beautiful beyond words. God the Father and God the Holy Spirit were impressed. Equally were they impressed when the Son begin to weep. Large tears fell from His eyes and mingled with the dust that fashioned the mighty angel. The Creator, One, weeping? What a sight. Being all knowing, He could read the future of this beautiful angel and see the first time he questioned the One. He watched as the future of Lucifer unfolded before Him. He saw his rebellion and ultimate expulsion from heaven. He followed his moral degeneration until he would stoop low enough to destroy his Creator. And so, the Creator, God, wept. Oh, He had the power to change him. He could have caused a wind to blow the form into the infinity of the universe and have started over. He could with one swipe, one word, wipe him from existence. He looked to the Father and the Spirit. Should He give life to one who would ultimately cause his death? Not only would Lucifer choose to rebel against God, but he would also lead billions to follow him in his rebellion. It would be so easy to not give him life. Should He do it? Should he continue? Yes! The Creator would do it. He would give this angel a chance to choose. All the subjects of this kingdom must be able to choose whether they would serve their maker out of love or not. The kingdom of the One would be a kingdom of love. Only through the free power of choice could the created subjects of this kingdom truly love their Creator.

The Son bowed low and placed His form over Lucifer, then life entered him. It happened in a moment. He wasn't and then he was. What wonder, what love. The One bringing into existence a being who would choose to destroy Him. But there would be others, millions of them, who would choose to remain true to their Creator. Sin would rise once but it would never rise a second time. So, the object lesson of the universe began. Life with the One God, or life and ultimately death without Him. For in Him and Him alone, the Three in One, is life eternal, life everlasting.

The occupants of that giant globe watched everything unfold. They watched the first look of adoration this mighty prince gave his Creator and saw the love that passed between the two as they roamed the realms of glory. They saw each angel as they came forth from the Creators hand, praising Him for His excellence and Glory. They saw the perfect order and harmony that existed then and entered the experiences of these angels as they sang their anthems of praise to the King of Kings. As soon as there was the first angel, Christ stepped down and became one with them. At this time, He was known as Michael the Archangel. Lucifer, Son of the Morning was the most exulted of the angels and stood next to Michael. In his innocence not a thought of rebellion marred his Nobel mind. Michael stood to the right of the great white throne; Lucifer stood to its left.

The congregation saw it all. They saw Lucifer's first doubts about the Creator. They saw him spread these doubts to other angels. They entered the pain Jesus experienced as He witnessed this being, He love so dearly turn in open rebellion against the throne of God. They saw the ultimate expulsion from heaven and were saddened at the results of sin. Everyone now understood that God's way of ruling was the only way to be truly happy. It was sad to see the great choir hall in heaven with so many empty seats. With one third of the angels gone, it seemed to leave a big void in the Holy City. They watched as the drama continued. The four living creatures left the immediate presence of the Father and with Jesus traveled to a place outside of Heaven. They saw Michael stretch forth His hand and instantly where there had been nothing billions and billions of independent bodies of matter drifting in a universe, all around Heaven, appeared. Jesus went to one of these bodies of matter and called out in a voice loud and clear.

"LET THERE BE LIGHT" Instantly the universe took on a new look. The light from around the throne of God went leaping out to these places the instant the words were uttered, and they were enshrouded in glory. On the second day The Creator spoke again.

"LET THERE BE A VAULT, BETWEEN THE WATERS, TO SEPARATE WATER FROM WATER" The Four Living Creatures moved out from the presence of Christ over the waters and divided the waters on the earth into two parts. A sheet of water now covered the world, and another surrounded it several miles higher in the sky. It was if someone had enshrouded this little speck of matter in a giant greenhouse. The waters above the earth filtered out the cold. The place became warm like a summers evening. On the third day He spoke, and land rose out of the waters and there were great lakes and rivers. He spoke again and, on this land, trees and flowers appeared with all manner of vegetation. As this was taking place the group were able to look in on the activities of Lucifer. He had been cast out of Heaven and with his angels, stood watching from afar off Michael's work as He brought the world into being. There was a sort of medium territory midway between earth and what was soon to become the sun, where these angels of darkness took their stand. They dwelt there in that limbo land as it were, quarreling and bickering, each fighting for the highest place next to their mighty leader.

On the fourth day the voice of the Creator called out. "LET THERE BE LIGHTS IN THE VAULT OF HEAVEN TO SEPARATE DAY FROM NIGHT AND LET THEM SERVE AS SIGNS BOTH FOR FESTIVALS AND FOR SEASONS AND YEARS. LET THEM ALSO SHINE IN THE VAULT OF

HEAVEN TO GIVE LIGHT ON EARTH." Instantly the sun stood blazing in the sky with all its brilliance. Throughout the universe trillions of suns shone in all their splendor and around them independent bodies of matter circled in perfect order and harmony.

The group watched as each day passed–bringing forth new wonders. They watched with tender regard as Jesus formed Adam from the dust of the ground. Many of the original occupants of various planets remembered their own creation and the first time they looked into the eyes of their Creator and gave shouts of glory as they saw these things. But amidst the glory there was sorrow. It was the second time Jesus wept. Again, the universe looked on with aw and wonder. At a time when the angels of heaven were ready to burst into joyful anthems of praise and exultation to the Creator wept. To look around Him, one would think there was everything to be happy about. The world, fresh from the hand of the Creator, was beautiful beyond words. Colorful flowers carpeted the evergreen meadows. Birds filled the air with their joyful songs. Thousands of animals frolicked among the giant trees. Tempting fruit hung in reach for all who were hungry. The streams and lakes were crystal clear. You could look in and clearly see all kinds of fish and water creatures. One stream was particularly beautiful. It flowed over a bed of pure white quartz. Sparkling from the banks were millions of beautiful gems. A group of diamonds caught the rays of the sun high above. Ruby and emerald lay next to each other in a pleasing pattern. Jesus had walked along this very stream earlier that day. Now He rested for a moment over His latest masterpiece. He had scooped some moist clay from the bank and had fashioned a form both powerful and beautiful. This form had an image close to the Creator's. It was truly amazing to watch the Master at work. He had first fashioned several strange organs then placed them side by side within the form. They were interconnected with several tubes. Then ever so gently the

Lord had covered them over with a thin layer of something called skin. He had fashioned two eyes and a nose. There was a mouth set with deep red lips, a mouth designed to bring glory to its Creator. It was truly overwhelming to see this form now nearly completed at the feet of The Word. And it was astonishing to see the form of the Son of God convulsing with deep sobs as He beheld the work of His hands stretched out in front of Him. Once before He had wept like this and that was when He had created Lucifer, Son of the Morning. The universe knew now why He had wept at the creation of the mighty angel. He had rebelled against His Creator and divided heaven. Would this new creation also rebel against the Creator? Would he join Lucifer in his plot to overthrow the government of God? The Creator lingered again before giving life to this new order of being. He knew this one He loved so much would also rebel. But His sadness was deeper and yet less somehow if that could be, deeper because the rebellion of Adam would cause the Creator Himself to leave His throne in heaven and be subjected to a cruel death by the hands of His created children. The sadness was less though because the Creator knew that unlike Lucifer, this being and many of his offspring would ultimately be reunited with Him. The number would exactly replace the number of angels that lost their place in heaven. So, He wept, yet it was not the same this time.

Then wonder of wonders. Jesus bent low and placing His lips over the nostrils of Adam, He breathed into them the breath of life and Adam became a living soul. Then the angels of God sang sweet anthems of praise to the Creator and all heaven rejoiced. But it did not erase the sadness of the Creator. He looked ahead and saw a tiny baby born to a virgin. He saw Him grow and be a perfect example of love. He saw Him finally hang up his carpenter tools and take up His work. He followed Him through three-and one-half years of agony and ecstasy. He saw cruel men finally nail the hands and feet of this God man to a cross. He saw the struggle of life and death while the fate of the world hung there in the balance between earth and heaven. Then He heard that wrenching cry, "it is finished," that forever doomed the rebellion of Satan.

After viewing the creation of Adam, the drama ceased to unfold. The images projected in the skies faded away. At the head of the assembly Adam approached the Creator. He bowed low before Him and then the Creator lifted that giant to his feet. As Adam began to speak, a quietness came over the place.

"What you saw in that drama is exactly what happened," spoke Adam. "I remember it as though it were yesterday. I remember looking up with wonder and seeing the loving eyes of Jesus looking into mine. I was thrilled as He took me around and showed me all the wonders He had created. Each animal was a blessing and a work of beauty. I named them all. That day was the happiest of my life, especially when Eve was brought to my side." At that time Eve came up and testified that all that had been seen was true."

"We were given a chance in a perfect world, but we wanted more," continued Adam. "We wanted to partake of the fruit of the forbidden tree thinking we would be like God. The talking serpent trick Lucifer played on us, was very clever. He is a master deceiver and we fell, but thanks be to God. Jesus came to our world and paid for the penalty of our sin. He took our death so we could have His life. Blessed be the name of the Lord."

At that the vast group gathered at the feet of Jesus, bowed low again and then rose as music swelled the globe. What a choir that will be reader. Billions and billions of beings singing praises to their Creator. Take me home Jesus. Don't you think it is about time for You to come? When that time comes, when we are on our way home to be with Christ, then and only then will the Creator rejoice with the angels as they sing songs to His glory. So, Jesus came.

He was called Immanuel God with us. For God did come down and take on the form of man. He lived and died so all who believe in Him should not perish but have everlasting life. And so today, Immanuel is here with us. God is with us through the person of His Holy Spirit, but a day is coming when God will no longer only be with us, we will be with Him. Us with God, our Creator, our Redeemer and our Lord, King of Kings, Everlasting Father, Prince of Peace.

After Adam and Eve testified all that was shown was true, the throng witnessed the story of sin from its beginning to end. It took days to see it all. Throughout the drama thousands of people rose and testified all that God showed in this panorama was true. The drama was interspersed with pleasant meals and time for the people of all these planets to become acquainted with whoever they liked. It was like a giant camp meeting.

Joy took Gentle back to the Holy City several times and showed her the beautiful palace Jesus had made for her with many other wonders of that glorious land. All the occupants entered the great city at least once. It was the first time for many. The beings of unfallen worlds rejoiced at the salvation of sinners. They did not envy them but expressed what a great privilege it must be, to ever be with Jesus. Many would have gladly traded places with the saints, but after viewing the pain of sin, wanted no part in it. One of those times when Gentle was with Joy in the Holy City, Jesus came up to the two. He smiled down at Joy then looked directly at Gentle. As this daughter of God looked into the eyes of Jesus, she felt the wonder of His love. Though she had never seen Him in person before He came to her planet, she knew Him and realized that He was acquainted with her intimately. With one swoop of His mighty arms, he picked her up and held her close to his chest like a child would hold a kitten or a puppy. The feelings that came over Gentle were like none she had ever known. "Safe in the arms of Jesus, safe on His gentle breast, sweetly His love surrounds me, sweetly my soul doth rest." Jesus knew of her secret desire. She had wanted so much to be in the arms of the Son of God at least once in her life, and here He was. He held her for quite a while as they walked on one of the golden streets. After a time, Joy reached up and grasp His massive hand. Then a very special thing happened. With His free arm, Jesus hoisted the little girl up on His broad shoulders and carried both girls for a time while they waved at many of their newly made friends. It was something both girls would remember and cherish for the remainder of eternity. Jesus just loved everyone, even the billions of inhabited beings of countless worlds, and made them very happy "for in His presence is fullness of joy, and blessings for evermore."

Back on the giant planet, the saga continued. The story of Salvation was seen from every angle until every person in that great throng had all their questions answered. Then the Holy City–that beautiful gem in the sky, brighter than any ten suns–lifted away from the giant planet and headed for another galaxy. Though it took nearly half a year, by that planets standard of time to understand it all, the weeks flew by far too quickly for Joy and her new found friends. But another galaxy must hear the story, there were millions of places to go yet. What new wonders would meet the little girl, Joy, and her friend, Trust as they traveled on, into the eternal, endless expanses of God's great Universe?

BIBLE TEXTS

"For all have sinned and fall short of God's glory."
Romans 3:23

"We are all infected and impure with sin. When we put on our prized robes of righteousness, we find they are but filthy rags. Like autumn leaves we fade, wither, and fall. And our sins, like the wind, sweep us away."
Isaiah 64.6

"For the wages of sin is death; but the gift of God is eternal life through Jesus Christ our Lord."

Romans 6:23

"Where sin increased, God's grace increased much more. So then, just as sin ruled by means of death, so also God's grace rules by means of righteousness, leading us to eternal life through Jesus Christ our Lord."

Romans 5:20, 21

"If we confess our sins, he is faithful and will forgive us our sins, and cleanse us from all unrighteousness."

1 John.1.9

"For by grace you are saved through faith; and not of yourselves: it is God's gift: Not of works, in case any should boast."

Ephesians 2:8. 9

"God has given us eternal life, and this life is ours in his Son. Whoever has the Son has this life; whoever does not have the Son of God does not have this life. I write you this so you may know that you have eternal life–you who believe in the name of the Son of God."

1 John 5.13

"For God so loved the world, that he gave his only begotten Son, that whosoever believeth in him should not perish, but have everlasting life."

John 3:16

"This is a true saying to be completely accepted and believed: Christ Jesus came into the world to save sinners."

1 Timothy 1:15

CHAPTER 20
BACK HOME AGAIN

Joy and Trust watched as the giant planet faded into the distance. Would they ever see their friends again? Maybe in a million years. There was so much to see and so many places to go. After viewing the panorama of sin and salvation, they had a much better understanding of God. They knew their place in God's plan. They knew what it meant to be His witnesses. They could see the end from the beginning and realized that things really had worked out for the ultimate good of all. The two flew around for a few hours enjoying the freedom that only flying can bring then went back into the city and entered the House of Trust. Joy always marveled at Trust's home. In fact, she spent so much time there she wondered if perhaps Jesus had not designed it with her in mind. She loved the garden pool outside the golden laced windows. She had made great friends with the swan that chose to live there. She could communicate with them even as she and Trust communicated with the parrots. But the parrots had chosen her palace as their home. Jesus had created a little room above her robe room for them. It had a little window that looked out over the waterfall. Their colorful red, green, and gold reflected perfectly in her mirrored walls. Today however the parrot pair were at the house of Trust.

"Joy, Trust, come see, come see," exclaimed the dual. The children did not hesitate. They followed the birds into the forest on the edge of the Garden of Eden. The forest in heaven is very different from the ones on earth. Here on earth, you cannot enter a forest without seeing shadows all over the place. In heaven there are no shadows. The brightness there illuminates everything clearly. The forest with their tall ferns, took on the form of a fantasy land. It was all very enchanted. The birds came to rest on a strange looking rock. Trust had entered this forest several times but never had seen this before. He was simply amazed. The rock was in the shape of a perfect sphere. In places he could look inside and see images. It was almost like the little rock that contained a likeness of Joy's tree house friend but much larger. After carefully examining it, Joy discovered it was a cover to a sub terrarium room. They wondered how they could move the stone though to get inside. Standalone answered their question by pecking with his beak on the top of the rock. It magically moved away from its place exposing a cave. The children entered the opening. They could see the makeup of the elements that formed the grounds of heaven. Unlike earth there were no layers of soil, however. The substance was hard like a rock. At the base of the room several tunnels went off in different directions. They followed one until it came to an end. They returned to another and did the same. All the tunnels ended. They went back out of the opening very puzzled. Trust looked at the parrot and asked.

"What is this, Standalone?"

"A tree," came the reply.

"No, no you must be wrong. This is not a tree but a rock."

"It is a tree," replied the bird. Now the children were really puzzled. Just about the time they were about to throw up their hands in wonderment, Celestania appeared. Joy was so glad to see the angel. She took a flying leap and jumped right into the giant angels' arms. She kissed him on the cheek and then ask the question that was uppermost in her mind.

"What is this rock and cave?"

"It is or rather was a tree."

"A tree," responded Trust. "That is what Standalone said it was. If it is a tree it is the funniest shaped tree I have ever seen."

"Come over to this side," beaconed the angel. The children did so, and he motioned for them to look in the interior of stone near the center. The children did and were amazed at what they saw. There inside was the image of a tree with the most beautiful fruit. The shape of the fruit was long and red. At the top it was golden in color but grew redder as it progressed toward the end. It was beautiful. Of course, they had more questions about this newest wonder in heaven.

In the panorama they had seen the Tree of Knowledge of Good and Evil. They had watched Eve as she neared this wonder. Now they put the two together. This was that tree or the place at least where that tree had been. When God created the earth, He had placed two trees in the garden. Each had a special purpose. One was the Tree of Life. It now stood beneath the throne of God at the center of the city. The other tree had been the Tree of the Knowledge of Good and Evil. It had been the tree where the ancient serpent had deceived the mother of the race. From this very spot, she had stood and talked to the serpent and eaten the forbidden fruit.

"So, this is where the Tree of Knowledge of Good and Evil stood," questioned Trust?

"Yes," replied the angel. "This is the very place. Jesus removed the tree from the garden, or rather entombed it in this monument as a reminder of the awful consequences of sin."

"That cave then must be where the roots of the tree were anchored into the ground."

"That is correct," responded the angel. "There were trees like this on all of the planets. Jesus gave each world a choice. They could follow Him or choose not to but if they chose to, the results would be separation from Him. You both have experienced that. In the ages to come anyone can come to this spot and see the medium through which

Satan gained access to humans. The tree will never again raise its branches toward the heavens. Its deadly fruit will never again be a temptation for some future citizen of the kingdom. Sin was destined to rise once but it will never rise a second time. Jesus has seen to that."

The children were amazed at this new wonder. Trust would now have a place to take the many visitors who would come to his home from planet to planet. The monument was so close to his home. He could bring them here time and time again and tell them the story of sin and salvation through Jesus. Somehow knowing the tree was embedded in rock was a comfort to the lad. Sin had been terrible. It was the one dark spot in the beautiful universe of God. It was a comfort to know it would never rise a second time. The five, left the spot and headed back to the House of Trust. The male parrot rested on the shoulder of Trust the female on the shoulder of Joy.

"The Knowledge of Evil was not good for Eve," spoke the lady parrot.   "You are right, Starlacia," responded Joy.

"The knowledge of evil is good for only one thing. That is to help us know how good, good is. Without a knowledge of evil we might be less satisfied with the good we now know."

Back inside the House of Trust, the party refreshed themselves on some of the fruit and drank long from the crystal glasses. The water of life, like the tree of life, vitalized their very beings. Even the parrots joined in the feast and quickly devoured a cluster of grapes, plucked from the vines in Trust's yard. It was nice to be home in the House of Trust. Heaven was home. Since heaven has no time the time in heaven passed in no time. The children visited thousands of galaxies and made friends all over the vast universe of God. But it was always good to be home in the golden city with Jesus. Were there still wonders to be seen in this city? Joy would find a wonder next to her very own palace. And the parrots would again be instrumental in leading her to it. But that would be later nearly at the end of her thousand years in heaven with Jesus when the city of gold would be relocated to earth.

As Joy traveled throughout the universe, she was attracted to the different kinds of music she encountered. There were so many instruments used and so few of them were small enough for her to play. Her fingers were so tiny, they would not cover the holes in the numerous flutes and others she collected. She kept on collecting them though and the music room in her palace soon had a large collection. In time she would grow large enough to use them, then she could play music to her hearts content. There was one instrument however she could play. It was small, something like a flute. There was a big difference though. It was adapted the language of birds. Joy hardly left it in her palace. Wherever she went, it went with her. She learned the songs of hundreds of birds. By studying their sounds, she grew quite apt at communicating with them. If she wanted to, she could call them to her. It was not unusual to see her walking with her bird flute and being surrounded by several the beautiful creatures. They would fly along with her and answer her notes.

Joy took her bird flute one day over to the home of her adopted mother. Nancy's palace was a wonder to behold. She loved glass and transparent gems. Her palace showed it. Jesus had selected for her several choice gems. These He had cut to reflect and transmit light. When you walked into her home you were dazzled by the glory of the place. Light reflecting off the various angles of the cut gems would send rainbows all over the room. If your eye passed through one of the beams, brilliant colors exploded into your head. There was a large garnet panel set in a frame of gold. The deep red/purple shone brightly and cast a colored hue on a crystal table laden with the many fruit Nancy picked from trees growing in the multiple terraces. There were two matching gems on either side of one window. They were rubies that were perfectly correlated. At times God's throne would revolve as the Ancient of Days looked out over the different directions in the city. When this happened, the bright rays from the throne of God would beam through these two-exquisite works of grander and send streamers of glory into the room. These beams would first fall on the golden mirrored walls then bounce back into other gems located in precise locations in the various rooms. A chain reaction would be set up and the home would vibrate with colors for a long time. That was not all though. Music also affected these gems. There was a violate opal that somehow had the molecular structure altered. When musical sounds were heard in the room it would vibrate at the frequency of the music and send out rays that would find a response in many of the other gems around the room. There was a large green, transparent gem resting on the center of the crystal table. It was cut in such a way that it could beam rays to other gems located around the room. Joy called softly to Nancy before entering to make her aware of her presence.

"Mother, are you home?"

"Yes, Joy, came the reply. "I am here."

"Do you have time to play some music with me?"

"Yes, I was thinking of coming over to your place with my harp just now. Please come in." With that the little girl entered and sat down on one of the soft cushions. Nancy got out her harp and soon soothing sounds were floating out the window of that glorious palace. She didn't know what possessed her, but Joy decided to call her bird friends. By the time she started calling them, the opal was sending rays of color all over the room in rhythm with the music. As the different measures of their songs came and went the gem sent out longer or shorter rays. It was awesome indeed to see and hear. Then it happened. Joy gave a call of a meadowlark and soon a pair of yellow birds flew in through the window. She called to the cardinals and they came also. She must have given the calls of at least 20 kinds of birds for soon they were all there in the palace of Nancy. As the music played and the rays pulsated, the birds flew around the room dodging or catching the rays. It was truly remarkable to see. There were birds of all colors of the rainbow and they migrated to the rays that matched their colors.

The concert went on for a long time. Grandmother and Grandfather came over to see the wonder. Grandfather was very musical also. He brought over an instrument that gave out a deeper base sound and soon was matching the rhythm of the song. Others came. All in all, about 25 people gathered near the door and outside the windows looking in at the wonder of it all. It was so much fun to see the birds fluttering in time to the music, flying up, down and around the flashing rays of light. A coral group composed the song of the birds and sang to the glory of God and several pleasant hours passed in the palace of Nancy.

So often we think of heaven as a place where we will set on a cloud and play harps or get bored doing nothing, but heaven is a real place. We will do real things there. Whatever we do on earth that is not of sin, will be done there. We will eat and walk, fly, and talk. We will have physical bodies and enjoy physical things. There is a human side of heaven. So often we focus on the spiritual side of heaven but there is another side also. On earth there is waste, in heaven nothing will be wasted. We will have glorified bodies with a vitality some 20 times greater than what we have now. Our minds will be much more active there also. Here we use only a small portion of our brain. There all of it will be available for our use. Our understanding will be complete. Our communication will be perfect also. We will understand and be understood. English will not be the language of heaven. Heaven has its own language. Imagine talking to your friends and having them understand completely what you are communicating.

On earth we enjoy physical contact. I am sure there will be several hugs and kisses in heaven. As far as physical relations go between men and woman, it is hard to understand how that will be changed. Jesus clearly stated there would be no marriage in heaven, but we would be like the angels. If that portion of our physical being is not present there, I am sure He will replace it with something more perfect. At any rate heaven will be beyond our wildest expectations. Nothing that will bring us happiness will be withheld from us. Jesus will see that all are satisfied completely. I know I shall be satisfied and if you have developed a relationship with Jesus to the point of wanting to be with Him for all of eternity, you will be satisfied also. That is why it is important to develop a friendship with Him while you are on earth. If you know of Jesus and He is not your friend on earth, how can you expect to spend eternity with Him in heaven or the earth made new? If He is not your friend and you want to develop a forever friendship with Him, read about Him. Read the Gospels. If you do not have a copy of Desire of Ages, by Ellen White, get a copy and read of His life on earth. This will help you to see He fully identified with all of us while on earth. He lived in our world and became one of us, eating at our tables, staying in our homes, walking our streets, and ministering to our needs. He is the same today. He will minister to our needs now and longs to establish a friendship with each one of us.

There is some who feel since there is a heaven there must be a hell. Evil must balance out the good, but in God's world such is not the case. God did not create evil. It originated in the heart of an angel. God created a perfect environment in heaven. Everything was there to assure the happiness of the angels. He also created a perfect world. Adam and Eve were given everything to assure their happiness. It was only as they wanted more, and took hold of sin that it took hold of humans and plunged us into this hell we now live in. For ages ministers of the gospel have painted pictures of a burning hell where God punishes the transgressors of His laws. This concept has caused many to hate God. If one day, as Revelation states, God shall wipe away all tears from their eyes and there will be no more pain, then a burning hell must be a misconception. How could we enjoy the beauties of heaven and the many wonders there if we could look across the gulf and see our former friends and loved ones engulfed in flames, wreathing in pain and agony?

God is a God of love. He is not some tyrant who zaps us the moment we step out of line. He wants to be our friend, forever and that friendship is based on love. He loves us and when we understand that we can then give Him love in return. There will be a lake of fire, a burning but that will come when sin and those who refuse to accept salvation meet with their end. That need not happen to any of us. God has written each of our names in the Book of Life. Our names can only be blotted out if we choose not to accept the gift of eternal life Jesus came and purchased for us with His own death on the cross. It was His blood that was shed for our sin. He took on the death we deserve so we might live the life He deserved, eternal life. Yes, heaven has a human side and Jesus will forever be a human with us. He gave up His divine form and took on the form of a man. Though we were created in His image, the fall of man changed the image of God. He will forever bear the scars of sin, the nail prints in His hands and feet. There will be the wound in His side and perhaps scars on His brow from the crown of thorns. He chose to dwell with us because He loved us. He takes no delight in our suffering. Indeed, He relieved suffering wherever He encountered it on earth. This is the real picture of Jesus we need to see. He is a Savior not a destroyer. He brings comfort, not pain. He is a God of love.

BIBLE TEXTS

"Then the Lord God planted a garden in Eden, to the east, and placed in the garden the man he had formed. The Lord God planted all kinds of beautiful trees there in the garden, trees producing the choicest of fruit. At the center of the garden, he placed the Tree of Life, and the Tree of the Knowledge of Good and Evil. A river from the land of Eden flowed through the garden to water it; afterwards, the river divided into four branches... The Lord God placed man in the Garden of Eden as its gardener, to tend and care for it. But the Lord God gave the man this warning: "You may eat of any fruit in the garden except the fruit from the Tree of the Knowledge of Good and Evil. Its fruit will open your eyes and make you know what is good and what is evil. The day you eat of its fruit, you will die."

Genesis 3:8-11, 15-17

"The angel also showed me the river of the water of life, clear, sparkling like crystal. It comes from the throne of God and of the Lamb and flows down the middle of the city's street. On each side of the river was the tree of life. It bears fruit twelve times a year, once every month; and its leaves are for the healing of the nations. Nothing that is under the curse of sin will be found in the city. The throne of God and of the Lamb will be there and his servants will worship him. They will see his face, and his name will be written on their foreheads. There shall be no more night, and they will not need lamps or sunlight, for the Lord God will be their light, and they will rule as kings for ever and ever."

Revelation 22:1-5

This is what the LORD says, I will return to Zion, and will dwell in the middle of Jerusalem: and Jerusalem will be called a city of truth; and a mountain of the LORD of hosts, the holy mountain. This is what the LORD says, Old men and old women will dwell in the streets of Jerusalem, and every man with his staff in his hand for a long time. And the streets of the city will be full of boys and girls playing. This is what the LORD of hosts says, If it is marvelous in the eyes of my remnant, shall it not also be marvelous in my own eyes? Says the LORD... Behold, I will save my people from the east and from the west. And I will bring them in, and they shall dwell in the middle of Jerusalem: and they shall be my people, and I will be their God, in truth and in righteousness.

Zechariah 8:3-8

CHAPTER 21
THE LAW OF GOD

There are many things to see and do in heaven. In the Bible, God's book of the recorded history of sin and salvation, there are many stories. If you have read the Bible and or attended church, you have heard of the stories of David and Goliath, Jonah and the whale, Balaam and the talking donkey, Sampson the strong man, Enoch and Elijah's translation to heaven and hundreds of others. Some of these stories were given for a better understanding of the mercy of God. Some of the objects in these stories were taken to heaven and preserved for a testimony to the truth of the Bible. The giant fish that swallowed Jonah was taken to heaven. It resided in one of the pools under the golden fountains at one of the intersections of the city's streets. The donkey that talked to Balaam, with the help of the angel of course, was also there. There were several items one could see that reminded the occupants of the other world. There was another very special item that was taken to heaven. It was the Ark of the Convenient or the Ark of the Testimony as others call it. If you do not know of it, I will share its story briefly now.

Joy and Trust were walking near a shiny temple one day. It was a beautiful place on a hill at the north end of the city. This temple rested on 4 pillars. It had a door and just outside the door was a golden plaque. On the plaque were engraved the names of the 144,000. These were the only people who could enter the temple. Next to the temple in the side of the hill was another building. I suppose on earth we would call it a museum. It contained many things along with a complete history of sin and salvation. In it you had access to the time capsule that contained the story of salvation. It was to this place that the children decided to go. As they wandered through the building they came to the Ark of the Testimony. The children took a special look at it now. For those who have not read about it in the Bible, it was a gold plated, wooden box that contained the actual law of God, given to Moses on Mt. Sinai. That law forms the foundation of God's throne. The law of God is so important that when Adam and Eve broke it, they were told that they must die. God's law could not be changed because He is unchanging. It is so important that Jesus had to come to earth as a man and perfectly obey the law of God and die the death we deserve so that we might inherit the eternal life that He deserved.

The children looked at the two carved angels on top of the ark and marveled. They were not exact copies of angels in heaven but more of a streamlined, symbolic form. The children could also see into the ark and view the tables of stone. On top of the ark, beneath the angel forms was the mercy seat. This ark represented God's throne. In heaven there were 2 covering cherubim that stood on either side of God. Before his fall, Lucifer was on the left and Jesus, or Michael as He was called then was on the right. After Lucifer sinned and was cast out of heaven, Gabriel took his place on the left-hand side of the Father. The ark contained what is called a mercy seat. It represented the mercy of God toward the sinner. When man sinned, Jesus stepped between the sinner and God so the sinner would not die. Jesus offered to pay the penalty for man's transgression of the law of God so man would not have to die. So, a model of God's throne was made on earth. It had the law of God at the foundation, the mercy seat where Jesus came between the law of God and the Father, the place where God resided and the covering cherubim. This ark was placed in the sanctuary of the wilderness. It was God's throne on earth. When that temple was dedicated, the glory of God took possession of the building. When the temple that Solomon built was finished, the ark was placed there also in the most holy place. God again came and His glory filled that temple also. But Israel did not follow the law of God. They broke every commandment and as a result, God allowed their enemies to come and destroy the temple and take many of the people away as captives. Just before the Assyrian's came, the Ark of the Testimony disappeared and was not seen for over 2500 years. It was hidden in a cave outside the inner walls of Jerusalem.

Many of you probably know what happened in the sanctuary service. But for those who don't I will tell you. God set up the sanctuary to show the nation of Israel that someday the Lamb of God, Jesus Christ, would come down to earth and die to bring salvation. The head of each family was supposed to bring a lamb once a year and sacrifice it to point forward to the coming of Jesus to be sacrificed. The priest would take some of the blood of the lamb and sprinkle it on the altar outside the temple. Once a year on what was called a Day of Atonement, the priest would offer a bullock on the altar to atone for his sins and take some of the blood and sprinkle it on the Ark of the Testimony on what was called the mercy seat. Then he would offer a goat for all the sins of the people and go back into the Most Holy place and sprinkle its blood on the mercy seat again. He would then take some of the blood and mix it with the blood washed off from the horns of the altar and place that on the head of another goat. This was called the scape goat and it represented Satan. That goat was led into the wilderness and left to perish, representing the thousand years Satan would spend on earth suffering for all the sins he caused people to commit. During this time of course, the redeemed were in heaven.

As Joy and Trust were looking at this Ark, they saw that there was some blood still on the mercy seat. About that time Celestania came in. He was good at this. The children had many questions by this time and the gentle angel was there to answer them.

"What is that blood on the mercy seat," asked Joy?

"Is it the blood of the bullocks and the goats," asked Trust at the same time?

Celestania smiled and looked at these two loved ones.

"Let's not ask so many questions so fast," he replied. "The blood you see is not the blood of the bullocks and the goats, Trust. That blood turned to dust and fell away long ago. The blood you see is the blood of Jesus Christ."

Trust was very silent when he heard that. His father had spoken much on the Sanctuary in the wilderness, so he was well familiar with the story. He knew the Ark of the Convenient had been removed from the temple that Solomon built shortly before it was destroyed. He knew it had been placed in a cave. He also knew about the blood of the animals that was sprinkled on it once a year but if this was the blood of Jesus, how could that happen? The Ark was not in the temple that Jesus visited. The Bible stated in all the gospels the most holy place of the temple that Jesus cleansed was opened at his death. An unseen hand ripped the veil that covered the Most Holy place from top to bottom as a symbol, representing that the earthly sacrificial system set up by God through Moses, had come to an end. So how could the blood of Jesus be applied to the mercy seat? The gentle angel let him ponder the question for what seemed a long time. Finally, it was enough. Looking deep into the eyes of the angel, Trust asked how?

"It was not God's intent that Jesus die on a cross," he answered. "God wanted Israel to accept the sacrifice of His Son as the Lamb of God. Jesus was supposing be sacrificed on the altar outside the temple as the Lamb of God. Isaac, the son of Abraham was a type of what Christ was supposed to do when God asked the patriarch to offer him up. But the Israelites did not accept the plan of God. They did not accept Jesus as the Lamb of God, so He died the death of a criminal on a cruel cross. God's first plan was not carried out. The symbol of the sacrificial system needed to be carried out though. So, God arranged it to happen. You see Trust, the cave where the ark was hidden was directly beneath the cross of Jesus. When the soldier thrust the spear through the side of Christ, blood and water came out and went through a crack in the ground and some of it ended on the mercy seat of the very ark that contained the law of God that He wrote with his own finger."

The children were astounded at this revelation. As they pondered this, they realized that God's providence was carried out through this symbol in a literal way.

"Do you remember how Uzzah died when he reached out to steady the Ark and keep it from falling, Trust?"

"Yes, I always wondered why God did that," replied the lad.

"The Ark with the Commandments was to remain undefiled by sin or sinners until it fulfilled its primary purpose. That primary purpose was to receive the very blood of Jesus," continued the angel. "The Ark had to be Holy even as the Blood of Jesus was Holy. There was no other holy, undefiled object on earth that could receive the undefiled sacrifice of the Savior. So, God arranged for the Ark to be in the right place at the right time. It is called the Ark of the Testimony because that is what it is to be. It is to be a Testimony to the fact that God's perfect law cannot be broken. Since it was broken though, the very commandments that God gave Israel in the wilderness needed to have the blood of Jesus applied above them on the mercy seat so man could be free from the law of death, through that blood and partake of eternal life. God preserved that ark containing the commandments for a purpose far greater then to receive the blood of bulls and goats. It was not destined to end up in a cave and be destroyed. It was especially preserved, outliving 3 temples so that it could receive the blood of Jesus. Shortly after you were asked to give your life for Jesus, Trust, the Ark with the commandments was removed from the cave and a lot of publicity given to it to show those still alive on earth that God did have a law that was still binding. When discovered, the blood was analyzed and found to be different than any human blood. It was the blood of a man who had no earthly father. Jesus had a heavenly father but no human one. God the Father was the One who brought about this union of God and man in the person of Jesus Christ. He provided a body for His only begotten Son. When these things were presented to the world, many of the people who heard your message, Trust made their decision to follow Jesus and accept the Law of God as the standard of righteousness rather than accept the mark of the beast. This was the third purpose of the Ark with its precious cargo, the Law of God. The fourth purpose was to be a testimony for all eternity that Jesus died. The proof is on the mercy seat. If we analyzed the blood there, and compared it to the Blood of Jesus now, it would be the same. There is no other blood like it in all the universe. It is totally unique to Jesus, the Lamb of God. It was preserved as a testimony that these things are true. It is His very own blood. There is no denying it. Never can it be said that the death of Jesus was a fable. He did all that He said He would, and we can know it is true because of this."

As the children and the angel left the museum, they had plenty to think about. Trust remembered a text from the Bible. "Thy way, O God, is in the sanctuary: who is so great a God as our God?" Psalms 77.13 Evil men controlled by the Satan tried to thwart God's plan of redemption, but God's will, was carried out. His purpose was accomplished in a truly remarkable way through this sanctuary object, the Ark of the Testimony. Someday they would ask the angel to show them the details of this event from within the time capsule but not now. Throughout the ages of eternity both Joy and Trust wondered if more of the love of Jesus would be revealed in different ways.

So, the weeks, months, and years passed, if heaven has weeks, months, and years. Time could well be on a different schedule there. Though a thousand years will pass on earth who knows what that time will be in heaven. The inhabitants of that glorious place traveled all over God's Universe. They always returned home though. The City was their home.

Now it was one of those beautiful times at home in the city of Gold, a time when all the residents of that celestial city were especially happy to be there. All had just spent a wonderful Sabbath with Jesus. He loved to be with His redeemed. It brought Him great pleasure to know they loved Him with an everlasting love. Joy and Trust were at the Palace of Joy this time when the parrots emerged from their private room. Joy was resting comfortably on her sponge cushion from the Planet of Trees. Trust was amusing himself with some of the trinkets the girl had collected from all over the heavens.

"Come, Joy, come, Trust. Come see another wonder." The two children followed the birds to the window. All four mounted the windowsill and flew down to the waterfall just below. Joy had been there so many times she knew where each gem rested. She knew each plant and flower. She had picked many flowers and set them in vases around her rooms. After she had enjoyed them for a time, she returned them to their mother plants, and they continued to grow and bring praises to their Creator. This time however one plant was missing. It was a special plant she had collected from a distant planet. Where was it? She decided to ask Starlacia.

"Where did that plant with the orange flowers go?"

"Come and see," replied the green and golden lady. The children followed the parrots under the falls. At the base of one corner there was a square stone.

"Could you remove the stone," requested the bird?

"Yes," replied the girl. She stooped to remove the stone and was surprised when the whole waterfall turned and disappeared into the wall. In its place was a beautiful section of ruby. It was a large one that dwarfed the girl.

The children were so taken back by this new wonder they failed to again see their favorite angel standing nearby. He had slipped in unnoticed. How many questions had he answered for these young children over the ages? Hundreds, thousands, perhaps millions. Now he read the questions in their minds again before they ever asked them.

"Where did the waterfall go and what is this ruby?" The angel smiled and went to another portion of the garden. He removed another square stone, then another, and another until the garden receded into wall and a whole panel of precious gems formed a colorful fortification. As the children looked out over the city, garden after garden was disappearing, and gem after gem taking their places. The city, the beautiful city was changing before their very eyes. With great wonderment the children looked on the scene. Then both questioned in unison.

"What is happening, Celestania?"

"The city is about to take another journey," he replied.

"But on all the other journey's nothing like this ever happened," noted Trust."

"Yes, I know, but this journey is one that will be different. This time the city will land on a planet. Before it always rested in the sky above the planets like another moon or perhaps a sun because of its brightness. During this journey however, it will come down and rest on the earth. The New Jerusalem is heading for earth soon."

The children shuddered at the thought of earth. They had spent far too long in that place. Now they would return. Then the panorama in the sky again came to mind and they saw the New Jerusalem coming down from God out of heaven and landing on earth. They remembered seeing the unsaved resurrected at the command of Christ. They saw them come up and surround the city. So, a thousand earth years had passed, had they? Was it really time to return and close out the reign of sin forever? Somehow the city looked more beautiful than ever with its panels of precious stones. Each stone reflected more of the glory of God. God had streamlined the great metropolis in preparations for its journey to earth. The living plants within this environment would never experience the harsh atmosphere of earth, at least not until it was created anew. The children felt a tremor deep underneath. The beautiful city was lifting off from its resting place. It was starting its decent toward the habitation of demons. They entered Joy's palace and looked at their reflection in the wall. They had grown quite a bit. They were still children though. When they stood next to the patriarchs, they still came only a little above their waist. There was still some physical growing they would do. But they would not grow up in heaven. They would grow to full stature in the earth made new. This journey then was the beginning of the end which would end with a new beginning.

BIBLE TEXT

"I don't want you to think I have come to destroy the law, or the prophets: I have not come to destroy either of them, but to fulfil them. For truly I say to you, Till heaven and earth pass away, not even a period or a coma will pass away from the law until all that is planned has been fulfilled. Whoever then shall break one of these commandments and shall teach others to do so shall be called the least in the kingdom of heaven: but whoever shall keep and do them, the same shall be called great in the kingdom of heaven."
Matthew 5:17-19

"And God spoke all these words, saying, I am the LORD thy God, which have brought thee out of the land of Egypt, out of the house of bondage. Thou shalt have no other gods before me. Thou shalt not make unto thee any graven image, or any likeness of anything that is in heaven above, or that is in the earth beneath, or that is in the water under the earth: Thou shalt not bow down thyself to them, nor serve them: for I the LORD thy God am a jealous God, visiting the iniquity of the fathers upon the children unto the third and fourth generation of them that hate me; And showing mercy unto thousands of them that love me, and keep my commandments. Thou shalt not take the name of the LORD thy God in vain; for the

LORD will not hold him guiltless that taketh his name in vain. Remember the Sabbath day, to keep it holy. Six days shalt thou labor, and do all thy work: But the seventh day is the Sabbath of the LORD thy God: in it thou shalt not do any work, thou, nor thy son, nor thy daughter, thy manservant, nor thy maidservant, nor thy cattle, nor thy stranger that is within thy gates: For in six days the LORD made heaven and earth, the sea, and all that in them is, and rested the seventh day: wherefore the LORD blessed the Sabbath day, and hallowed it. Honor thy father and thy mother: that thy days may be long upon the land which the LORD thy God giveth thee. Thou shalt not kill. Thou shalt not commit adultery. Thou shalt not steal. Thou shalt not bear false witness against thy neighbor. Thou shalt not covet thy neighbor's house, thou shalt not covet thy neighbor's wife, nor his manservant, nor his maidservant, nor his ox, nor his ass, nor any thing that is thy neighbor's."

Exodus 20:1-17

"Look at what kind of love the Father has bestowed upon us, that we should be called the sons and daughters of God: Because we are his, the world does not know us, because it did not know him. Loved ones, now we are the sons and daughters of God, and we are not yet what we will become. This we do know though, when he shall appear, we shall be like him; for we shall see him as he is. And every man that has this hope in him purifies himself, even as God is pure. Whoever commits sin transgresses the law: for sin is the transgression of the law. And you know that Christ was revealed to take away our sins; for in him is no sin. Whoever abides in him sins not: whoever sins has not seen him, neither known him. Little children let no one deceive you: he that does righteousness is righteous, even as the Son is

righteous. He that commits sin is of the devil; for the devil sinned from the beginning. For this reason, the Son of God was revealed, that he might destroy the works of Satan. Whoever is born of God does not commit sin; for God's righteousness is born in him: and he cannot sin. In this the children of God are distinguished from the children of the devil: whoever does not do righteously is not of God, neither is he that does not love his brother. For this is the message that you heard from the beginning, that we should love one another."

1 John 3:1-11

"I know that I am a sinner through and through when it comes to my old nature. It doesn't matter what way I turn. I can't make myself do right. I really want to do what is right and good, but I always end up sinning and doing what is bad. When I want to do good, I don't, and when I try not to do wrong, I go ahead and do it anyway. Now if I keep on doing what I don't want to do, it is plain to me where the trouble lies: sin still has an evil grip on me. As far as my new nature is concerned, I really love to do God's will, but there is something else deep inside me, way down in my lower nature, that is warring against my mind and wins the battle, making me a slave to the sin that is still within me. So deep inside I am still enslaved to sin. You can see now how it is: my new nature tells me to do right, but the old life that is still inside me loves to sin and forces me to do bad things. This is a terrible predicament to be in. Is there anything that can deliver me from the deadly effects of my lower, sinful self? Thank God! It has already been done for me by Jesus Christ our Lord. He has set me free."

Romans 7:18-25

CHAPTER 22
EARTHWARD BOUND

The city was moving again. Joy and Trust flew high in the air as it pulled away from its resting place in heaven. They remembered the last time the city relocated. At that time, the whole planet moved but this time it was different. This time just the megalopolis moved. Several of the saints advanced to the top of the walls. They were entering Orion now. The children never ceased to be amazed at this beautiful splendor in God's great universe. Its distance across was incomprehensible. You could take 30,000 of our solar systems and put them side-by-side in the entrance of Orion and still have more room. Soon the Horse Nebula came into view. It stood towering thousands and thousands of miles above the city. From heaven's viewpoint, it did not look like a horse at all, only a column of dark red and black. Astronomers feel Orion is the birthplace of stars. Could Jesus the Creator, still be creating stars or suns? There were many stars around Orion. Some were giant blue suns others were red. The children noticed a brilliant green one. This was rare. They had traveled through several galaxies and seen only a few green stars.

The city was moving quite rapidly now, approximately five times the speed of light. In time it slowed. Beneath them, far away in the distance, was earth. The saints on the top of the wall watched as it grew closer and closer. There was another observer also. His name was Lucifer. For one thousand years, he and his angels had been trapped as prisoners on planet earth. Now the hated city had arrived. Lucifer despised it more than ever. He hated everything in it. The hated the Father. He hated the Son, and he hated the saints. They were untouchable now. He may have been able to control them earlier but not now. They had gained the victory over him through the blood of Jesus Christ. Never again would they fall to his temptations. As he watched the city approaching the earth, he and his comrades knew the time of their end was near. For over seven thousand years they had been granted life. A portion of that time had been lived in the city of gold with Jesus and the Father. They remembered the days of their innocence. They remembered singing in the vast choir around the throne of God. But now what a change. Their energies had so long been bent toward evil, all traces of the goodness of God were removed from them. The once proud leader, Lucifer in his current state was much changed from his former time in heaven. He was still a mighty prince, but his once noble brow commenced to recede at his eyebrows and what looked like skin appeared to hang in loose wrinkles over his giant frame.

He must not let the saints see him this way. He must not let the wicked who would be resurrected see him as he was, a fallen angel. He summoned his utmost power, and a bit of his original glory came to the surface of his being. His stooped shoulders straightened. He transformed his robes to purest white and took on the appearance of a mighty king. He must look as much like Christ as possible. But in some ways, he would differ from the Creator. He would have no nail scars in his hands. There would be no wound in his side. No thorny scars would mar his brow. Though the interior robes would be of shining light, inside was total darkness. That had to be covered, he must look like a mighty king. He decided to wear a cloak of brilliant red, trimmed in gold. On his head would rest a crown of glory. His fallen angels followed his example. They presented themselves in the most pleasing forms. They would go to their doom at least looking like mighty, powerful beings. It was a solemn time for them. It is only natural for a living being to want to preserve the life it has been granted. It is with reluctance we lay down our duties and go to our rest. Ahead of these angels of destruction was no rest. They knew there would be a lot of agony to bear as they faced their fate. As the end drew near, they determined with their leader to not yield to the destiny they had been handed. They congregated together in little groups using their highest mental powers to devise a way of escape. Was there a way? Was it all true? Everything Jesus had said He would do earlier, during their time of existence, He had done. As they recalled the ages that had passed, they could find no place He had failed. There was no weakness in Him. He had done and probably would do just what He said He would do but while there was life there was hope. They would not yield easily to the higher powers that seemed to be controlling them now.

The city came to a stop about five miles above earth. The saints on the top of the walls looked out over the world. It was a scene that would long be remembered. In ages to come this picture of earth would come up again and again. Everywhere the eye rested was havoc and ruin. The proud cities were broken down. Jagged canyons were visible all over the earth. There were long cracks on the surface that extended for miles and miles. Laying on top of the ground were the dusty, skeletal remains of the wicked. They lay just where they had fallen. Not all life had been destroyed at the coming of Jesus. There were rodents running ramped over the face of the earth. There were rats and moles along with bats and the despised creatures of earth. For over five hundred years, large glaciers had formed over the earth carving out canyons and valleys while pushing up gigantic mountains. These had resulted from the darkness that had covered much of the world. The dust in the air, the smoke from the volcanoes and fires had caused it. Then as the air cleared, the sun had returned and during the last five hundred years the snow had slowly melted. In some place's vegetation had returned. There were areas of green where these changes had occurred. But within these areas the thorn and thistle grew in abundance. All nature was cursed it seemed. But then why not? The author of all that was anti-Christ had nothing to do for the last thousand years. Why not attempt to invent more foul and destructive plants. Perhaps they could be used to help in the destruction of the hated sect who would return to transform the earth once again into a place of habitation. As the redeemed looked below the city, they saw the Mount of Olives. This was the place Jesus would return to. He promised to return even as He went into heaven.

Jesus, now accompanied by His loyal angels, descended toward the earth. Christ went first. As His feet touched the top of the mount, the earth began to move. The Mount of Olives split and parted moving outward, forming a great plain. At the same time the area where Jesus feet were standing rose higher and higher forming a tall plateau. Several of the ancient cities were covered over. All of Israel and most of Jordan were covered. So were Lebanon and the Sinai Peninsula with parts of Syria and Saudi Arabia. The great plain also stretched over the site of ancient Egypt. The saints watched as the giant pyramids were crumbled to dust at the power of the advancing ground. The plateau pushed out and covered over half of the Mediterranean Sea. The prophecy of Obadiah was finally fulfilled. At Petra he had prophesied that one day Jerusalem would cover this city and now the time was about to come. The New Jerusalem was about to descend on the place made ready for it. At this time, the redeemed left the metropolis and took up positions at the edges of the great plain. They were again arranged in companies according to their tribes.

It was strange to touch earth again. Trust stomped his feed on the planet that had given him birth. Dust rose into the air. It had been so long since he smelt it. He looked up toward the great city. It was huge. It blocked out most of the sky. He was awed by the power of a God who could move more than mountains. He could move planets and cities. Nothing was impossible to Him. Then accompanied by the sounding of trumpets and a great noise, the city came slowly earthward. As it advanced, Trust found himself raising his voice with the those around them.   "The city, the great city is coming down from God out of heaven!" As it touched the vast tableland, there was the sound of fusion and it became one with the mountain. No power aside from God could move it from its place now.

Satan and his hosts of evil angels were awed by the splendor of this event. The city stood as a golden pyramid resting on the top of a great mountain. It rose high above the earth and stood gleaming in the light of the setting sun. The sun was no match for its splendor though. It paled into insignificance at the glory of God. There would be no night on earth ever again, at least not on this side of earth. The light illuminating from the city would shine forever and ever over the land of the free.

As Lucifer observed the saints so happy and radiant outside the city, he wanted to go up and crush out their life. He hated them with an intense hatred. They had been his until they accepted the salvation offered by Jesus. They had taken he and his angels places in that great city. He now would have to suffer for all the sins he had caused them to commit. His suffering would last for days, weeks, perhaps even months. If he could just cause it all to go away, he might consider some changes now, but it was no use. They were protected by the divine power of Christ. He could never have any power over them again. Neither could he undo what he had done when he once turned his back on loyalty to his Creator. Joy snuggled close to Nancy and grasped her hand as they advanced toward their gate. She had grown in her time away from earth. She was now nearly nine foot tall and came a little below the shoulder of her adopted mother. She had developed into a creature of stunning beauty. No one was happier. She was a bright and starry gem giving praise and glory to the King of Kings. The heavenly adventure had been good to her. Her understanding of God was nearly complete. As they entered the gate they again headed for their palace in the sky. At last, all were inside the city. Those inside would not go out again until the recreation of the earth, neither would any from the outside enter.

Outside this glorious place were the angels of darkness and the remains of the fallen. Jesus also entered the city with His angels and ascended to the throne. From that position high above, He looked out over the earth and in a voice that penetrated the souls of the deceased, called them to life. His proclamation rolled out over the earth and it trembled as a blade of grass shaken in the wind. From all sections of the globe, they came forth. There were billions and billions of them. Among them were those of the ancient race who were lofty in stature, the same size as the redeemed within the city. In contrast to these were those of the last generations who appeared as dwarf, adult children. There was a great difference in their appearance. When Joy was resurrected from the dead, she had been given a glorious, new body. No marks of sin remained. There were no deformed legs, no blinded eyes. There was no trace of death in her but as these wicked came from their resting places, they appeared even as they had entered. The lame were still lame. Those with disease still had its effects occupying their bodies. There were a couple of exceptions to this. Those who died blind were resurrected with their vision intact. The first person they saw was Jesus, the one who had called them from their resting places. The ears of the deaf had also been opened to hear. They had heard the voice of God calling them forth and with that sound, their hearing had been restored. The wounds of the wounded were somewhat healed, enough to keep the blood within its vessels. But sin and its effects still reigned supreme. After calling them from their graves and places of destruction, Jesus and his attendants disappeared. The mighty host of resurrected ones looked around for someone to instruct them as to what to do now. They were not disappointed. A powerful prince arrived on the scene. He looked very much like the one who had called them from death. He was brilliant. His inner robes were dazzling and white and few could tell the difference. After raising them back to life had this prince come to them to grant them their kingdom? All waited in expectancy.

Yes, he told them he had brought them to life to give them their kingdom, their reward. He pointed to the great city on the mountain and told them that was their home. He told how it was built to last forever. There was one problem though. A group of unworthy beings had taken possession of it. They were foreigners from another world. He told of their small numbers. He said he had built the city, but it had been wrested from his hands in an unfair battle. At the time he tried to defend the city he was outnumbered two to one. He told how he and his comrades had fought valiantly and had left only when forced. Now things would be different. The odds were stacked in his favor. On his side were billions and billions of warriors. They outnumbered the group within the city by odds of over a thousand to one. On his side were all the great generals of the ages. Men of superior battle strategy. Plus, he and his agents were familiar with the city. They knew every part of it. They could easily overthrow its inhabitants. They would be destroyed in a quick battle. Then the masses could go up and inhabit the city of gold. He told of the riches and treasures within its walls. He told of the food that grew in abundance. None would ever hunger again. Within the city there was a tree that would cause them to live forever. Death would never again come to them. To those who had been resurrected twice already, this appeared to be great news. Death was hard enough the first time, to experience it three times would be dreadful. Then the great prince of darkness gave even more promises. He said he would heal them of their diseases. He then went from person to person. At his touch they were strengthened. Life surged through them. He removed the curse his own hands had installed. Shouts of glory and praise ascended from their lips. In time all were touched. A great expectancy permeated the air. There would be eternal life for all. All they had to do to gain it was remove from existence those who were keeping it from them.

Now the angels of darkness begin to consult with the former leaders of the world. A great army was formed. In that army were men who had never lost a battle. The great intellectuals were engaged to form weapons of destruction. They had weapons that would shoot beams of energy into the unsuspecting guardians of the gates. These were powerful enough to microwave them without destroying the vegetation and the structures there. Battle plans were set up. Those outside the city would then enter and destroy the ones within. They would go up and inhabit this paradise. Its treasures would be theirs. Its supply of food would feed the billions. Its life-giving tree would assure an everlasting existence. The mighty prince would rule as king of kings and lord of lords. And so, the day for conquest was set. There was a feeling of excitement as it approached. The mightiest of the army would go first. They would be followed by those of less stature and strength. Behind them would come the strongest of the women. They would be followed by the weaker and at last the children and aged would come. Beyond the aged, on the fringes of the army, the stealth bombers, missiles, and airborne weapons were ready if any of the residents somehow slipped through to freedom. Such a conglomeration of weapons had never been amassed before nor ever would be. The ranks were drawn up. The battle was about to begin.

BIBLE TEXTS

"Then the Lord will go out and fight against those nations, as he fights in the day of battle. On that day, his feet will stand on the Mount of Olives, east of Jerusalem, and the Mount of Olives will be split in two from east to west, forming a great valley, with half of the mountain moving north and half moving south... On that day living water will flow out from Jerusalem, half to the eastern sea and half to the western sea, in summer and winter. The Lord will be king over the whole earth. On that day there will be one Lord, and his name the only name."

Zechariah 14: 3, 4, 8, 9

"Then I saw a new heaven and a new earth, for the first heaven and the first earth had passed away, and there was no longer any sea. I saw the Holy City, the New Jerusalem, coming down out of heaven from God, prepared as a bride beautifully dressed for her husband. And I heard a loud voice from the throne saying, "Now the dwelling of God is with men, and he will live with them, They will be his people, and God himself will be with them and be their God. He will wipe every tear from their eyes. There will be no more death or mourning or crying or pain, for the old order of things has passed away." He who was seated on the throne said, "I am making everything new!"

Revelation 21:1-5

"Come, I will show you the bride, the wife of the Lamb." And he carried me away in the Spirit to a mountain great and high, and showed me the Holy City, Jerusalem, coming down out of heaven from God. It shone with the glory of God, and its brilliance was like that of a very precious jewel, like a jasper, clear as crystal. It had a great, high wall with twelve gates, and with twelve angels at the gates. On the gates were written the names of the twelve tribes of Israel. There were three gates on the east, three on the north, three on the south and three on the west. The wall of the city had twelve foundations, and on them were the names of the twelve apostles of the Lamb. The angel held in his hand a golden measuring stick to measure the city and it was a square as wide as it was long; in fact, it was in the form of a cube, for its height was the same as its other dimensions–1,500 miles each way."

Revelation 21:15-17

CHAPTER 23
THE LAST BATTLE

The walls of the New Jerusalem were 216 feet thick. The mathematicians outside the city had figured how much power would be needed to melt through them if that became necessary. It was decided the gates would be easier to penetrate. The Bible stated they were made of pearl. Twelve giant lasers had been constructed. They were positioned adjacent to each gate. The heat produced from these beams would melt anything. To the inhabitants outside the gates, the materials making up the walls of the city were foreign to earth. They had never seen anything like it before. They wondered why none of the outsiders had climbed the base of the mountain to try and enter. The walls were like glass. As they looked through them, they saw the inhabitants of this metropolis busily going about their activities within. Many telescopes had been reconstructed and brought to different locations outside the city. As the people looked, they saw wonders never before imagined. The interior of the city was so bright, they had to put filters on these scopes, or their eyes would be blinded. The rainbow above the city was very colorful. Truly this city was a work of architecture constructed by no earthly builder. Its sheer size was an impossibility for human achievement. Supernatural forces were at work here or so much time had passed, man had evolved to a wonderful state. For most they felt there was a god but who was he? Was he the prince dressed in red of another prince with pure white hair and fiery eyes?

The saints within the city were as much interested in those without as were the outsiders interested in those within. Some of the saints would come to the walls or ascend to the top of the wall and with perfect vision, peer over the activities of the vast sea of human life below them. In that group were mothers, fathers, husbands, wives, children, brothers, sisters, aunts, uncles, and friends. Tears were shed as many spotted these loved ones without. Even though there was a vast difference in the wicked and the righteous, there was still a bond. All were human. All were decedents from the same father and mother, Adam, and Eve. As Adam looked out over the vast ocean of the lost his heart was most heavy. He above all others took the blame for their loss. He kept saying to himself.

"If I had only obeyed, if I had not taken of the forbidden fruit, there would be no outsiders now." He was contemplating this theme again when Jesus came up to our noble father and placed His arms around him. The two walked the streets of gold in silence for a while. The Creator could read every thought going on in the mind of this mighty patriarch. He knew the struggle he faced and longed to take it from him. Soon he would but Adam would suffer on for a time. Adam well knew he had been forgiven. Forgiveness was not his struggle. It was the woe and pain he saw. When he had died some six thousand years earlier, the world was still in its infancy. Gigantic forest covered the planet. There were no jagged mountains. Quiet streams flowed from sparkling springs. The animals, though they feared man had been so beautiful. The earth was still a paradise when he passed on. While he slept the wickedness had increased more and more with each passing year. Some men and women were entirely controlled by the enemy but there could still be seen some noble traits in their beings. In the panoramic views, Adam had seen the earth wasted by flood and fire. He had seen paradise change to stark desert. He had seen humanity degenerate to only a fraction of their original vitality but seeing it in the panoramic scenes was not like looking on it face to face. Conditions on earth were so pitiful now. The true cost of his sin had hit him full force when he caught his first view of the numberless throng of the wicked. It was like every sin that kept them out of the city was his sin. Had not Christ strengthened him for this last, inner battle, the experience would have been too much for him.

The two had been walking in silence for what seemed like hours. Now they were at another one of the gates. At last Adam raised his eyes and looked again on the sea of human woe. Then he saw him. Could it be? Yes, it was. There at the edge of the vast throng was Cain, his first-born son. He thought back over the millennia. He remembered the awe and wonder he felt as he held that son in his arms for the very first time. He remembered the joy in his wife's eyes as she looked at her little one. Could this be the redeemer that was promised? He remembered caring for this little child. He taught him the names of all the animals. He showed him every type of fruit. Cain loved to garden. In those early days he would take long trips away from their home in search of new varieties of fruit. When he found some, he would bring back a branch and in time he had an orchard filled with the wonders of that world. Adam also remembered the birth of Able. That too had been a time of joy and then Seth. Able took to spiritual things much better then Cain. When Able heard the story of how the redeemer would come and restore the earth, he longed with his whole heart for that day to hasten. He remarked time and time again how good God must be to consider saving fallen man from eternal death. But when Cain heard these stories, his heart was hardened. He blamed God, he blamed his father, he blamed his mother, he blamed his brother, and he blamed the serpent. Every time he saw one of those loathsome creatures, he wanted to kill it. He hated the sacrifices of the lambs. He hated the blood and despised the thorns and thistles. If any of his fruit trees developed thorns, he considered it cursed and took it out and burned it. Adam remembered trying to get Cain to turn to God but more and more he set his face against him. Now the father of our race looks out on the face of his firstborn for the first time in over six thousand years. All the emotions welled up within and he found himself weeping uncontrollably. Then he fell at the feet of Jesus and taking both wounded hands in his own looked up through the tears and ask.

"Why?" Jesus wrapped His arms around him and wept too. That was answer enough for Adam. The second Adam, though He knew why was asking why also once again. The Father looked down on them and sent a ray of glory from the throne. It penetrated the heart and soul of those two Adams and a peace came over them. Soon all tears would be wiped away and that was a comfort.

From outside the city Cain looked up toward the gate and saw Jesus and his father. He too remembered the days of his youth. Where had he gone wrong? Had he been so much a sinner to blame God? Was the murder of his brother more unforgivable than the sin of his Father in eating of the fruit? In a way was not Adam responsible for all the deaths that had taken place. His sin seemed the greater, yet he was inside the city and Cain was without. He too asked why? Everyone in that great throng had asked why? What was so evil about their lives that would keep them out of the city of gold? Hatred welled up within them along with anger. Was there a chance they might someday enter one of those gates and partake of the glories of that city? With renewed vigor they set about their activities and went over and over various battle plans. Finally, they were convinced this was a winnable war. They could do it. They must do it. They would do it. Look how weak the so-called ruler and redeemer was. He was weeping there at the gate. This was not a king; this then was their weakest link. A god with that much compassion could not possibly bring himself to the point of destroying His own created beings. Cain looked on his father and despised him. Time and time again he had pointed his little and then little, bigger fingers at his father and told him it was all his fault. Each time he said that it had cut Adam with a wound that grew ever deeper. For over 900 years not only Cain, but the entire world had pointed the finger until he had withdrawn from society. Seth now came up to his father. He too looked out and saw his older brother. Cain cried up from the base of the mountain.

"Father and brother Seth. We are going to come up and enter the city soon. Then you will be torn from limb to limb by these people. They all blame you. It was your sin Father. That is the reason why we are here. You have no right to the city or its beauties. You deserve to die, and you will. I will not raise my hand against you as I did Able. These around me will deal with far less mercy than I. They can have you. I have given them permission to deal with you as they see fit. You will pay for all the pain you caused us." Cain's taunting threats died away as he and his comrades turned and disappeared into the crowd. Adam would see his son Cain one more time and that would be all. He wiped a tear away from his eye. Jesus lifted him to his feet and turning their back on the millions without, headed for the tree of life. To the father of our race, it seemed even larger than he remembered.

Adam took one of the fruits in his hands. He remembered eating of that fruit in his paradise home. Now he looked at the variety that was growing. It was a deep red fruit. It had a soft smooth skin like a nectarine but was translucent. For just a moment he thought about taking it to Cain. But as he remembered the hatred coming from his son, he knew happiness could never come to Cain inside the city. He had chosen another master. It was the Prince of Darkness. He took a few bites and shared it with the Master. Then they parted company. Adam headed back to the Garden of Eden and looked up his wife Eve and told her all about seeing Cain. She too wept as she thought back on those early years with this son they had loved so much.

Lucifer now looked at the city then at the vast army gathered around it. It was almost time for the battle that would end all battles. He made his rounds to all the lasers and the captains of hundreds, thousands, and millions. He told each one to bid their troops eat a good meal. They must have strength to win this battle.

After the ice had begun to melt, a new species of plant emerged and quickly began to cover the barren landscape. It was a vine that spread by root, seed, and wind. Within a matter of years, it had covered the earth. It also happened to be edible. The roots under the ground produced a starchy tuber a little smaller than the potato. The flower also produced a seed pod that was very sweet. These plants had sustained the populace for the last several weeks. There were other plants that were edible, and the rats and bats were also eaten by some. There was no large game left, only rodents. So, the people longed for some of the fruit they had seen within the city. There were bees and from time to time their store of honey was found. When such a discovery came the sweet syrup was taken to the leaders to be dispersed among them. The only other fruit outside the city were some berry varieties and wild grapes. The great oceans had some aquatic life left, but they were mostly the scavengers of the sea and not all that tasty. It was time for a real meal from within the city. It was time for the last battle.

The signal was given, and the troops began their advance. Slowly like a dark sea the wicked moved toward the gleaming walls. They came from everywhere. There were billions and billions of them. No man could number them there were so many. Every man woman and child who had ever lived save a few who were as if they had never been, were alive. None had died since the special resurrection. God was on earth and would not allow death. Would he now sustain them in battle? He had risen them once, could he do it again if any were killed? He claimed he could, and he would.

"Be brave and courageous. Fight as if you cannot fail. Victory will be ours. We will win." So, with those words of hope ringing in their ears they moved forward, closer, and closer to the city. The great planes were reaving their engines. The missel launchers were at the switches ready to propel their deadly cargo within. The great microwave lasers were powered up waiting for the final command to fire.

As Jesus saw the armies advancing, He commanded that the gates be shut. The great gates of pearl emerged from the walls and came together without making a sound. The army kept advancing. Then they stopped. No command had been given to stop. Lucifer raised his voice and sent it out over the vast throng.

"Continue to advance he cried but none obeyed. All eyes seemed to be transfixed on a spot high above the city. Jesus had emerged on a throne high and lifted up. Beside Him was the Father. His eyes glowed like coals of living fire. Jesus had stood up and His form was massive. It appeared to fill the whole sky. His nail scarred hands were raised. None could go any further for the one who spoke the universe into existence had made the command to halt and He was God. The people could clearly see that now. This look alike who had claimed to be their creator was an imposter. He was not God at all. When the realization of this came to the people without, a great wail arose.

"We are lost. Our cause is hopeless." At the sight of Jesus with His hands raised high, every knee bowed, and every tong confessed that Jesus was Lord. Everyone but Lucifer. He stood boldly and defiantly at the center of people refusing to bow. Jesus now looked at the deceiver. For a moment Lucifer quivered at his presence then gained his composure. If he were god as he claimed why would God kneel to God? Then in a voice awful and terrible Lucifer threw his accusations into the face of the Son of God.

"You created all of this, Son of the highest. You are to blame for sin. You have no right to keep us from the treasures of the city. We deserve our place within just as much as those you stole from us. We demand entrance to the city. Give us our inheritance. We have suffered enough. Life everlasting is our just reward. We were nothing but puppets in your hand. You forced us to live and foreordained some of us would die. You are unjust in doing this. You made us what we are."

Jesus did not answer the accusations of Lucifer. Across the sky a giant scroll was slowly being unrolled with unseen hands. As it opened all could look within and see there perfectly recorded, every deed, every word, every action they had ever made. They could see where mercy pleaded with them to turn from their wicked ways. They could see where the heavenly angels had directed them to seek righteousness and shun that which was evil. All could see there engraved in permanent writing the deep, dark secrets of their life. They could also see where the deceiver had led them astray, time and time again.

"We have been fools they cried. We followed the wrong master." Next to the scroll the decalogue appeared in the heavens. There was seen the Ten Commandments written with the finger of God. As the wicked looked on the measure of God's standard, they realized how far they had fallen short of the glory of God. Every sin burned deep within their souls. It was clear where they had veered from the path of right. At the sight of the awful law of God, the kneeling multitudes, both within and without the city fell prostrate on their faces and cried in one voice.

"The Lord, He is God. The Lord, He is God. Blessed is He that comes in the name of the Lord." The words from the wicked were not out of sorrow from the sins they had committed nor were they sorry their sins had caused the death of the Son of God. The words were spoken out of a realization of who God really was. Again, as one looked out over the sea of fallen humanity, none save Satan–that old serpent, dragon, and devil–still stood. His angels had all prostrated themselves at the feet of Jesus. But not Satan.

Early on in his rebellion he vowed he would never again bow to the Son. He had kept his promise. Now the vast throng rose and looked again in the sky.

A new picture had appeared. A star shown over a stable. Two parents bent over their infant son. His face shone and all could see He was the Christ, child. There was no doubt. They watched as his life unfolded. Those who taunted him in his childhood and made fun of his questionable birth, saw their part in the drama. As he grew, the priest and rabbis who tried to mold him in the ways of tradition, saw their part in the scene. They saw his baptism and the Holy Spirit descending like a dove and resting on his head. They saw the wilderness temptations and the part Satan played in trying to move Him from the path of righteousness. Jesus never faltered. He was victorious on all accounts. They saw His ministry. Those who were the recipients of Jesus healing touch remembered the thrill they had experienced as virtue had entered them. They saw the final days of His earthly work. Judas watched with horror as he saw himself betray the Son of Man. Each member of the trial clearly saw with fear and trembling the part they had played. Then He was crucified, and each saw themselves acting their part, recorded in perfect exactness.

As His cry "It is finished, Father into Thy hands I commend My spirit!" ripped across the vaults of heaven, all beings within and without of the city again fell to the ground and acknowledged that God was just in his dealings with them. Again, all but Lucifer bowed. He had set his face against God and refused to bow. Then the last wonder appeared in heaven. In the hand of the Father was another scroll. John in Revelation puts it this way.

"Then another book was opened, and it was the Book of Life." Revelation 20:12. The Father handed the scroll to the Son. Everyone within and without the city watched with silent anticipation. They could see that seven seals had been placed on this scroll. Six of the seals had been opened. One yet remained. It was understood that this book had been written thousands of years earlier, then sealed up with these seven seals so none could tamper with its contents. When John saw this book in vision, he wept when no one was found worthy to open it. Then Jesus had been found worthy. As the seals were opened one by one, major events had taken place in heaven and on earth. John had wept because that scroll would tell him if he was found worthy of salvation. The Book of Life contained all the names of those who would be granted eternal life. John longed to see if his name was written there. And so, as the scroll was handed to Jesus, all knew it was heavens final roster. If your name graced its pages, you would be granted a right to the eternal glories of the ages to come. As Jesus took the scroll in His hand, He opened the last seal. John also told us when this happened there was silence in heaven for the space of a half an hour. And so, it happened. As this scroll–The Book of Life–was unrolled under the first one–The Book of Records–all eyes were riveted to its unfolding drama. This scroll, or The Lamb's Book of Life, was written on both sides. Those within the city saw one side of the scroll, those on the outside saw the other. Those on the inside would see their sins blotted out. They were remembered no more. Those on the outside would have their names blotted out. But they did not know this yet. So, all wondered, would their name be written on its pages? Before the scroll began to unroll, Jesus announced it. His voice was awesome and rolled across the heavens with the sound of a million thunders. The very earth shook from its power and all knees became weak.

"People of all ages of the earth. Earlier you heard Lucifers accusations that the Father and I were unfair. We are accused of creating some of you for damnation and others for glory. See for yourselves. The Father wrote out the entire history of earth long before it was ever created. He saw each one of you and knew what choices you would make ages before you were ever born. He recorded it all with perfect exactness, then sealed it up with seven seals so none could open and see. He wrote about the rise and fall of Lucifer. He wrote about the sin of your first parents. He told of the flood and of My life on earth and your response to My salvation. For those of you outside the city, as you looked at the scroll of records, you saw where time and time again, by your own choice, you refused the mercy of God and continued in disobedience. You all knelt and admitted We were just in our dealings with each one of you. Now compare the scroll the Father wrote before the foundations of the earth were laid with the scroll of records. You will find them exact in every detail. Though the Father had foreknowledge of everything that took place, you will see, He forced none to obey or disobey. You will see where Lucifer's accusations are unfounded and totally false. For at the end of this scroll that was written before time, you will see even this drama that you are now a part of, recorded in every detail, even down to the exact words of Lucifer. The Book of Life will show more than the Book of Records. On the inside you will see recorded the names of those who will inherit eternal life. On the outside you will see there are names blotted out of this book. You will see where at the beginning of your life; your name was written down. You were all given the same chance. When you appeared on the scene you were given the chance to partake of the salvation I freely offered. If your name has been blotted out of the Book of Life, you will see it was clearly your own choice. You made that choice day by day in your acceptance or rejection of My sacrifice to pay the penalty for your sins. Read and see for yourselves and may the Father stand vindicated, without fault before you."

As the announcement of Jesus ended, the entire earth became silent. The giant scroll was unrolling. At first the observers could see heaven as it was before Lucifer was even created. They watched as he came forth from the hand of Christ. They saw his rebellion and eventual expulsion from heaven. Then the earth was formed, and man created. As the scroll unrolled it matched the scroll of records in every detail. There was not a period or a comma out of place. Truly God was all knowing. The ages unfolded and each looked at their name. They saw where it had been written down. They saw each had been given the same chance to accept Salvation. As the scroll opened further and further, the watchers became more tuned in to what they saw. Was their name written there, or would it be blotted out. The book of records had not given this information. It had not shown who of the inhabitants of the New Earth would receive eternal life, and who would not, because they had not been judged yet. The Book of Life, though the same as the Book of Records up to a point, contained more information. The Book of Records ended with the end of the world. The Book of Life continued. It showed the events that had taken place in heaven. It showed Satan bound with his angels to the earth for a thousand years while the saints enjoyed the presence of Christ. Faithfully recorded there were the events that had transpired before the wicked were resurrected. It showed the great city coming down from God out of heaven. With disappointment and anguish those outside of the city saw the lies of Satan plainly revealed. He had not built the city. It had not been taken from his possession. He was not God as he claimed to be. Now the scene of judgment came, and each saw recorded in perfect exactness the events that had just passed. They saw Jesus announcement recorded word for word, exactly as it had appeared. They saw the accusations of Satan written with perfect accuracy. Then the book showed what would happen next. The scroll was turned inside out. The names of those who would dwell in the City of God were listed. It was turned back again to the viewers outside the city. With awful distinctness they saw where their names had been blotted out. Then came the purifying fire that cleansed the earth from sin and destroyed all those workers of iniquity. As the wicked saw their fate recorded before it ever took place, they once again bowed and acknowledged that Jesus was King of Kings and Lord of Lords. Though God knew of all these things, He never forced any to accept or reject Him. If they were lost, it was because they had chosen to reject His offer.

Lucifer's attention was most intense. He was aware of his part in the drama. He knew of the sins he had caused each to commit. As he saw his history painted in perfect accuracy, he knew his cause was lost. He saw along with the entire world; he and he alone was the culprit. It was not God's fault. It was not the fault of Christ. He had been the one who started this evil reign, and he alone. God's finger pointed directly at him. For ages he had placed the blame on God and had led multitudes to do the same. Now the total picture was opened for all to see. He could not escape the reality of it. His life of deception was exposed, and the deceiver was fully unmasked. Lucifer, this great prince, was none other than the devil, and destroyer of souls. As the scroll revealed the very words, he had spoken just moments earlier, he had to acknowledge that God was God, and He was just in his dealings with sin and sinners. The Bible said that every knee would bow, and every tongue confess that Jesus Christ was Lord. As his part in sin was clearly revealed to all, he finally knelt and acknowledged that God was just and Jesus Christ, was Lord. What else could he do?

The scroll was fully opened now. Everyone could look ahead and see their future written by the finger of God. As Satan looked and saw the consuming fire, he determined one more time to not yield the battle. He jumped to his feet and rushed into the midst of his followers. With the fury of a million demons, he tried to arouse them to battle, but he had come to his end and none will help him now. Where just moments before the finger was pointed at God and the people within the glorious city, they now pointed to Satan. Mobs of men and demons lunged at him and attempted to rip him to shreds. The saints who were looking on turned their backs. Many went to their homes in the city and wept. There was no joy now in that celestial city for the fire of God's wrath had begun to fall. Most of the wicked were consumed in an instant, but some suffered on and on for days. The purifying fire of Jehovah rained down on the unsheltered heads of those outside the city. It lasted for hours. Long after all had been brought to ashes, Satan suffered on. As long as one atom of his being existed, he suffered. On him was placed the sins of all the saints inside the city, but the sin which caused him the most anguish and pain was the murder of Michael, the Son of God. For this he suffered on and on until at last nothing remained. It must have seemed like forever to that Prince of Darkness. But the Bible tells us he will come to his end and be ashes under the feet of the righteous. Sin had finally been eradicated. It would never rise a second time for if any had any questions as to whether God's way was best, they need only go to The Book of Life, and there recorded for all to see, was the sad story of sin. After seeing it once, who would ever wish to have it raise its ugly head again. The consequences of sin had run their course. Never again would any wish to return to the life of bondage. Good had triumphed.

BIBLE TEXTS

"Then I saw a scroll in the right hand of the One sitting on the throne. It had writing on the front and back sides. It had been sealed closed with seven seals. And I saw a mighty angel. He called with a loud voice. 'Who is worthy to break the seals and open the scroll?' but there was none found worthy in heaven or earth or under the earth who could open the scroll and look inside of it. I wept and cried because there was no one who was able to open the scroll. Then one of the elders said to me, 'Do not weep! The lion from the tribe of Judah has been victorious. He is the heir to David's throne. He is able to open the scroll and loose its seals.' Then I saw a Lamb standing in the center of the throne and the four living creatures were around

it. This Lamb looked like it had been slain. It had seven horns and seven eyes. The seven eyes are the seven spirits of God that are sent into all the world. The Lamb came and took the scroll from the right hand of the One sitting on the throne. After taking the scroll, the four living creatures and the 24 elders bowed down before the Lamb. Each had a harp. They were also holding golden bowls filled with incense. These bowls are filled with the prayers of God's saints. And they all sang a new song to the Lamb. 'You are worthy to open the scroll and break its seals, because you were killed; and with the blood of your death purchased men from every kindred, tribe, language and nation. You have made them a kingdom of priests for our God. They will live and reign with you and rule the earth.'"

Revelation 5:1-10

"And when he opened the seventh seal, there was silence in heaven for about the space of half an hour."

Revelation 8:1

And nothing shall enter it that defiles, neither does works of evil, or tells a lie: but only those whose names are written in the Lamb's book of life.

Revelation 21.27

"The beast that you saw was and is not; and will ascend out of the bottomless pit and go into perdition: and they that dwell on the earth, whose names were not written in the book of life, written from the foundation of the world, shall wonder when they behold the beast that was, and is not, and yet is."

Revelation 17:8

"*Then I saw an angel come down from heaven with the key to the bottomless pit and a heavy chain in his hand. He seized the Dragon–that old Serpent, the devil, Satan– and bound him in chains for 1,000 years, and threw him into the bottomless pit, which he then shut and locked, so that he could not fool the nations any more until the thousand years were finished. Afterwards he would be released again for a little while. Then I saw thrones and sitting on them were those who had been given the right to judge. And I saw the souls of those who had been beheaded for their testimony about Jesus, for proclaiming the Word of God, and who had not worshiped the beast or his image or accepted his mark on their foreheads or their hands. They came to life again and now they reigned with Christ for a thousand years in heaven. This was the first Resurrection. The rest of the dead did not come back to life until the thousand years had ended. Blessed and holy are those who share in the First Resurrection. For them, the Second Death holds no terrors, for they will be priests of God and of Christ and shall reign with him a thousand years. When the thousand years end, Satan will be let out of his prison. He will go out to deceive the nations of the world and gather them together, with Gog and Magog, for battle–a mighty host, numberless as the sand along the shore. They will go up across the broad plain of the earth and surround God's people and the beloved city of Jerusalem on every side... And I saw a great white throne and the one who sat upon it, from whose face the earth and sky fled away, but they found no place to hide. I saw the wicked, great, and small, standing before God; and the Books were opened. And another book was opened which was the Book of Life. And the wicked were judged according to the things written in The Books, each according to the deeds they had done.*

The oceans surrendered the bodies buried in them; and the earth gave up the dead in them. Each was judged according to his deeds. And Death and Hell were thrown into the Lake of Fire. This is the Second Death–The Lake of Fire. And if anyone's name was not found recorded in the Book of Life, he was thrown into the Lake of Fire... Fire from God in heaven will flash down on the attacking armies and consume them. Then the devil who had betrayed them will again be thrown into the Lake of Fire burning with sulfur where the Beast and the False Prophet are."

Revelation 20:1-15

"You have been in Eden, the garden of God (Lucifer); every precious stone was your covering, the Sardis, topaz, and the diamond, the beryl, the onyx, and the jasper, the sapphire, the emerald, the carbuncle, and gold: the workmanship of your throat and of your voice was prepared in you on the day you were created. You are the anointed cherub that veiled God's glory. I made you so: You were upon the holy mountain of God; you walked up and down in the midst of the stones of fire. You were perfect in your ways from the day you were created, till iniquity was found in you. By the number of your products, they have filled you up with violence, and you have sinned: therefore, I will cast you as a profane thing out of the mountain of God: and I will destroy you, O covering cherub, from the midst of the stones of fire. Your heart was lifted because of your beauty, you have corrupted your wisdom by reason of your glory: I will cast you to the ground, I will lay you before kings, that they may behold you. You have defiled thy sanctuaries by the number of your iniquities, by the iniquity of your traffic; therefore, will I bring forth a fire from the middle of you, it shall devour you, and I will bring you

to ashes upon the earth in the sight of all of them that behold you. All those who know you among the people shall be surprised at you: you shall be a terror, and never will you be anymore."

Ezekiel 28:13-19

"Surely the day is coming; it will burn like a furnace. All the arrogant and every evildoer will be stubble, and that day that is coming will set them on fire," says the Lord Almighty. "Not a root or a branch will be left to them, but for you who reverence my name, the sun of righteousness will rise with healing in its wings, and you will go out and grow up like calves released from their stall. Then you will trample down the wicked; they will be ashes under the soles of your feet on the day when I do these things," says the Lord Almighty.

Malachi 4:1-3

CHAPTER 24
A NEW HEAVEN AND A NEW EARTH

After the purifying fire had done its work, Joy and Trust flew to the top of the wall of the great city. Jesus commanded the gates to be opened. He took His place next to the Father on the throne. Then raising both hands to the sky cried in a loud voice that rocked the globe.

"Let there be a new heaven." It was amazing to see the effects of His command. A mist rose up out of the parched earth and formed a ring of water that surrounded the earth, high above the city. Such a ring existed before the great flood that had destroyed the inhabitants in the time of Noah. The effect of this ring of water was most wonderful. Once heated, it kept the earth at an even temperature all over the globe. The north and south poles were as warm as the tropical parts of the world. Scientist often wondered why giant creatures had been found frozen with tropical plants still in their mouths and stomachs. This was why. It turned the whole of earth into a tropical paradise, a giant greenhouse. When man had become so wicked that he filled up his cup of iniquity, three giant asteroids had pelted the earth. They hit with such force the ring of water was partially vaporized. The vapors fell to the earth as rain and the remaining water above the earth came down and flooded it. None had survived save the family of Noah and those animals within the ark. After a time, God caused a great wind to blow and pile up the waters. Without the warm ring of water above the earth to provide even heat, the poles became cold. As the winds blew against them, the polar caps were formed. In time, dry land appeared again, and Noah and his cargo repopulated the earth.

After reforming the ring of water above the earth,

Jesus issued another command and the panels that had hidden the plants within the city from the harsh atmosphere of earth, appeared again. The gardens grew and waterfalls once again flowed from their appointed positions all over the city. Their beauty again graced the golden metropolis. The New Jerusalem was so tall, the upper portion of it would have been void of oxygen except for the preserving power of God Almighty. Now the time had come for the recreation of the earth. Joy was so happy she flew close to the throne of God and thanked Jesus for returning the gardens and waterfalls. He looked at her with eyes of love. She had been such a treasure. He beaconed her to come near.

"Do you remember when you asked Me if you could stand by my side when I created the New Earth," He asked?

"Yes, I remember Jesus," she replied. "How could I forget."

"The time has come, Celestania for this to be done. Come with Me." She followed Jesus as He left the city. One more person had made that request. It was the mighty Adam. Long had he waited and longed for the day when his Creator would restore earth to its former beauty and remove the curse of sin. He too had asked if He might stand next to the second Adam as He recreated the earth. Somehow to have that happen would help ease the pain his sin had caused within. His request was also granted. He joined Joy and Jesus now outside the city. Joy was a little over half his height. He looked down at her and smiled.

"You are so beautiful, Joy. You have made all of heaven rejoice. You have been a precious blessing to all of us." With that he picked her up and placed her on his powerful shoulders. She was a little higher up than Jesus now, and liked the view very much.

Outside, as she looked down, she saw the earth perfectly round. All the jagged cracks were gone. All the rocky mountains were burned smooth. The earth appeared as a giant ball of bronze. As far as her eyes could see it stretched on and on. Not a living thing appeared anywhere outside the city. There were no more seas. There were no more people out there. The entire population of heaven now mounted the walls and stood looking with amazement at the spectacle in front of them. You could see where many had been weeping. Jesus took His hand and swept it across the sky.

"Let the former things pass away," He cried with a powerful voice. Instantly all sorrow was gone. With just a few words He had wiped away all the pain, all the tears and instilled unspeakable joy into the hearts and minds of all His subjects. It was a miracle. As the realization dawned on that happy throng that sin was forever gone, a shout of victory swelled the ranks of the redeemed. The angels struck a note. The harps came out and with skillful fingers the great orchestra of heaven played music to the glory of the Father, the Son, and the Holy Spirit. They were uplifted and elevated. God's kingdom had been made sure. The praise lasted for hours. Its melodies rang out across the barren earth and echoed back a thousand times over. Adam put the girl down and he and Joy joined in the happy celebration. Life everlasting was here, and it was now. There would be no more sorrow, no more pain, no more curse for the former things had passed away at the command of Jesus. At last, the praises ended, and Jesus walked out over the metallic globe with his two companions.

Once again as in a time seven thousand years earlier, He spoke. The first thing He did was go to the four corners of the Holy City. With His hands, and finally His voice, He commanded the River of Life to flow out from the city. As He spoke, a rushing sound came and the pure water passed through the walls, forming four rivers. The four rivers branched out to the north, south, east, and west. They flowed down from the mountain and banks were formed in the earth. He set their boundaries with His mind and the rivers obeyed. Then he spoke trees, flowers, birds, and animals into existence. Joy witnessed it all first hand. At His command, when each new marvel appeared, she let out exclamations of wonder and amazement. Adam again hoisted her to his shoulders and smiled as each curse was replaced by beauty and splendor. Jesus was a master artist. His voice could create the most beautiful things. Some of the birds He called into existence, flew to him, and rested on His shoulder. One came to rest on the head of Joy. Another flew to Adam. He gave it a name. He called it Ecstasy after the little girl Joy. The animals came too. He gave them names also. Some of the animals were new to all the people watching. Adam had no problem finding names for them. When they came to a beautiful lake surrounded by a lawn of living green, and flowers of radiant beauty, he began to call the fish by name. There were beautiful ones. Some were of brilliant colors. Others had long flowing fins that guided them gracefully through the water. As the trees and flowers pointed their leaves and petals toward Christ, a sweet fragrance arose and surrounded the trio. The air had the sent of spring, washed clean after a warm rain. It was beautiful, simply beautiful. The last little creature had been spoken into existence. The earth was restored more lovely than at its beginning. The celestial city shone like a mighty diamond, rising from its foundation on the mountain. The rainbow appeared ten times brighter. The winding rivers reflected the ashier blue of the sky. Then it was done. This was the home of the redeemed for all eternity.

Looking with satisfaction over the new earth, Jesus pronounced that it was very good and so it was. In all the vast universe of God no place existed that was more beautiful. What made it most beautiful though was the fact that Jesus was there. This was His kingdom. This gentle King would reign for ever and ever as King of Kings and Lord of Lords, or would He? Jesus entered the city. He bid His friends farewell and mounted the throne, again taking His position next to the Father.

As everyone became silent, the voice of Jesus rolled out over the city and continued throughout the new earth.

"Beloved, you who have chosen Me as your Salvation, behold your reward. The earth created new, is yours. Go out and take possession of it. There is room enough for everyone. You have your city homes that I built for you. Now go and select your country habitation. The universe is yours; its treasures are there for your enjoyment. You are free at last. Whatever your heart desires to do, do it. Go now and make a way for yourselves. I will dwell with you forever and ever. I will walk among you and help you plant your vineyards. If you like, I will help you build your homes. I will eat at your tables and dwell in your presence. I am yours even as you are Mine. Go now and fill the whole earth and prosper. Once each week you will return to the city. It will be on the Sabbath day. We will worship together at the feet of the Father. Behold. All that you see is yours go now and take possession of it."

Once again, the inhabitants of heaven prostrated themselves at the feet of Jesus. He was their King, and none could be a better one. He now turned to the Father. From His pure white robe, He pulled out a golden key. He handed it to the Ancient of Days and spoke to Him.

"Father, You gave Me this key a short while ago. You gave Me the authority to do whatever I thought necessary to close the chapter of sin and restore to You the kingdom claimed by Satan. I purchased these subjects once with My blood. They accepted My sacrifice. Now I have prepared a habitation for them. They will go out and build houses and inhabit them. They will plant vineyards and partake of their fruit. No one will build a house, and another come and inhabit it. There will be no more sickness or pain or sorrow or crying for the former things have all passed away. Will You accept the work I have done for You? I did all that You asked. They wish that I rule over them but Father. I long to dwell with them not as their King but as a brother. I want to help them build their new homes. I want to eat at their tables. I want to love them for eternity to come. I do not want to rule over them but live with them. You are the ruler. Here is the key you gave Me. It is the key to this kingdom. You, Father be All in All. You be King of Kings and Lord of Lords. I will be one of your subjects. I gave My life that these might be here with Me forever. Will you grant that I may dwell with them rather than rule over them? That is what I really want to do. I want to be one with My own."

"Yes Son," replied the Father. "Go and dwell with those you have redeemed. Be a brother to them. Go help them plant their vineyards and orchards. Help them build their homes. Dwell with those You have come to love. I grant your request. You may have whatever You want within this universe. Go and do even as you have requested." With that Jesus handed the key back to the Father and went down and joined some of His friends. They made their way to the nearest gate and walked out of the city to select a home among the beauties created for their pleasure and enjoyment. The universe was finally free from the curse. God the Father was the supreme ruler of all. He watched as His beloved Son vanished into the distance with his friend. Abraham was that friend. He had finally found the country, that city whose builder and maker was God. He was no more a pilgrim and stranger in his own land, he was finally home. Jesus fulfilled His promise to this patriarch. His descendants were indeed numberless as the sands of the sea. From Abraham, Jesus would move on to others, and still others until each person was graced with His presence. On earth they had walked with this King through the eyes of faith. Now they would walk with Him in the earth made new, face to face. In a short time, all the children would be grown. They would build their own homes, and once each week, on every Sabbath Day, they would return to the city and worship God. This New Earth would travel throughout the universe of God. As it neared the various subjects of the inhabitants of other worlds, they would come and fellowship with the redeemed of the Lord. If they happened to be near on the Sabbath day, they would join in the worship service of God. The kings of the universe would bring their light into this vast city of God for ages eternal. Truly the Father would be All in All.

Joy entered the House of Trust. She loved to go there. Next to her own palace it was her most favorite place in all the universe. She loved the blue stone that formed its walls. She loved the silver door that perfectly reflected her likeness as a mirror. She loved the cobblestones of hematite going up to the door. The crystal chandelier with its hundreds of diamonds, never ceased to amaze her. Outside the window, the swans were swimming in the beautiful pond. The flowers Jesus had arranged around the waterfall were perfect. As the two set on some of the elaborate furnishings, they thought back over the last thousand years and marveled. Their view of heavenly things had changed a great deal. They were mature young people, nearly adults. The former life on earth was just a shadow in their minds. Joy could not recall the pain she had suffered. Neither could Trust. He could not even sorrow at the thought of the loss of his Mother. The former things had passed away. There was just too much good to dwell on the evil that could not be recalled.

"Do you want to start building your country home now, Trust," asked Joy?

"Not yet," came the reply. "I want to travel. I would like to see a few thousand homes before I design my own. I have no idea of what is even possible. In my travels though, I would like to collect things for my new home. What about you Joy? What do you plan to do?"

"O, I would just love to travel, especially if it could be with you. Do you mind if I tag along? I would love to so much, and you are the best friend I have ever had. There are none who I would rather travel with."

"I was hoping you would say that Joy," responded Trust. "I love you so very much. There is none I would rather spend eternity with then you. You are truly my very best friend." He went over and gave the young lady an affectionate hug. She snuggled down in his strong arms and smiled.

"Let's do something together before we go wandering off to the unknown reaches of the universe, Trust. Let's travel around on this new earth and see all the wonders Jesus has created for us here first. While we are checking out this place, we can look for a location to establish our new residences. When we find just the perfect spot, we can lay claim to it and as we collect wonders from planets all over the universe, we will have a place to take them. We will have a country paradise away from our homes in the city. What do you say?"

"There is nothing I would rather do Joy. You have spoken the desire of my heart. Unlike our homes in the city, we can in time, build our country habitations right next to each other. And your idea of laying claim to our own plot of land is just perfect. I am sure if Jesus is here, the New Earth will be a model of perfection. There is likely no place in the universe as lovely and wonderful as this world now that it has come fresh and new from the hand of God. Let's go and look for our homestead. I feel like flying."

"Me too," chimed the young lady. With that they were out the great silver door of the House of Trust and winging their way higher and higher into the heavens. Beneath them the earth spread out in a beautiful garden. Eden extended as far as they could see. Graceful mountains and rolling hills advanced out over a land carpeted with trees and flowers. Lakes and streams branched out from the center of luscious valleys of splendor and beauty. They could see the four branches of the River of Life as it wound in and out over the earth. There were wonders too many to tell of. As they looked down, they, saw families already at work on their own country paradises. There were some who loved the city of gold. They did not want to be far from it. They were comforted by the massive walls rising high into the heavens. They wanted to see the travelers from other world as they brought their treasures to the King of Kings. They wanted to be near the Tree of Life and the great white throne of God. So, they set their faces toward the great city. Others wanted to be away from the hustle and bustle and busy traffic that would surely surround the celestial metropolis. They looked for secluded areas away from the eyes of the universal travelers.

For days and days, the young people traveled, taking in the wonders of this new world. There was a variety of beauties. One thing was certain, both Joy and Trust wanted to build on the side of a mountain or at its uppermost peak. Trust was used to the giant trees next to his home in the city. He loved high places. He supposed he would build his home elevated in the air. Within the city Joy was very high up in some of the upper strata of rooms. She wished for an area a little closer to the earth. Perhaps a place carved out of the mountain like some of the beautiful homes of Adam's descendants. At last, they spotted a tall mountain off in the distance. Graceful hills rolled up to it. Stately palm trees swayed back and forth around its parameter. It was high enough to view much of the surrounding area. And far, far away they could catch a glimpse of the great city towering into the heavens. They went down for a closer look. As they landed a doe, and a buck came up to them. The buck went to Trust and nuzzled him with his nose. The doe went to Joy and rested her head on the shoulder of the young lady. Over the years, the young people had learned to communicate with the animals. They now carried on a conversation with them. It was simple communication but pleasant. The animals welcomed them to their mountain and expressed the hope of a long relationship. They led them to a small opening in the rocks. Inside was a most glorious display of crystals. They were deep purple, almost pink. The top of the cave was made of translucent rock. The light penetrated it and illuminated everything within. Joy at once fell in love with it. Along the walls of the cave were natural shelves. She envisioned her growing collection of treasures inside the city and immediately adopted this new cove as a possible storage place and display cabinet. Trust climbed to the uppermost peak of the mountain. He looked off toward the great city. His gate was not quite in view. He needed to be up a little higher. He flew up in the air and found the perfect spot some five hundred feet higher. Could he build a palace five hundred feet in the air? Already the home of his dreams was coming into his mind. In time he would see it all perfectly constructed, then he would begin building it. Perhaps Jesus would be by his side and help with the engineering. That would be so nice. He made his way back to the cove where Joy was and smiled at her with his best look.

"I love this place, Joy. It is perfect. I really think we are home now."

"It is not home yet Trust," she replied. "But it will be. We have a great start. I love this little cave, the mountain, and our animal friends. I love the view and I think I want to build my home adjacent to this little cove." Trust continued smiling as he thought out loud.

"You are so right about that. This place does have a view or will have." And so, eternity had begun for two children of the King. Everlasting life was their inheritance. Throughout the ceaseless ages to come, they would embrace this moment and remember when they were fully home. Their wanderings were over. Universal love permeated everything.

So begins the story of two who found rest in the country of God. What about you reader? There is a place for you here on earth, in the future when it will be recreated anew. There is room enough for your family too. Eternal life is yours for the asking. There have been times earlier in this little book when I appealed to you and prayed with you. If you long for that day when sin and sorrow will be forever in the past, if you ache for the eternal city of God, if you want heaven and the earth made new to be your ultimate home, make plans to be there now. The invitation stands. The Father wrote your name in the book of life before you were ever born. It can be blotted out only if you choose not to accept the salvation Jesus offers. Accept it now with me. Let's plan to meet under the tree of life at the feet of Jesus and there forever dwell with our Lord and Savior, Jesus Christ. That is my prayer for you.

Yours in Christ Jesus,
Donielle

BIBLE TEXTS

"And I saw a new heaven and a new earth: for the first heaven and the first earth were passed away; and there was no more sea. And I John saw the holy city, new Jerusalem, coming down from God out of heaven prepared as a bride adorned for her husband. And I heard a great voice out of heaven saying, 'Behold, the tabernacle of God is with men, and he will dwell with them, and they shall be his people, and God himself shall be with them, and be their God. And God shall wipe away all tears from their eyes; and there shall be no more death, neither sorrow, nor crying, neither shall there be any more pain: for the former things are passed away.' And he that sat upon the throne said, 'Behold, I make all things new.' And he said unto me, 'Write: for these words

are true and faithful.' And he said unto me, 'It is done. I am Alpha and Omega, the beginning, and the end. I will allow any who are thirsty to drink freely from the fountain of the water of life. He that overcomes shall inherit all things; and I will be his God, and he shall be my son. But the fearful, and unbelieving, and the abominable, and murderers, and prostitutes, and sorcerers, and idolaters, and all liars, shall have their part in the lake of fire and brimstone: This is the second death.'"

Revelation 21:1-8

"And behold, I come quickly; and my reward is with me, to give every man according as his work shall be. I am Alpha and Omega, the beginning, and the end, the first and the last. Blessed are they that do his commandments, that they may have right to the tree of life and may enter in through the gates into the city. For without are dogs, and sorcerers, and whoremongers, and murderers, and idolaters, and whosoever loves to tell lies. I Jesus have sent my angel to testify unto you these things in the churches. I am the root and the offspring of David, and the bright and morning star. And the Spirit and the bride say, 'Come.' And let him that hears say, 'Come.' And let him that is thirsty come. And whosoever will, let him take the water of life freely.

Revelation 22:12-17

The Palace of Trust and House of Joy
(Epilogue, an Allegory)

The time had come for Jesus to help build the Palace of Trust and House of Joy. Many years had passed on new, planet earth since Jesus had recreated it. Most of the citizens of this kingdom had settled down into their routine of Everlasting Life. They had built lovely homes and planted the most beautiful gardens imaginable. From the valleys and hillsides surrounding the city of gold, spectacular edifices had been constructed. The redeemed had enjoyed fellowship with Jesus as He did whatever was helpful in each individual case. He was loved by all and He loved all. He had no favorites. Each person there was a most precious possession. They were twice His. He had created them and then bought them back. From the glorious land, the Rock of Salvation, rising out of Mount Zion, stood as a memorial to the entire universe. Universal peace was here and now. The former life had been forgotten. Only as was necessary in sharing salvations story was any of it recalled. Planet earth was always on the move. It traveled from one galaxy to another. As numerous planets were visited, the witnesses of earth told and retold the story of Jesus. The panorama was seen by all. After seeing the results of sin, none ever wanted it to return. And so, the endless ages of eternity rolled on and on.

Joy and Trust were no longer children. They had matured to the full stature of God. Trust came a little below the shoulder of Adam. Adam came a little below the head of Christ and Joy a little below the head of Trust. She had developed into a creature of grace and beauty. Her wings were delicate and dainty. Her dark eyes shown out with a fire of peace and passion that captivated any who took the time to look deep within them. On her head, beneath her crown of glory, another crown of long black hair silhouetted her face. It came down in gentle curls and fell softly on her shoulders. All the women in the New Earth were beautiful but even by heavens standards she was gorgeous. There was no marriage in the New Earth but had there been that option, Trust would have married her. He loved to show her off to everyone he could. The two were very happy in their friendship. Something banded Joy to this gentle young man in a bond closer than most friendships could ever experience. Joy's taste had changed some. As she visited more and more of the universe of God, she matured in Christ to the point of utmost perfection. Trust also was a friend of Jesus. He had developed into a fine man. He was always giving. If any came to him, he freely offered whatever he had. Nothing was withheld. He gave, and gave, and gave, but found he could never out give his Lord. Now as Jesus stood talking to these two beloved ones, they unfolded their plans for the homes of their dreams. It was quite a project they cut out for themselves. Their homes would be somewhat united but still separate. It would take years, and years to do but then time was no longer of any consequence. They had eternity to complete it if need be. They ushered Jesus to the spot they had chosen for this wonder of the new world. It was on a little mountain. The two had shaped a portion of it, hour after hour. They had collected samples of earth from each planet they visited. These samples had been piled one on another and formed a most unusual shape. A great arch rose out of the ground and fashioned a thruway in the elevation. As one entered it, they could look up and see many treasures. There were strange, exotic plants arranged in delicate patterns of color and texture. Joy had collected a great assortment of dainty, and delicate flowers. Trust had selected larger, bolder ones. These had been woven in and out among those of the lady to form rivers of color. Now Trust opened his desire to Jesus. He wanted to suspend or hang a palace in the sky above the arch. It would be transparent and look like a precious stone glistening in the sky. He wanted it designed to capture and reflect the glorious rainbow that surrounded the throne of the Father. As Jesus heard of these plans, He smiled. This palace would be most challenging. He discussed the design with His friends, and they decided rather than hang the palace in the air, it would be supported by two, ultra-thin pillars or legs of transparent material. They would be long and deep at the base but fine and delicate at the uppermost point where they joined the main structure. It would be a place to remember. It was time for the work to begin. Jesus came into their presence on one of those finer days in this new world, if one day can be finer than another? He loved these children dearly. He placed an arm around them and as He did, they felt a deep love flowing from Him. In His presence was fullness of Joy and Trust beyond measure. He was, Life and this Life was, the Light of the New Earth. It illuminated everything. The eyes of these two beloved ones shown with the glory of Jesus. His image was perfectly reproduced in them now. The three were as one.

Jesus turned His attention to the project at hand. Trust was still bent on placing his palace five hundred feet in the air. Jesus bid the two come with Him. They made their way to the Mount of Perfection. It had been fashioned grain by grain over the centuries as the saints on the New Earth grew up in the grace of Christ. Jesus took the chisel of truth and the hammer of knowledge and begin to whittle away at a portion of the mountain. In time He had carved out a five-hundred-foot pillar. It was about twenty feet square at the base and ten-foot square at the top. He carved a second pillar to the exact same proportions. Then with the help of a few citizens, they transported them to the mountain. One pillar was named Trust, the other Joy. They placed them in position and then Jesus fused them to the earth. At the mount of Sanctification, Jesus again took up the hammer and chisel and carved out a floor. This was transported to the mountain and put in position on the pillars. The height of Trust's palace was now established. He took Joy up to see the view. She loved it. As she looked off in the distance, she saw her beloved city rising out of Mount Zion. She saw the colorful rainbow and heard the voices of the celestial choir echoing across the rolling hills as they sang praises to God. One of the branches of the River of Life flowed into the valley beneath their homestead. It was so clear and beautiful. Holding Trust close in one arm and Jesus in the other, she told them this was one of the happiest moments of her life.

"It is so beautiful up here," she said. "I could stay here like this forever and be eternally happy." After that Jesus, Joy and Trust continued building the home day after day. The walls of this palace were carved from the vaults of grace. Its roof was cut from the sky of purity. The windows were transported from the island of goodness. The inside walls were made from the material of excellency. There was a ceiling of righteousness that curved up to form a cathedral style arch of blessing at each end. From this Jesus hung the lights of redemption and salvation. From their collectibles the young people furnished the place with a chair of honor and a sofa of dignity. When completed it was beautiful beyond words. Beneath the arch where the pillars met the ground, Trust wanted grape vines. Jesus was the Vine and he and Joy were the branches. They wanted to remember their constant dependency on Christ. After these vines were planted, and in time grew up the pillars till they reached the top, Jesus again came to the home of these two special ones. This time He did a very wonderful thing. He fused the Vines with the pillars. The pillars of Joy and Trust became united with the Vine of Christ to form living columns. Only Jesus could bring life out of perfection. He alone was the Creator.

The columns now appeared to be carved from living plants. They drew water up with them. The young people could go to the tip of the pillar and pour a cool, refreshing drink any time they pleased. Trust could also reach out one of the windows and pick delicious grapes of glory where they either ate them or squeezed juice from them to refresh themselves or some visitor. It was a most marvelous creation. Joy had taken up piano music. Trust sought out a skillful craftsman and had him come and build a crystal piano of effervesce. As the lovely lady played the piano, Trust would often bring his harp back from the city of gold and join her in giving praise and glory to God. Joy brought several of the musical instruments she collected from all over the universe. The acoustics in the palace were perfect. They tried many instruments. They selected several combinations and became proficient at each one. In time their sound became so well liked, people would come from miles around to listen to a concert. The Palace of Trust took a long time to complete but on a special preparation day, before a special Sabbath to the Lord, it was finished. That Sabbath it was dedicated by Jesus Himself. Many came to partake in the celebration.

After taking a break from the work on Trust's palace, Jesus returned one day and offered His services in building the House of Joy. She had waited a long time for this day. Her taste was quite simple but elaborate at the same time. Unlike the Palace of Trust, who built his country home high in the heavens, she wanted hers close to the earth and made from the elements of earth. She loved animals. From that first visit years, and years ago, when the doe and the buck welcomed them, her animal farm had grown considerably. She liked the big cats. A pair of tigers had taken up residence not far from the entrance to the cave. A lion and his mate had claimed a place beneath the pillars that supported the palace. A black cat with green eyes and a lighter colored twin had claimed their resting place above the cove on top of the arch. Joy wanted her home to look like the mountain. Jesus began to weave together the flowers of beauty and loveliness. After a few moments of instruction, Joy found herself weaving them also. The delicate patterns that came from the hands of these two individuals were amazing indeed. After forming the walls of these weavings, they decorated the interior with gladness and delight. They interspersed charm with bliss, and happiness with serenity. The combination was beautiful indeed. Everyone loved The House of Joy. In time all was finished. Then like His home with Mary, Martha, and Lazarus, in the first earth, this combination of Palace and home became a home away from home for the Master, with Joy and Trust in the earth made new.

As the ages rolled on and on, The Palace of Trust, and the House of Joy hosted many of the great celebrates like Adam and Eve, David and Bathsheba, Sampson, Paul, the apostles, and all the Twenty-Four Elders. Many of the One Hundred and Forty-Four Thousand entered it and marveled at its beauty. There were many others. Abraham, Isaac, Jacob, Joseph, Noah, Enoch, Methuselah, not to mention Samuel, Daniel and his three companions. These occasions were most enjoyable when Jesus was able to be there with them. Eternity was far better than life on the first earth but being with Jesus was the best!

What a friend we have in Jesus. What a privilege is ours to be counted worthy to share this eternal brotherhood with Him. Eternal life is ours for the taking. It is God's gift to us through His Son, Jesus. Blessed be the Name of Jesus. Holy and Righteous is He, and worthy of all praise and glory. To be with Jesus is to be in paradise. We can be with Him reader. He loves each one of us more than we can ever understand. We can be over comers through the power He freely offers. He took the death we deserve so that we might inherit the life He deserves. We can overcome simply by accepting the sacrifice Jesus made on the cross. "For

God so loved the world that He gave His Only Begotten Son, that whosoever believes in Him, should not perish but have everlasting life. (John 3:16) That life is ours for the asking.

These are the rewards then; Jesus will give to all who overcome. They are found in Revelation chapters 2 and 3.

"As for the one who conquers, I will make him a pillar in the temple of my God; he will be secure and will go out no more; and I will write my Fathers' name on him, and he will be a citizen in the city of my Father–the New Jerusalem, coming down from heaven, from my God; and he will have my new Name inscribed upon him."

This is what Jesus says: "I will let everyone who conquers sit beside me on my throne, just as I took my place with my Father on his throne when I had conquered."

"Everyone who conquers will be clothed in white, and I will not erase his name from the Book of Life, but I will announce before my Father and his angels that he is mine."

"If you overcome and to the very end keep on doing those things that please me–I will give each of you what you deserve–I will give you power over the nations. You will rule them with a rod of iron just as my Father gave me the authority to rule them; they will be shattered like a pot of clay that is broken into tiny pieces. And I will give you the Morning star!"

"Strive with all diligence to be victorious for if you are victorious, you shall eat of the hidden manna, the secret nourishment from heaven; and I will give you each a white stone, and on the stone will be engraved your new name, a name that no one else knows except the one receiving it".

"Remain faithful to me on earth even if it means dying for my name. If you do, I will give you the crown of life–an unending, glorious future... you will not be hurt by the second death."

"Finally, if you conquer, if you are victorious, you will have continual access to the Tree of Life which is in the Paradise of God." Amen!